About the Authors

Me
Lor
area
tion
inve
in
Res
Fin

Eev
trai
the
ST
and
act

Studies in International Health Policy and Practice

Profound changes are taking place in the field of international health. New problems and challenges are arising – the ongoing spread of AIDS (in Asia in particular), the rapid ageing of populations in the South and North, the emergence of new strains of drug-resistant diseases, the breakdown of ordered government in some parts of the world and the persistence in the industrialized countries of minorities caught in a poverty trap with its attendant epidemiological problems. New agencies have come to the fore in making international health policy, notably the World Bank, and with them a squeezing of state health expenditure and a corresponding new emphasis on private sector health service delivery. Independent NGOs continue to criticize the pharmaceutical industry and the impact of structural adjustment and other economic and technological developments on people's health. This is the context in which Zed Books is developing its health studies list to examine issues of health policy and practice in a changing global political and economic context.

The Blue Room: Trauma and Testimony among Refugee Women
INGER AGGER

Trauma and Health Under State Terrorism
INGER AGGER AND SOREN BUUS JENSEN,

Private Health Providers in Developing Countries: Serving the Public Interest?
SARA BENNETT, BARBARA MCPAKE, & ANNE MILLS (EDS)

Women and Disability
ESTHER BOYLAN

Problem Drugs
ANDREW CHETLEY

A Healthy Business? World Health and the Pharmaceutical Industry
ANDREW CHETLEY

The Politics of Essential Drugs: The Making of a Successful Health Strategy
ZAFRULLAH CHOWDHURY

Medicine Betrayed: The Participation of Doctors in Human Rights Abuses
BRITISH MEDICAL ASSOCIATION

Population and Reproductive Rights: Feminist Perspectives from the South
SONIA CORREA

The Pesticide Hazard: A Global Health and Environmental Audit
BARBARA DINHAM

Lethal Laws: Animal Testing, Human Health and Environmental Policy
ALIX FANO

Participatory Research in Health: Issues and Experiences
KORRIE DE KONING AND MARION MARTIN (EDS)

Torture: Human Rights, Medical Ethics and the Case of Israel
NEVE GORDON AND RUCHAMA MARTON (EDS)

Family Planning and Reproductive Rights: A Feminist Report
ELIZABETH HAYES AND ANITA HARDON (EDS)

Drugs Policy in Developing Countries
NAJMI KANJI *ET AL.*

Women and Health
PATRICIA SMYKE

Making a Healthy World: Agencies, Actors and Policies in International Health
MERI KOIVUSALO AND EEVA OLLILA

The Circumcision of Women: A Strategy for Eradication
OLAYINKA KOSO-THOMAS

The Use of Epidemiology in Local Health Planning: A Training Manual
AXEL KROEGER *ET AL.*

Vaccination Against Pregnancy: Miracle or Menace?
JUDITH RICHTER

Ageing: Debates on Demographic Transition and Social Policy KASTURI SEN

Empowerment and Women's Health: Theory, Methods and Practice JANE STEIN

The Politics of Public Health
MEREDETH TURSHEN

Motherpower and Infant Feeding
PENNY VAN ESTERIK

Health Policy: An Introduction to Process and Power
GILL WALT

Making a Healthy World

Agencies, Actors and Policies in
International Health

Meri Koivusalo and Eeva Ollila

STAKES

HELSINKI

Zed Books Ltd

LONDON & NEW YORK

Making a Healthy World
was first published by
Zed Books Ltd., 7 Cynthia Street, London N1 9JF, UK
and Room 400, 175 Fifth Avenue, New York, NY 10010, USA
in 1997

Published in Finland by STAKES,
National Research and Development
Centre for Welfare and Health,
Siltasaarenkatu 18, P.O. Box 220,
FIN-00531, Helsinki, Finland, in 1997

Copyright © Meri Koivusalo and Eeva Ollila 1997
Cover design by Andrew Corbett
Typeset by Long House, Cumbria, UK
Printed and bound in the United Kingdom
by Biddles Ltd., Guildford and King's Lynn

A catalogue record for this book
is available from the British Library

US Cataloging-in-Publication data has been applied for
from the Library of Congress

ISBN Hb 1 85649 493 4
Pb 1 85649 494 2

Distributed in the USA exclusively by St Martin's Press Inc.,
175 Fifth Avenue, New York, NY 10010, USA.

Contents

List of Boxes

Preface

Three principles – social justice, equality and respect for human dignity – have influenced our views and formed the starting point of our analysis in this book. We have emphasized critical and controversial issues in health policy and drawn attention to issues that deserve a closer look. While the health of nations may deteriorate rather quickly, as has been seen in some of the Eastern European countries, it should be acknowledged that real changes towards greater well-being and better health for all are often slow, and we have not meant to undervalue the importance of continuous effort in international cooperation to achieve these goals. Errors are both inevitable and human. Nevertheless, we think that it would be a pity not to recognize errors and to learn from them.

In the international health field power relations and the division of labour among the actors are under scrutiny, and in many countries health systems are in turmoil. Even though other international actors and organizations, such as the North American Free Trade Agreement (NAFTA), the European Union (EU) and the Organization for Economic Cooperation and Development (OECD) are of relevance, the main emphasis in this publication is on the United Nations organizations. Our review is based mainly on published literature, and certainly there are many key aspects which we have not covered in this book. We have considered the different international actors primarily in the light of their stated policies and critical analyses of these policies, without a full account of practice in each case. While the gaps in health within countries should be acknowledged, we have paid more attention to health policies concerning the poorest countries. We have used the expressions 'Third World countries' or 'developing countries', although we recognize the problematic connotations of these terms.

The purpose of this book has been to provide critical insights and views – and not a mere presentation – of the actors and issues in the field of international health. The book is a revised version of an earlier work published by the National Research and Development Centre for Welfare and Health in Helsinki in 1996 under the title *International Organizations and Health Policies*. It has been updated and edited, and three new chapters have been added.

The book owes much to Director General Kimmo Leppo from the Finnish Ministry of Health and Social Affairs, who initiated the study process leading to its publication. His introduction sets the scene, and he has supported and commented on most of the other material. We also owe gratitude to all the people who made the publication of the first edition possible, helping us in gathering material, commenting on the drafts, and editing the manuscript into a book. Comments by Andrew Green of the Nuffield Institute of Health and Robert Molteno of Zed Books led to substantial changes in this second edition. We owe special thanks to Ilmari for his patience during the process, and to those who have taken such good care of Ilmari while his mother has been at work.

Abbreviations and Acronyms

AIDAN	All India Drug Action Network
AIDS	Acquired Immune Deficiency Syndrome
AMRO	Regional Office for the Americas (WHO)
ARA	Analysis, Research and Assessment Division
BI	Bamako Initiative
CDR	Division of Diarrhoeal and Acute Respiratory Disease Control
CHDR	Child Health and Development Revolution
COHRED	Council on Health Research for Development
CONRAD	Contraceptive Research and Development Programme
CSDR	Child Survival and Development Revolution
DAC	Development Assistance Committee (OECD)
DALY	Disability Adjusted Life Year
DAP	Drug Action Programme
DPM	Drugs Policies and Management Unit (WHO)
DPT	Diptheria–Pertussis–Tetanus
EBFs	Extrabudgetary funds
ECOSOC	Economic and Social Council of the United Nations
EFTA	European Free Trade Area
EHA	Emergency and Humanitarian Action Programme
EPI	Expanded Programme on Immunization
ESAF	Enhanced Structural Adjustment Facility
EU	European Union
EURO	European Regional Office (WHO)
FAO	Food and Agriculture Organization
FHI	Family Health International
FP	Family planning
GATT	General Agreement on Tariffs and Trade
GDP	Gross Domestic Product
GEF	Global Environment Fund

GNP	Gross National Product
GOBI	Growth monitoring and promotion – oral rehydration therapy – Breast-feeding and Immunization
GOBI-FFF	Growth monitoring and promotion; Oral rehydration therapy; Breast-feeding and Immunization; combined with Family planning; Female literacy and Food supplementation
GPA	Global Programme on AIDS
GPV	Global Programme on Vaccines
HAI	Health Action International
HDI	Human Development Index
HFA	Health for All
HIV	Human Immune Deficiency Virus
HRP	UNDP/UNFPA/WHO/World Bank Special Programme of Research, Development and Research Training in Human Reproduction
IARC	International Agency for Research on Cancer
IBRD	Internation Bank for Reconstruction and Development
ICH	International Conference on Harmonization of Technical Requirements for Registration of Pharmaceuticals for Human Use
ICO	Intensified Cooperation with Countries in Greatest Need
IEC	Information, Education, Communication
IFC	International Finance Corporation
IFP	Indicative Planning Figure
IFPMA	International Federation of Pharmaceuticals Manufacturers Association
ICPD	International Conference on Population and Development
ILO	International Labour Organization
IPCS	International Programme on Chemical Safety
IPPF	International Planned Parenthood Federation
IRPTC	International Register of Potentially Toxic Chemicals
IMF	International Monetary Fund
IUD	Intra-uterine device
IUSSP	International Union for Scientific Study on Population
IYC	International Year of the Child
JCHP	Joint Committee on Health Policy (WHO, UNICEF)
MAI	Multilateral Agreement on Investment
MaLam	Medical Lobby for Appropriate Marketing
MCH	Maternal and child health
MIGA	Multilateral Investment Guarantee Agency
NAFTA	North American Free Trade Agreement
NGO	Nongovernmental organization

OCP	Onchocerciasis Control Programme
OECD	Organization for Economic Cooperation and Development
OIHP	Office Internationale d'Hygiène Publique
OED	Operations Evaluation Department
OHS	Organization and Management of Health Systems Division
ORS/ORT	Oral rehydration solution / therapy
PAHO	Pan American Health Organization
PATH	Programme for Appropriate Technology in Health
PHC	Primary health care
PUMA	Public Sector Management Programme (OECD)
RDB	Regional Development Bank
SAF	Structural Adjustment Facility
SSC	Strategic Support to Countries in Greatest Need Division
STAG	Scientific Advisory Group
STD	Sexually Transmitted Disease
SUNFED	Special UN Fund for Economic and Social Development
TDR	Tropical Diseases Research Programme
TNC	Transnational corporation
TRIPs	Trade-Related Intellectual Property Rights
UCI90	Universal Child Immunization by 1990
UNAIDS	United Nations Joint Programme on AIDS
UNCTAD	United Nations Conference on Trade and Development
UNDCP	United Nations International Drug Control Programme
UNDP	United Nations Development Programme
UNEP	United Nations Environmental Programme
UNESCO	United Nations Educational, Scientific and Cultural Organization
UNHCR	United Nations High Commission for Refugees
UNICEF	United Nations Children's Fund
UNIFEM	United Nations Development Fund for Women
UNIPAC	UNICEF Packing and Assembly Centre
UNFPA	United Nations Population Fund
UNRISD	United Nations Research Institute for Social Development
USAID	United States Agency for International Development
VHAI	Voluntary Health Action of India
WFP	World Food Programme
WHA	World Health Assembly
WHO	World Health Organization
WSC	World Summit for Children
WTO	World Trade Organization

1
Introduction

Kimmo Leppo

On the nature of health policy

In principle, health policy should not be very different from other fields of public policy in terms of either research or action (Wilensky *et al.* 1987). It deals with goals and means, policy environments and instruments, processes and styles of decision making, implementation and assessment. It deals with institutions, political power and influence, people and professionals, at different levels from local to global.

Policies are always based on two elements in varying degrees and different shapes: values and evidence. Values express what is desirable or acceptable to those who decide on policies. Evidence or lack of it reflects the fact that there is always some sort of theory or understanding, however rudimentary, of the determinants and consequences of health and illness, as well as measures to influence them.

The values on which policies are based may be explicit, clearly enunciated, or they may be implicit, only to be derived or deduced from the content of the policies being pursued. Values may be expounded to guide and influence policy choices in reality, or they may be there for rhetoric only. Policy analysis must decide what values are involved and to what extent. Without exception, however, values are present. There are no policies without values, even if policies often are presented as neutral or value-free, without explicit value premises.

The centrality of values lies not only in setting the guiding principles for societal action – what goals and whose interests are being served, and who should be the beneficiaries – but also in setting the scene and laying down the perspective for analysing and choosing between policy objectives and options. The substance of policy choices and priorities is guided by an understanding of the key variables and relationships among the health phenomena in question. This understanding is based – again, explicitly or implicitly – on theoretical,

1

empirical or experiential knowledge that necessarily must be organized by certain fundamental assumptions about how the world works and how human action is shaped in time and place. And this is where values enter the picture again: they determine to a large extent the choice of issues raised, the focus, weight, or neglect given to them, and the measures considered feasible or legitimate to deal with them. In short, agendas for health policies, as for other policies, are set by vision and values on one hand, and the understanding of causal mechanisms involved and their amenability to change on the other.

Fundamental variations in value orientation and in understanding health in social development

Perhaps the most basic distinction that exists in various views about health as a policy objective, is whether health is seen as an intrinsic societal and human value, good in itself, or as an instrumental value towards other goals, such as economic growth. The question is about the place of health in the hierarchy of social values. Those who stress health as an important social and human goal in itself tend to emphasize its relation to basic human rights, distributive justice and social equity.

Another important distinction that runs through many debates is about how health is conceived. First, is it looked upon as an individual phenomenon, or in the context of population or society? It goes without saying that in any meaningful debate about policies, one should adopt a population perspective of the levels and distributions of health phenomena at that level. Second, there are widely differing views about what constitutes health and how it should be measured. Perhaps the most influential tradition has been medical and epidemiological, where health is conceived as an absence of disease. Increasingly, however, health is seen in its social context, as a human capacity to cope with the environment and everyday life.

Both social and medical conceptualizations are useful for health policies. Despite their differences in outlook and measurement of health, they lead to similar views about how the health of populations is determined. This in itself – understanding the determinants of levels, trends and distribution of health – is crucial. It is widely understood that the major determinants of health and disease are wealth and poverty, availability of clean water and sanitation, entitlement to proper food and nutrition, level of general education and the status of women (Gray, 1993). In addition to these, the hazards of modern lifestyles have grown rapidly in importance (changing diets, urbanization, traffic, substance abuse). This is why health policies should be intersectoral in nature.

Compared with such determinants of health, the role of health care or health services is of secondary importance. Even if access to health is determined mainly by other factors, however, access to health care is important as a policy objective. It does make a difference to people's quality of life and security, and to the promotion of health and the prevention of disease. Only sustainable and well-functioning health systems can implement effective disease control programmes. The resources devoted to health go mainly into services, and it is not without consequence how they are organized.

In recent years strong evidence has accumulated to show the fundamental significance of social equality and social cohesion for health (Wilkinson, 1996, Blane *et al.*, 1996). It is not the richest countries which have the best health (in terms of lowest mortality) but those that have the smallest income difference between rich and poor. This underlines the importance of egalitarian social policies for health development, a point constantly stressed by international bodies seeking to bridge the gap between rich and poor countries (for example, WHO 1995a, 1996a). But it is worth putting forward in discussing national policies as well. There are revealing variations in health levels between nations that address equity differently as a social policy goal. For instance, Costa Rica or Sri Lanka are far better off in terms of health than Brazil, despite the rapid economic growth of the latter. Whether wealth creates health depends on how it is distributed.

It goes without saying that, based on the findings above, the expected focus of health policies would be long-term endeavours for overall socio-economic development in which health would have an integral part. Health would not be seen in isolation but as a part of egalitarian social policies, including the gradual building of sustainable health systems. Agendas for policies, however, are not all that rational and well-founded in real life.

Dominant themes in current health policy debates

One of the great paradoxes in the history of health policy is that, despite all the evidence and understanding that has accrued about determinants of health and the means available to tackle them, the national and international policy-making arenas are filled with something quite different. While all history and experience show that public health must be a public responsibility, and that health systems can only be financed efficiently and equitably by either Bismarckian or Beveridgean principles, we are in the middle of an epidemic of reforms based on various forms of market principles. At the same time, when policymakers rightly question the evidence base of many present-day clinical practices, at a larger system level of policies and practices all over the world we witness sweeping recommendations and reforms of questionable feasibility, effectiveness and equity. Why is that?

Presumably it is a matter of distorted vision and values, in addition to neglect of evidence. Many prevailing economic doctrines are out of touch with reality and major policy challenges (Krugman, 1994, 1996; Kuttner 1996, Heilbroner and Milberg 1995; Hutton 1995), and health policy is dominated by the short-termist vulgar economism to be found in almost any arena of public policy and management. This will be balanced in due course (Maynard 1995; Evans 1996; Evans 1997) and we can see the pendulum already swinging back (WHO 1997a).

Another major tension in recent health policy debates relates also to the prevailing short-termist concept of efficiency in health policies and programmes. There is a clear tendency, particularly among donor institutions, to insist on narrowly conceived vertical disease control programmes with expected quickly demonstrable results, without due emphasis on sustainability and the build-up of infrastructures (Vaughan *et al.*, 1995).

The international scene and this book

The report on which this book is based was initiated in 1994 as part of the work involved in preparing the ground for the strengthening of Finland's contribution to international health policy. The international health scene was in a state of flux. It was thought that one useful, quick and feasible way of updating ourselves on key issues in a rapidly changing policy environment would be to take stock of recent international literature in the field.

First, in order to identify the dynamics and moving forces in international health policies and systems, it was important to look at key *actors* among the international organizations. Here, the aim was documentation and analytical description of policy aspects of major organizations, with particular emphasis on the United Nations family.

Second, there was a need to look at certain major policy issues in the current health policy debate. It was thought that particular attention should be given to topical issues such as Health for All (HFA) and comprehensive primary health care (PHC), as opposed to more selective and vertical approaches, and to issues of equity, health improvement and efficiency in so-called health reforms, especially those arising from topics such as essential drugs or reproductive health. All these issues, it was thought, will remain on the policy agenda for years to come.

It was hoped that such a combination of perspectives – on actors and issues – would illustrate similarities or differences, and synergisms or antagonisms, in the roles, missions and policies of different actors. A deliberate choice had to be made regarding the contents of the review. Any choice is partly arbitrary, and the main criterion for inclusion was anticipated policy relevance.

It gives me special pleasure to introduce the report to a much wider audience than was originally planned. I hope the reader will share with me the importance of synthesizing existing knowledge through a systematic account based on a public health perspective and explicit value premises.

2

The World Health Organization (WHO)

WHO is the specialized United Nations agency charged with the 'attainment by all peoples of the highest possible level of health' (WHO, 1994a). The organization came into existence as the result of international cooperation over cholera epidemics and the International Sanitary Conferences. The first International Sanitary Conference was convened in Paris in 1851, and the more permanent organization, the Office International d'Hygiène Publique (OIHP), was set up, also in Paris, in 1907. The first permanent international health organization was actually the Pan American Sanitary Bureau, which was established five years earlier. In the 1920s the League of Nations proposed the formation of a health organization, which met its demise with that of the League. In 1946 the International Conference of Health was convened, with 51 members and 13 non-members of the United Nations represented. The first World Health Assembly was held in 1948. (Siddiqi, 1995; WHO, 1958)

WHO was given a decentralized structure, because the structure of the preceding organization was regionalized within the League of Nations, and because of the existing regional organizations in Europe and America: the OIHP and the Pan American Sanitary Bureau. The Pan American Sanitary Bureau and the Pan American Sanitary Conference formed the Pan American Sanitary Organization, currently known as the Pan American Health Organization (PAHO). While PAHO functions as a regional organization of WHO, it is also a separate and distinct organization in its own right, with its own budget and personnel. The other regions and regional offices are Europe (Copenhagen), Eastern Mediterranean (Alexandria), Africa (Brazzaville), South East Asia (New Delhi) and Western Pacific (Manila). The decentralized structure of WHO, however, has been a subject of debate since the first World Health Assembly (Siddiqi, 1995; WHO, 1958).

The work of WHO is based on its constitution, which assigns equal importance to the normative, coordinating and directing role of the Organization, on one hand, and to its technical cooperation role on the other (Box 2.1.).

Box 2.1 The constitution of WHO
(WHO 1994a)

The States Parties to this constitution declare, in conformity with the Charter of the United Nations, that the following principles are basic to the happiness, harmonious relations and security of all peoples:

Health is a state of complete physical, mental and social well-being and not merely the absence of disease and infirmity.

The enjoyment of the highest attainable standard of health is one of the fundamental rights of every human being without distinction of race, religion, political belief, economic or social condition.

The health of all peoples is fundamental to the attainment of peace and security and is dependent upon the fullest cooperation of individuals and States.

The achievement of any State in the promotion and protection of health is of value to all.

Unequal development in different countries in promotion of health, control of disease, especially communicable disease, is a common danger.

Healthy development of the child is of basic importance; the ability to live harmoniously in a changing total environment is essential to such development.

The extension to all peoples of the benefits of medical, psychological and related knowledge is essential to the fullest attainment of health.

Informed opinion and active cooperation on the part of the public are of the utmost importance in the improvement of the health of the people.

Governments have a responsibility for the health of their peoples which can be fulfilled only by the provision of adequate health and social measures.

Organization

Membership of WHO is open to all states. The governing body of the Organization is the World Health Assembly (WHA), which meets annually to review the Organization's work and to decide on policy, programme and budget (United Nations 1992). In the WHA all members are represented, preferably by persons representing the national health administration of the particular member state. The WHA nominates the members of the Executive Board and appoints the Director General. The 32 individual members of the Executive Board are chosen for three years, taking into account the geographical distribution of member states. The Director General appoints the staff of the Secretariat and, subject to the authority of the Executive Board, acts as the chief technical and administrative officer of the organization. Each regional organization consists of a regional office and a committee composed of representatives of the member states and associate members in the region (WHO 1994a).

It has been noted that within the WHO structure, the members of the Executive Board with a professional background may not have as much influence as the regional level government representatives (Godlee, 1995a). It is also built into the WHO constitution that the Executive Board members serve in their personal capacities, whereas the regional committee delegates represent their governments (WHO, 1994a). The regular budget is first allocated to the regions, which in turn have considerable independence in distributing the funds (Roemer, 1993). The role and exercise of power in the regional offices has been of concern in many evaluations, and claims of politicization of the regional offices have been presented. The strength of the WHO country offices and WHO operations at field level have also been criticized and there have been calls to move more power from the regional to the country level (COWIconsult, 1991; Peabody, 1995). The increase in extra-budgetary funding has also been connected to the donor's wishes to allow more control over spending (Peabody, 1995). The ability of WHO to manage its decentralized democracy (regionalized structure) has been questioned, with claims that the Organization needs to reform its regional structures and make them more accountable both financially and politically (Godlee 1994a).

Over the years, the number of members of WHO has risen to 190 (WHO, 1994b). In the WHA, power is shared on the 'one state – one vote' principle. Although potentially the Third World member states of WHO can override any unpopular resolution, this potential power is counterbalanced by changes in WHO finances. The Third World member states have called increasingly for greater levels of technical assistance, and by 1966 more than half of the budget was devoted to operational activities in less developed countries. According to Walt (1993), this has put the member states in two categories: donors and recipients. The major industrialized countries of the West have great influence within WHO. They have shifted their favour over the past decade, and it has been suggested that the decision-making power be weighted according to the size of the state – measured by population and financial contribution (Lee and Walt, 1992). In addition to voting or funding, power in WHO may be exercised through other channels such as nongovernmental organizations (NGOs) with consultative status or professional and scientific communities. The process of the formulation of the Infant Formula Code, the international code to limit marketing of infant formulas especially in developing countries (WHO, 1981a), may be considered as a good example of the transnational exercise of power by nongovernmental actors, such as pressure groups, networks and industries.

Finances

The budget of WHO includes the regular budget, consisting of assessed contributions by governments, and the extrabudgetary funds, which are made up of voluntary contributions. The regular budget of WHO approved an effective working budget level of US$ 822 million in 1994–5. This represents a decrease of 3.55 per cent in real terms when compared with the approved programme budget for 1992–3 (WHO, 1994b). In 1990 the total WHO regular budget of US$800 million amounted to less than one per cent of the expenditure on health in developing countries (World Bank 1993a). In size, the WHO regular budget is comparable to the budget of the Helsinki University Hospital. It has not grown in real terms since the early 1980s. The major contributors are the USA (25 per cent), Japan (11.7 per cent), Germany (9.18 per cent), France (6.13 per cent) and the United Kingdom (4.77 per cent) (Vaughan *et al.*, 1995). The regular budget for the programme year 1996–7 is US$ 843 million and the programme budget for the financial period of 1996–7 is US$1.836 million in total, with an estimated 6.84 per cent decrease due mainly to the decrease in extrabudgetary funds (WHO, 1995b).

The extrabudgetary funds consist of voluntary donations from governments (79 per cent since inception), other UN agencies, including the World Bank (6 per cent), and other sources, including nongovernmental organizations and the private sector (15 per cent). The major government donors to extrabudgetary funds have been the USA, Sweden, the United Kingdom, the Netherlands, Norway, Denmark, Japan, Canada, Italy and Switzerland. The largest donors, the USA and Sweden, have together provided 27 per cent of the total extrabudgetary funds (Vaughan *et al.*, 1995). The extrabudgetary funds have grown continuously over the past two decades, and in recent years have been estimated to amount to over half of the total budget of WHO (Stenson and Sterky 1993). Most of these funds go to programmes in health promotion and disease prevention and control (Vaughan *et al.*, 1995). According to Walt, the current structure of WHO financing, with its significant amounts of voluntary contributions, tends to raise demands for transparent financial management, and financial issues and budgets often dominate meetings between donors and the WHO Secretariat. There is a tendency to spend more time on financial discipline and budgets than on definition and formulation of policy (Walt 1993).

The WHA and the Executive Board are the only organs within the WHO not receiving extrabudgetary funds. Between two thirds and three quarters of all extrabudgetary funds and about 10 per cent of the regular budget funds have been allocated to nine major programmes. Those nine programmes in 1995 were (Vaughan *et al.*, 1995):

- The three cosponsored programmes: Tropical Diseases Research Programme (TDR), Onchocerciasis Control Programme (OCP), Special Programme on Research, Development and Research Training in Human Reproduction (HRP);

- Five large regular programmes: Emergency and Humanitarian Action Programme (EHA), Global Programme on Vaccines (GPV, former Expanded Programme on Immunization EPI), Division of Diarrhoeal and Acute Respiratory Disease Control (CDR), Action Programme on Essential Drugs (DAP) and Tuberculosis programme (TUB); and

- Global Programme on AIDS (GPA).

On the basis of the 1994–5 programme structure, 51 other programmes received the rest of the extrabudgetary funds and about three quarters of the regular budget funds. It has been noted that while most donor governments remain remarkably stable in their selection of programmes for their extrabudgetary funds, they retain flexibility in the volume of funds allocated, only making commitments for one year at a time. The Swedish decision to reduce its funding in 1995 illustrated the need for a broad funding base for the extrabudgetary programmes, as several of them are substantially reliant on one or a few donors (Vaughan *et al.*, 1995). In 1994 it was decided to transform the GPA to UNAIDS, a programme cosponsored by WHO, UNDP, UNICEF, UNFPA, UNESCO and the World Bank (Bailey, 1994). UNAIDS started in January 1996.

There seems to be some incoherence within the donor countries on the allocation of extrabudgetary funds and policies concerning WHO: the allocations to extrabudgetary funds usually fall under the mandate of development cooperation, whereas WHO policies in general are dealt with by the Ministries of Health (Vaughan *et al.*, 1995). This incoherence may place WHO in a different position from other international agencies as far as the allocation of funds is concerned. This also has implications for policy development in bilateral development cooperation, as WHO policies are often clearly promoted by the Ministries of Health, but may receive lower priority in the respective Ministries of Foreign Affairs responsible for development cooperation. Even though WHO is not a development agency, its global policies, strategies and knowledge base are in danger of being undermined by the increasing efforts towards donor coordination on health policies taking place at forums where donors are represented by functionaries in the field of development cooperation.

Accountability

In principle the WHA voting system makes WHO accountable to all member states. Nevertheless, the possibility of directing funding through extrabudgetary funds has provided another mechanism of funding with implications for accountability. Governments have been requesting also more accountability from the individual WHO programmes for their extrabudgetary funds, rather than requesting this from the Organization as a whole (Vaughan *et al.*, 1995).

Policy

In its early years, WHO was stable and pragmatic, largely disease-oriented and dominated by medical professionals. It was possible to find political consensus in the WHA, with the emphasis being on major disease burdens to which new technologies seemed to be providing solutions. Until the mid-1970s, WHO was able to avoid conflict largely by taking a specifically technical approach to its work. It became increasingly evident, however, that the disease approach to health policy was problematic. Failure in the malaria eradication programme was one example of this (Walt, 1993).

The failure of malaria eradication resulted in an evaluation of the disease-oriented health policies being practised and the formulation of more horizontal policies based on a primary health care approach. These policies were articulated internationally in the 1978 Alma Ata Declaration, and with the adoption of a broader interpretation of the relationships between health, development and community participation (WHO, 1978). In the 1980s the debate on health policies agreed in theory on the fact that the vertical services should be integrated with the comprehensive primary health care policies originally introduced in the Alma Ata Declaration. The additional allocation of funds from the regular budget became problematic after the decision to freeze the regular budget in 1981, however, and the extrabudgetary funding has been allocated more to the disease-oriented programmes than to the programmes supporting the development of health services (Vaughan *et al.*, 1995). Some WHO programmes, at both headquarters and country level, were run in a vertical fashion, and programmes such as CDR and the EPI were relatively centralized and not integrated into primary health care. According to Walt (1993), the extent to which this has been due to the undermining of primary health care policies by bilateral donors supporting these programmes remains unclear; nevertheless, it seems that there were also significant and avoidable contradictions within the Organization. This may be found in the rhetoric of demedicalization, for example, accompanying increasing dominance of doctors. Also, the division whose major responsibility was the implementation of primary health care was never given the top-level leadership and support that it needed in order to integrate activities across WHO (Walt, 1993).

The period from the mid-1970s to the end of 1980s was characterized by the transformation of WHO into a more political organization. By the mid-1970s, a change in health policy had led to a broader interpretation of the relationships between health and development, a trend which culminated in the primary health care approach. An International Code on infant formula foods was passed by the WHA in 1981 (by 118 votes to 1: the USA objected). The next 'political battle' was fought over essential drugs policies. As the United States is the largest contributor to the agency's funding, its stated objection to both the infant formula code and essential drugs policies made the issue problematic (Walt, 1993). In the early 1980s the cancelled publication of a study on the global alcohol industry created further controversy (Selvaggio, 1984). In 1986 the WHA consensus condemned the distribution of free and subsidized breastmilk substitutes to maternity wards and hospitals (WHO, 1987a). The infant food campaign also brought consumer groups into WHO – to challenge the multinational companies (Walt, 1993). Nevertheless, there have been claims of increasing influence by industrial firms as representatives of nongovernmental organizations (NGOs) – for example, through their participation in the consultations on infant feeding within WHO (Allain, 1991; see also Chapter 10). In 1996 the WHA voted unanimously for the stronger implementation of the baby milk code and against the involvement of commercial interests in its supervision and evaluation after problems had been reported in several countries.

During the 1970s and 1980s WHO was part of the larger politicization debate which involved several United Nations agencies and focused on politically sensitive issues within the WHA and the perceived ineffectiveness of the agency. In 1976, the debate on health care among Arabs in the Israeli-occupied territories led to accusations by the US ambassador that WHO was becoming 'politicized'. In the 1980s politicization claims related to resolutions on 'Health conditions of the Arab population in the occupied Arab territories, including Palestine', 'Repercussions on health of economic and political sanctions between States' and 'Liberation struggle in southern Africa: assistance to the frontline States, Lesotho and Swaziland' (Siddiqi, 1995). The WHO report on the health impact of nuclear war also created tensions, with different views clashing on the importance of the issue to the concerns of the Organization (Siddiqi, 1995, Williams, 1987).

As far as the different regions are concerned, it has been noted that the

Health for All initiative has had its greatest impact in the European region, though the European countries originally resisted the interference of WHO and perceived the HFA policies as an initiative for the Third World only (Godlee, 1995b). The European region of WHO has also been active in developing and promoting the Healthy Cities project (Tsouros, 1995; Kickbush, 1989). The Healthy Cities project and the Ottawa Declaration on Health Promotion in 1986 resemble the Alma Ata Declaration in their emphasis on a broader collective approach to health and intersectoral action, but take an even broader public health perspective on the issues. The Ottawa Declaration has been followed by subsequent conferences on Healthy Public Policies (Adelaide in 1988), Health Promotion in Developing Countries (Geneva in 1989) and by the Sundsvall statement on supportive environments in health (Anon, 1991).

The period since Hiroshi Nakajima took office in 1988 has been characterized by a return to a more technological and managerial approach (Walt, 1993). Nakajima has been expected to favour the viewpoints of the USA and Japan and, as the former director of the Nippon Roche research department, to be more sympathetic to the pharmaceutical industry. The election of Nakajima to the presidency has been criticized heavily and openly. An editorial in the *British Medical Journal* reported that the international donors would consider transferring funds to other agencies, such as the World Bank, if Nakajima were re-elected in 1993 (Godlee, 1993a). The criticism of Nakajima has focused on communication and managerial issues, but there have also been allegations of corruption and dominant national interests in the actions of the Director General (Godlee, 1993b; *Lancet*, 1995a). Since his re-election in 1993, Nakajima's position has not become easier, and there has been increasing criticism in a series of articles in the *British Medical Journal*. At the World Health Assembly in 1995 Nakajima also faced attacks by a number of African delegations on his statements concerning the abilities of Africans (Godlee and Carnall, 1995). Some countries have also shifted their support: for example, Sweden is a major supporter of the Joint United Nations Programme on Aids (UNAIDS) for the fiscal years 1995–6 (Awuonda 1995).

Much attention has been paid recently to WHO's move from the 'full menu' health policy approach to a more focused attack on priority areas (Godlee, 1997a). There is also a danger, however, that in this priority setting process some key elements in the definition of WHO policies may be surrendered to other organizations, further limiting WHO's capacity to act as the global health organization. In some circles there has been active discussion of the implications of other international health agencies, and how the division of labour between these agencies can be improved (Frenk *et al.*, 1997; Rockefeller Foundation, 1996). But, to what extent will the aim of dividing responsibility for health issues enhance, in practice, the fragmentation linked with the disease-oriented approach? Will it merely legitimize a role for other agencies in health policy issues? If WHO has spread its resources too thinly, the reasons for this may lie in the magnitude of the resources as well as in the limited professional resources available for analysis, evaluation and synthesis work. While there clearly is a need to increase the flexibility and responsiveness of WHO, this should not be achieved through dismantling the Organization.

The WHO core policy of Health for All is under a renewal, and the revised HFA policy will be discussed by the WHA in 1998. In January 1997, the Executive Board held a meeting on the issue which endorsed the value base of HFA policies as well as the necessity of reinforcing the WHO leadership in global health policies (see Chapter 8). The year 1998 will be crucial for WHO's future as well as its role in making global health policies. In addition, as Hiroshi Nakajima has announced that he will not seek another term, a new Director General will be chosen in 1998 (Walgate, 1997). While the 1996 Report focused on communicable diseases and the 1997 World Health Report on non-communicable diseases, there has been a renewed emphasis on developing health systems and healthy public policies in 1996-7, with implications for future action within the organization.

Concerns and constraints

The confusion over mandates has been brought up in several studies (Lee *et al.* 1996; Nordic, 1991; Frenk *et al.*, 1997) The Nordic study on the United Nations agencies (1991) suggests a clearer division of labour between the specialized and development agencies. The study concludes that the traditional normative and informative roles of specialized agencies have been reduced while their technical cooperation activities with developing countries have increased. As these activities are largely supported through voluntary contributions, this development has meant that the funding base of the agencies has become increasingly reliant on outside sources.

The functions of WHO are often described as a mixture of normative activities and technical assistance. Often these are interpreted erroneously as a separate entity. The normative functions are referred to in the constitution as 'directing and coordinating international health work' (WHO, 1994a). The normative activities have been described as those developed and carried out at regional and global headquarter levels, which define the scientific and technical excellence bases of health programmes, and which provide the necessary leadership, information, organization, promotion and coordination. They deal with ideas, values, goals, standards and advocacy, and influence the health programmes of all member states (Sterky *et al.*, 1996a).

Research capacity and contact with research institutions are important to a knowledge-based organization like WHO. Attention has been drawn recently to WHO's research capacity, from 'counting the dead by the year 2000' to more effective analysis of multidisciplinary research into health, health services, and health policies at global and national levels (Sterky *et al.*, 1996b; Frenk *et al.*, 1997; Seventh Consultative Committee, 1997; Brown, 1997). Capacity to research and analyse is important: it would be problematic if WHO were to be responsible mainly for biomedical research, while research on health policies, health services and the health impacts of other sectoral policies became the domain of other actors. There is clearly a demand for WHO to provide a research synthesis and clearing house function as a basis for normative guidance on policy level choices and issues of sustainability and equity in health. The Ljubljana conference in the European region is an example of such activities (WHO, 1996b).

In future, increasing cooperation in the field of research may be expected, involving not only United Nations agencies but also private funds and other nongovernmental organizations such as the Council of Health Research for Development (COHRED). There is concern, however, over sources of funding (conventional public sources vs. industry-related funding), due to the role of research work in the orientation of future health policies and technological development. Research which is focused predominantly on biomedical issues will provide predominantly biomedical solutions. Large policy choices may be influenced by the private research financing and support they attract during product development. If WHO is to fulfil its function as a normative and rule-setting agency and provide services on policy analysis, research and assessment, it is important that sufficient independent resources, both human and material, are guaranteed. Otherwise there is a danger that WHO research work may provide public support to private interests or fashionable research areas which may act against rather than support the aims and the value base of the organization.

Technical and normative functions

Some donors believe that WHO has shifted too far towards implementing programmes and in the process has become increasingly irrelevant to their interests. Nevertheless, the normative role of WHO and the continued provision of technical assistance are likely to remain important functions of the organization (Lee and Walt, 1992). There have been pressures to construct a more country-based role, along the lines of the development agencies, and this option has been under scrutiny in WHO during the 1990s. Many less developed countries have had concerns about the quality and quantity of the assistance offered. WHO is said to be slow and cautious in responding to countries' needs (Lee and Walt, 1992). It has been argued that WHO should undertake a fundamental review of the role of regional offices and should strengthen non-medical professional resources (COWIconsult, 1991; Peabody, 1995). According to a Danish study, despite WHO's advocacy of a health policy approach, the organization in practice has failed to take the lead on the country level. At field level the WHO role as a lead agency has been limited to selected global programmes, and lack of analytical capacity and of willingness to engage in critical policy dialogue has prevented WHO from acquiring greater influence on other donors' policies in the health sector. As the level of technical skills in many countries is currently rising, more management and capacity-building advice are needed – but WHO's centralized structure and lack of formal authority and professional capacity at the country level have contributed to its marginalization (COWIconsult, 1991).

In the Nordic study, WHO was found to have the greatest orientation towards technical cooperation activities (75 per cent) among the specialized agencies (Nordic, 1991). It has been argued that WHO should limit its role as a channel for technical assistance and should strengthen and clarify its normative and research-oriented role. It is suggested that WHO should make better use of the conventions, regulations, recommendations and reporting mechanisms on questions such as the regulation of advertising and labelling of pharmaceuticals in international trade. There is concern, too, over the minor (2 per cent) share of regular budget resources allocated to research. The specific research programmes TDR and HRP are dominated by a biomedical and clinical approach. It is suggested that WHO could have a normative function as a research council and a role as a coordinator of global scientific efforts, a clearing house for scientific information, a quality controller, a watchdog on ethics and an advocate for under-researched areas of global significance (Stenson and Sterky, 1993).

Finances and extrabudgetary funds

In spite of the emphasis on budgetary reforms and zero budget growth in past years, the WHO is to a large extent value for money to its member states. It is clear that effective, well-researched and sustainable global level activity is compromised severely by a level of funding comparable to a well-equipped university hospital. WHO personnel number around 5,000, half the amount of the sales force of a large pharmaceutical company (*Financial Times,* 1997). The need for funding may increase the temptation of private partnerships and sponsoring, which is problematic with respect to equity, normative functions and the orientation of global health policies, as well as to WHO's role as a public interest organization. It needs to be considered whether enhancing private partnerships may imply not only diversion of priorities and the vulnerability of WHO's normative role, but also the misallocation of public funds. This does not mean that the private sector can be ignored: there is a clear need for improvement in WHO's liaison with it, including a need for clear policy and transparency in practice.

Concerns have been raised about the effect of the large proportion of extra-budgetary funds (EBFs) on the scope of the Organization's work. According to a study sponsored by several member states, EBFs have played an essential role in contributing to WHO's comparative advantage, namely its global role in policy formulation and development, both for common global needs and in support of technical cooperation with low-income countries. Whereas WHO's direct role in providing countries with assistance, including those activities supported by EBFs, may be comparatively small, the indirect benefits to other international organizations using WHO 'products' have been considerable. The study concludes that there should not be any overall reduction in the EBFs contributed by donors to WHO. In addition, given the importance of reforming health systems, additional EBFs should be contributed in order to strengthen such aspects of technical cooperation, and to encourage pro-grammes giving more attention to this aspect of their work. It was further emphasized that the Organization has not taken the necessary corrective action to achieve sufficient integration between programmes, nor has it given adequate support to making primary health care strategies more responsive to the changing policy context. EBFs were found to have contributed to the emphasis on vertically managed programmes and on disease control activities. Donor involvement was found to have had many beneficial effects on management practices, particularly in those programmes with a large volume of EBFs, through clearer objectives, more transparency and better account-ability. Thus, according to this evaluation, the main issue is not the effects of EBFs on the Organization, but rather the lack of authority and leadership exerted by the WHA, the Executive Board and the Director General over the whole Organization. Such leadership would affect the use, distribution and accountable management of all funds, including extrabudgetary funds (Vaughan *et al.*, 1995).

Crisis and leadership

In addition to criticizing the Director General, several authors have com-mented on the crisis of WHO in the 1990s. They have stressed the need for WHO and the importance of the agency's regaining its role and significance in international health policies (*Lancet*, 1995a; Walt, 1993; Godlee, 1994b; Godlee, 1994c). The most visible critique of WHO has probably been that contained in the *British Medical Journal* series (Godlee, 1994a–d; Godlee, 1995a–d; Smith 1995). The WHO response regarded this as the start of a campaign for a Director General candidate and attacked what it considered to be biased sources, interpretations and mistakes in the series (Kickbush, 1995).

It is clear that not all of the critique is constructive and that the critics may have very different aims. The different interest groups in the health policy area – including professional and scientific groups, other development organizations, NGOs and, especially, the health-related industries – may have their own contrasting aims for the future work of WHO (or any of the other international organizations discussed elsewhere in this book). For example, the alcohol and tobacco industries, as well as some of the pharmaceutical companies, might have no objections if WHO were to concentrate more on disease-oriented priorities and operational activities in developing countries. Some of the criticism focusing on the bureaucratic aspects and inefficiency of WHO is tied in closely with general criticism of the United Nations. Nevertheless, the large number of rulings against WHO and PAHO by the International Labour Organization (ILO) Administrative Tribunal over the past six years are cause for concern, as they reveal an inadequate regard for the rights of staff members and have consequences for the standing, resources and effectiveness of the organizations themselves (Samson, 1995).

In the 1980s and 1990s, the bilateral agencies have turned increasingly to the World Bank for policy guidance on issues concerning health care development in developing countries. The Bank will have substantial support among donors and a significant role in coordinating the policies to be implemented. Especially since the publication of the *Investing in Health* World Development Report in 1993 (World Bank, 1993a), the World Bank has been acknowledged as the leading agency in health sector development (*Lancet,* 1993a). Whether or not the increased health-related activities of the World Bank are a result of WHO advocacy – as has been claimed by WHO representatives (Kickbush, 1995) – this trend seems to be putting WHO into the position of the leading specialized agency on biomedical and clinical issues, and turning it towards low-profile action as a cooperative and ancillary technical agency carrying out international health policies. According to Stenson and Sterky, the other actors (the World Bank, UNICEF and the European Union) have taken on important roles in areas such as policy analysis, health economics and health planning and management (Stenson and Sterky, 1993).

Cooperation and partnerships

WHO receives funding from other United Nations agencies for its extra-budgetary programmes, most notably from UNDP and UNFPA (Vaughan *et al.,* 1995). It also participates in joint initiatives (Safe Motherhood, for example) and cosponsored programmes (EPI, HRP, TDR) with other international organizations, indicating an issue-specific level of cooperation on both formal and informal levels. WHO also shares intersectoral activities with the

FAO in Codex Alimentarius and with the ILO and UNEP in the International Forum on Chemical Safety. In addition, it is claimed, the World Bank and UNICEF have taken over the coordination role from WHO and the UNDP in the UN Initiative on Africa in health reforms, in spite of the fact that WHO and the UNDP have the official mandate (Buse and Walt, 1996). There is an increasing tendency for United Nations organizations to look for partnerships and cooperation in programmes, initiatives and activities. All partnerships are not equal, however, and mere participation does not necessarily imply that one has a say in the definition of policies and priorities, or in the planning and implementation of programmes.

Cooperation with industry has been evident in the OCP, for which the drugs were donated by the manufacturer, and in the active approach to finding more private sector support for the funding of new financial arrangements for health within the TDR and inter-agency health research initiatives (Godal, 1994). In 1994 WHO also announced a partnership with the International Federation of Pharmaceutical Manufacturers (IFPMA) to combat AIDS by the means of research, development, marketing and distribution of HIV/AIDS drugs and vaccines (WHO, 1994c). The ethical aspects of research practices on AIDS in developing countries, however, have raised controversy between WHO and some multinational companies in 1997 (Johnston and Nicoll, 1997). WHO, according to its constitution, has norm and standard setting functions in health-related issues. In order to perform that task, WHO needs to remain sufficiently independent of those industries on whose conduct the norms and standards have concrete effects. There has been concern over the position and role of the manufacturing industries in the International Programme of Chemical Safety (IPCS) (Watterson, 1993; Abrams *et al.*, 1996). In the late 1980s the development assistance given by WHO has been seen as supporting a stronger role for transnational companies (TNCs) (Lee, 1995). As described in Chapter 10, already the TNCs have undertaken the task of harmonizing and norm-setting for the licensing documentation on drug policies, while WHO has been given observer status. The problem of support by industries has also been brought up in relation to choices and the development process concerning the oral rehydration therapy strategy (Werner *et al.*, 1997).

In addition to relations with the private sector, there is also a need for improvement of WHO practices in liaison with NGOs. The foundations for collaboration were laid in 1948 at the first health assembly, at which a statement of principles was adopted to guide WHO's formal and informal relations with NGOs. The statement of principles established a formal status, defined as an official relationship with WHO, and set out procedures for admission to this relationship (United Nations, 1994b). Between 1949 and 1969, the number of NGOs with official consultative status rose from 18 to 82

(Lee and Walt, 1992). The role of the NGOs was extended in the late 1970s, when WHO began to call on the expertise of the nongovernmental sector (Walt, 1993). In 1994 the NGOs maintaining official relations with WHO represented a large variety of international-level organizations ranging from professional, scientific, biomedical and general development organizations to those representing health-related industries (United Nations, 1994b). While WHO work with nongovernmental organizations has been continuous and on certain issues is very close, there could be more scope for improving and extending the relations to more policy-oriented organizations with special reference to the Southern, more recently formed NGOs and their coalitions. WHO mechanisms for dealing with NGOs could be broadened in terms of requirements, procedures and dialogue. In the environmental field liaison mechanisms have been structured around liaison centres:, considering the multitude of NGOs working in the health and social sectors, such an approach might be as relevant in these areas.

Challenges and future prospects

In 1993 the WHA endorsed a report from a working group on WHO response to global change (WHO, 1993a). This report included 47 recommendations which were implemented between 1993 and 1996. Further questions have been posed, however, in relation to these changes and the extent to which they have become institutionalized. One of the latest reform visions is that of the Swedish WHO project, which foresees a less centralized, less hierarchical Global Health Organization, more streamlined and 'planetarized', with smaller units clustered around a Global Health Assembly resembling the current WHA (Sterky *et al.*, 1996a). Further suggestions for organizational changes and reform will emerge, and there is no doubt that there are many structures and practices in WHO in need of reform. Reform proposals have emerged from the organization itself (Godlee, 1997b). There is, however, a danger that a constant process of reform will become merely a new means of streamlining and tightening power within the organization, with less effectiveness, increased sidetracking and a predatory organizational culture.

WHO has reacted to the growing need for more visibility and for publications aimed at a broader public by initiating an annual *World Health Report* since 1995. The first of these, *Bridging the Gaps* (WHO, 1995a) is to be welcomed as an initial step in disseminating WHO knowledge and in public advocacy concerning health. The Division of Intensified Cooperation with Countries in Greatest Need (ICO) can be seen as a response both to country-level needs in less developed countries and to demands for a broader and more dynamic approach in WHO policies, including professional competence in health economics (ICO, 1995).

In 1996 further administrative reorganization had led to a new health systems development programme structure, with three main Divisions: Analysis, Research and Assessment (ARA), Organization and Management of Health Systems (OHS) and Strategic Support to Countries in Greatest Need (SSC). The new core allows a more coherent and integrated development of health systems within WHO. In order to meet expectations, however, the organization needs to prioritize its allocation of regular and extrabudgetary funds more effectively. The grouping of programmes concerning the health of women, adolescents and children, as well as those concerning reproductive health and nutrition, under a single Division (Family and Reproductive Health), is another example of administrative reorganization.

It is clear that the role of WHO as a global forum on health-related issues and decision making could be strengthened and more emphasis placed on the development and monitoring of international codes. It may also be argued that WHO has underestimated its potential role in global advocacy on health and in monitoring equity in health and access to health care. WHO seems inadvertently to narrow its role, becoming the World Health Ministries Organization instead of the World Health Organization. In order to fulfil its role as a knowledge-based organization, WHO needs capacities to analyse, synthesize and act on health policy issues of a complex social, cultural and political nature. Its complement of professionals is not very large and, in certain key policy areas such as health systems development, it is clearly inadequate.

There is scope for WHO as a global forum and proactive actor in global health policies if the Organization is both willing and able to go beyond its more technically interpreted role. At a time when industries have increasing opportunities to make their influence felt, the status of WHO's normative role should be of concern. WHO's role in assessing the development of health services, health technologies, choices in treatment and ethical or legal issues – as well as the health implications of trade policies, multilateral agreements, multilateral development plans and programmes or sectoral policies – could be increasingly important. Although the international atmosphere is not supportive of regulatory tasks, increasing globalization will necessitate an emphasis on international agreements and global organizations capable of reaching beyond national, regional or commercial concerns.

Visible, fast and sophisticated phenomena often take precedence in the media. There is thus a danger that the work of WHO will be guided by its reputation in high-tech medical research, disease eradication, vaccination programmes and curative treatments for major diseases. While this may secure a mandate for WHO as a technical agency in the biomedical field, the priorities and general context of action are defined elsewhere. The search for specific cures and preventive measures tends to dominate the biomedical professional approach. Disease-oriented approaches emphasize vertical programmes, however, and can undermine functioning health infrastructures, which form the basis and prerequisite for more sustainable results as well as for effective implementation of the more vertical programmes. Furthermore, the bio-medical approach often ignores the broader environmental and social context, a neglect which is conducive to the reemergence and spread of the diseases that have been 'cured'.

The WHO task force on health and development has identified four target areas: (1) equity in health and market forces; (2) the quality of life and health security of specific population groups; (3) accountability for health; and (4) health and peace (WHO, 1994d). Whether and how WHO should address the issues concerning health and development in the broader context remains a crucial question for WHO's future orientation. If the determinants of diseases are defined by global, national and local level processes beyond the health services, it is clearly within WHO's mandate to assess, advocate and in some cases even to intervene. This is of relevance especially to the global-level policies, rule-making and agenda-setting of organizations such as the World Trade Organization (WTO) and multilateral agreements such as those on environmental issues. The WHO Task Force on Health in Development, in its report to the WHO Executive Board, presented its vision of WHO providing advocacy for a global culture of health based on 'health security', reducing inequities in health status, determining global standards and norms on technical and ethical issues, formulating criteria to guide policy and decision making in matters related to health, acting as a catalyst for policy making, providing clearing-house services for researchers, and being, in general, the 'health caretaker and conscience' (WHO, 1997b).

In the ninth general programme of work covering the period 1995–2000, the four policy orientations which provide the WHO framework are: (1) inte-grating health and human development public policies; (2) ensuring equitable access to health services; (3) promoting and protecting health; and (4) preventing and controlling specific health problems (WHO, 1994e) Leader-ship issues have caused concern in the 1990s and a new Director General will be elected in 1998. The challenge faced by the Organization will not be met by replacing the regional directors and the Director General. The real challenge is to increase the accountability of WHO's own practices to reflect its policies more truly. In order to act as the international public health agency, committed to reducing existing inequities in health and promoting access to health care, WHO not only needs to accept the value-based nature of its work, but also needs to gain more understanding of the broader determinants of health equity and access in the contexts where the health policies are practised.

3

The World Bank

The establishment of the World Bank and the International Monetary Fund (IMF) was agreed at the same meeting in Bretton Woods in 1944 (Mason and Asher, 1973). The World Bank consists of the International Bank for Reconstruction and Development (IBRD) and the International Development Association (IDA), but also includes the International Finance Corporation (IFC) and the Multilateral Investment Guarantee Agency (MIGA) (World Bank, 1995a).

The IDA is in practice a fund administered by the World Bank. Its creation was a major step in the evolution of the World Bank itself, marking the beginning of the transformation of that institution from something resembling a bank into a development agency. Unlike the IBRD, which could meet its resource requirements through bond issues in capital markets, the IDA's resources were limited to governmental budgetary contributions (Mistry, 1995). The IDA was established in 1960 to provide assistance primarily to the poorer developing countries on terms that would bear less heavily on the balance of payments than those of the IBRD. It shares the World Bank staff and operates under its rules, with control and decision making resting with the main contributors (World Bank, 1981). Before the IDA was established there were proposals for a Special United Nations Fund for Economic and Social Development (SUNFED), which would differ markedly from the World Bank in the sense that control would be shared equally between 'major contributors' and other members, and funds would be available largely as grants on 'soft' terms. The debate over SUNFED led to the establishment of the United Nations Special Fund (subsequently constituted as UNDP) as the principal channel for United Nations technical assistance and to the IDA as a soft-loan window for the World Bank (Adams 1994).

The World Bank operates worldwide and in 1995 it had 178 member countries (World Bank, 1995a). In contrast with the other development organizations working in the health area, such as WHO and UNICEF, the

Box 3.1. Extracts from the Articles of Agreement of the International Bank for Reconstruction and Development (IBRD) and International Development Association (IDA)
(Mason and Asher, 1973; IDA, 1960).

IBRD
Article 1. Purposes
The purposes of the Bank are:

(i) To assist in the reconstruction and development of territories of members by facilitating the investment of capital for productive purposes, including the restoration of economies destroyed or disrupted by war, the reconversion of productive facilities to peacetime needs and the encouragement of the development of productive facilities and resources in less developed countries.

(ii) To promote private foreign investment by means of guarantees or participations in loans and other investments made by private investors; and when private capital is not available on reasonable terms, to supplement private investment by providing, on suitable conditions, finance for productive purposes out of its own capital, funds raised by it and its other resources.

(iii) To promote the long-range balanced growth of international trade and the maintenance of equilibrium in balances of payments by encouraging international investment for the development of productive resources of members, thereby assisting in raising productivity, the standard of living and conditions of labour in their countries.

(iv) To arrange the loans made or guaranteed by it in relation to international loans through other channels so that the more useful and urgent projects, large and small alike, will be dealt with first.

(v) To conduct its operations with due regard to the effect of international investment on business conditions in the territories of members and, in the immediate postwar years, to assist in bringing about a smooth transition from a wartime to a peacetime economy.

The Bank shall be guided in all its decisions by the purposes set forth above

Article IV. Operations
Section 10. Political activity prohibited
The Bank and its officers shall not interfere in the political affairs of any member; nor shall they be influenced in their decisions by the political character of the member or members concerned. Only economic considerations shall be relevant to their decisions, and these considerations shall be weighed impartially in order to achieve the purposes stated in Article 1.

IDA
Article 1. Purposes
The purposes of the International Development Association are to promote

economic development, increase productivity and thus raise standards of living in the less-developed areas of the world included within the Association's membership, in particular by providing finance to meet the important development requirements on terms which are more flexible and bear less heavily on the balance of payments than those of conventional loans, thereby furthering the developmental objectives of the International Bank for Reconstruction and Development and supplementing its activities.

The Association shall be guided in all its decisions by the provisions of this Article.

World Bank does not have a clear mandate for health as such, and therefore its role in health matters needs to be legitimized by other arguments, preferably economic. Its original mandate is governed by Articles of Agreement, in which the roles and the aims of its actions are defined (Box 3.1) According to the Articles of Agreement decisions in the World Bank should not be made on political, but strictly on economic grounds. The Bank staff includes over 5,000 professionals, but the professional staff working on the areas of population, health and nutrition number about 300, with a small core staff with an educational background and long experience in health (Buse, 1994; Vaughan *et al.*, 1995).

Organization

Since the 1980s the World Bank has regarded itself as the major funding agency for population and health issues (World Bank, 1980). The World Bank is officially one of the United Nations agencies, but in practice it has kept a greater distance. According to Bradlow and Grossman, the Relationship Agreement between the Bretton Woods institutions and the United Nations, while acknowledging that the Bretton Woods Institutions (the World Bank and the IMF) are specialized agencies of the United Nations, requires them to 'consider' United Nations decisions and recommendations (Bradlow and Grossman, 1996) – though the United Nations was never allowed to play any significant role of supervision and coordination in relation to the World Bank and the IMF (Adams 1994).

In the World Bank, the share of voting power is determined by the amount of funding. The voting power is exercised by a Board of Governors, which used to number twelve, but whose size has been raised to 24 as more and more countries have joined the Bank. Even though voting power is formally vested in its Board of Governors, greater authority is delegated to its 17 Executive

Directors. Each of the five members of the Bank having the largest numbers of shares of the Bank stock is allowed to appoint an Executive Director (Brown, 1992). Despite the increasing number of governors, the ten richest countries still have over 50 per cent of the voting power. In the IBRD the share of votes of the USA, Japan, Germany, France and the United Kingdom was almost 40 per cent and in IDA slightly over 40 per cent in 1994. Finland, Sweden, Denmark, Norway, Latvia, Lithuania and Iceland share one governor, together with 4.6 per cent of the votes (World Bank ,1994a).

Finances

IBRD members finance the organization through subscriptions to its capital stock, but only 10 per cent of each member's subscription is actually paid into the Bank. Most of the money lent (90 per cent) is raised by IBRD borrowing in private capital markets. This corresponds to the portion of each member's capital subscription, which is payable only in the event that the Bank needs the additional funds to meet its financial commitments to borrowers ('callable capital'). The IBRD loans recycle funds borrowed in private capital markets, and because of this the institution must charge a rate of interest for its loans which corresponds to market conditions. The IDA's resources come almost entirely from voluntary contributions by donor governments. The funds contributed at any given time do not last very long, and so there is a need for additional contributions, called 'replenishments', every few years (Brown, 1992). In the 1980s and 1990s debt repayments have also meant that an increasing amount of funds has been cycled back from the developing countries. In addition, while IDA loans are given on softer terms, IDA funding comes to a large extent from the same sources as funding to other United Nations agencies. This means that, in principle, these funds could be used through another multilateral channel. In 1995, the largest subscriptions to capital stock in World Bank were made by the USA (17.5 per cent), Japan (6.4 per cent), Germany (5.0 per cent), France (4.7 per cent) and the United Kingdom (4.7 per cent) (World Bank, 1995a). The same countries were also the major subscribers and contributors to IDA in 1995 (World Bank, 1995a).

World Bank funding in the areas of health, nutrition and population increased rapidly in the late 1980s from US$103 million in new commitments in 1981–4 to an annual average of US$1.307 million during the fiscal period 1991–4 (World Bank, 1994a). It has been claimed that, through cofinancing, the Bank controls more funds than its lending portfolio suggests. In 1991, 29 projects were approved in the health sector at a total value of US$3.3 billion, less than half of which was committed by the Bank (Buse, 1994). In addition to the funds committed by the World Bank and other donors, the policies and projects of the World Bank tie substantial amounts of funds in the recipient countries. In 1980 the Bank financed on average 40 per cent of its projects, with the larger part of funding raised by the developing country from its own resources (World Bank, 1981). The IBRD loans must be made to, or guaranteed by, the government concerned, and IDA credits are made only to governments (World Bank 1981).

The World Bank's operations as a bank also shape its policies and actions. As a bank, the World Bank needs to lend if it is to maintain its profitability, whereas with a net negative transfer of resources it may not be considered as a development institution. Consistently since 1987 the IBRD has recorded net negative transfers (after taking interest payments into account, it has been extracting monetary resources from its borrowers rather than providing them), and these have escalated from about US$1.5 billion in 1987 to over US$8.6 billion in 1994. These transfers were large, particularly in the case of those to Latin America and East Asia. The World Bank soft-loan window, the IDA, which provides funds on highly concessional terms, has recorded substantial positive overall net transfers, however, which until 1990 enabled the World Bank as a group to show positive overall net transfers. Nevertheless, in the fiscal years 1992–4 transfers for the whole group were negative, and in 1994 amounted to US$3.9 billion (Mistry, 1995).

While the World Bank's role as a financing institution creates pressures to lend, the organization seems to incline towards the path of a development institution in terms of policy analysis and advice. This, on the other hand, raises the issues of its mandate in relation to the United Nations specialized agencies and whether the World Bank should or can provide policy prescriptions in broadly different areas such as education, health, social services, transport, the environment and rural development.

Accountability

The accountability of the IBRD is reflected in the fact that it obtains most of its funds through borrowing in the world's capital markets (World Bank, 1981). The share in funding and the weighted voting system indicate accountability towards the major contributors. Lending practices within the World Bank may also be seen to be more accountable in terms of economics and efficiency and not necessarily as much in other terms such as long-term development results or equity. Moreover, in general, the governments are to be considered as accountable for the outcome of World Bank projects and loans, though there is an increasing trend for the World Bank to be held accountable, due to the loan conditions and its major role in the formulation and implementation of the projects and policy changes.

Policy

According to Ayres, the dominant ideology, widely shared throughout the Bank, may be identified as that of neoliberalism. The principal objective of such neoliberalism is economic growth. The domestic route to growth is seen as capital accumulation (through savings and investments), while the external route is export expansion and diversification. The ingredients of neoliberalism that derive from these basic goals – and are reflected in most Bank documents, publications, and interviews with Bank staff and officials – include fiscal and monetary probity ('getting the prices right', or removing obstacles to the free-market determination of prices, wages, interest rates, user charges for public services, and so forth); a sound currency; external economic equilibrium; expert dynamism; economic stability; and, permeating all of these, a favourable investment climate. Deviations from any of these elements constitute deviations from prevalent Bank norms and are likely to be the subject of dialogue between the Bank and the deviating country. It was found, however, that the vast majority of World Bankers flatly reject the notion that these ingredients indicate an ideology. In their view, as expressed in repeated interviews, all of this is neutral. It is simply sound economic and financial management, technocratically orchestrated and applicable to any kind of economic system, be it capitalist, socialist, the 'third way', or whatever. This technocratic neoliberalism is tenacious; certainly it has not been discarded as a result of the reorientations, actual and proposed, of Bank activities since 1973 (Ayres, 1983).

Ayres's observations date to the times when the World Bank was committed to the more socially oriented redistribution with growth agenda; in the 1970s this included an emphasis on poverty alleviation. During the early 1980s the poverty orientation declined and the economic policies became tougher, until in the mid-1980s there were increasing calls for the protection of the vulnerable during the process of stabilization and adjustment. During the late 1980s and 1990s issues such as poverty, environment and health reemerged on the agenda, most notably in the published World Development Reports and increased funding allocations (World Bank, 1989, 1992a, 1993a). In some areas, such as health and social development, there have been different emphases and policy prescriptions within the organization as well as open recognition of problems, such as those amongst countries in transition (World Bank, 1996a). In general, however, the World Bank policies in the 1980s and 1990s do not indicate that substantial shifts have taken place in the policy orientation of the organization as whole (World Bank, 1987; Gibbon, 1993; Brohman, 1995; Bloom, 1991; Laurell and Lopez-Arellano, 1996; Smith, 1996).

The World Bank's focus on lending and priorities has changed over the years. In the 1950s and 1960s the project-based lending was primarily for infrastructural and industrial investments. In the 1960s and 1970s the projects branched out into the financing of agriculture and also to the social sector (education, population, nutrition and health). In the 1980s direct funding of health was started, but this decade was one of policy-based lending in terms of structural and sectoral adjustment programmes. In the late 1980s and 1990s newer development priorities (such as environmental protection, gender sensitivity and good governance requirements) have been incorporated as a result of pressure from developed country governments and NGOs (Mistry, 1995).

The World Bank focus on lending and activities has also been linked to the preferences of the World Bank presidents. Robert MacNamara broadened the World Bank agenda and activities in the 1960s and 1970s. In spite of the stated poverty focus, however, the increased lending and the orientation of lending practices resulted in many problem projects and criticism of World Bank project lending in the 1980s (Payer, 1985; Rich, 1994; Ayres, 1983; Mosley *et al.,* 1991). In the 1980s the World Bank directors had a lower public profile, but in the 1990s the choice of James Wolfensohn as President raised expectations amongst the critics of the World Bank, especially in relation to greater emphasis on dialogue with nongovernmental actors and emphasis on poverty and social issues. Wolfensohn has been well placed *vis-à-vis* the influential actors in the international community and resource base, with current or past formal links to the Bilderberg group, the Population Council and the Rockefeller Foundation (World Bank, 1997). In addition to building up a more 'human face' for the World Bank, the Wolfensohn policies have also been oriented towards promoting private sector development (Wolfensohn 1996), which has drawn attention to the increasing role of the private sector parts of the World Bank group, namely the IFC and MIGA. According to Caufield, Wolfensohn has launched specific efforts to change management within the organization. However, his determination to make the World Bank efficient and responsive has not been matched by a coherent vision of what the World Bank should be doing to achieve the poverty reduction which he has spoken about so often. Neither has he addressed the contradictions which have led to increasing indebtedness and exacerbated the gap between the rich and the poor (Caufield, 1996). Focus on the private sector may not only mean less funds for public sector development, but also that more attention is diverted towards private sector actors and health projects.

Part of the World Bank policy dialogue is conducted through research and country-specific or sector-specific analysis. The World Bank research work is broad and forms an important part of the policy process in legitimizing the policy prescriptions suggested. Changes in health policies (such as the introduction of fees and the development of population policy) have also been used as part of the loan conditions and aims for sectoral loans (Sai and Chester, 1990; Cassels and Janovsky, 1992; Okuonzi and Macrae, 1995). The major role of the World Bank in development cooperation ensures a receptive ground for policy dialogue. The World Bank involvement in research work and donor coordination also gives additional strength to its policy prescriptions.

Health policies

The World Bank entered health policies through population policies, following public statements by President MacNamara in which he argued that the high rate of population growth was the greatest single obstacle to economic and social development and was, moreover, undermining the effective employment of scarce development funds. The first Bank loan to the population sector followed in 1970. As there was no population experience among the existing staff, the new Population Projects Department was placed under the general supervision of the Central Projects Staff – the Bank's 'Quality Assurance Unit'. The reorganization of the Population Projects Department as the Department of Population, Health and Nutrition was carried out largely with the idea of offering new and nonclinical bridges to family planning (Wolfson, 1983).

The funding of the population, health and nutrition sector was part of the World Bank's poverty-related activities, in line with the general emphasis of the World Bank. The World Bank's promotion of redistribution-with-growth strategies, aimed at redistributing funds towards the poorest, was close to the initiatives made by other agencies with 'basic needs' goals (Ayres, 1983). The World Bank adopted a formal health policy in 1974 after several years of informal activity in the sector. In the first health policy, operations were limited to components of projects in other sectors, reflecting concern at that time about the feasibility of low-cost health care systems, and uncertainty about the World Bank's proper role in the sector and about how its activities should relate to those of WHO (World Bank, 1980).

In the early 1980s the World Bank started direct lending in the area of health, justifying this on the grounds of its country programming and sectoral analysis. Direct lending on health was to be used to help ensure the success of emerging national programmes to expand the coverage of health care. The role of health programmes in poverty alleviation was emphasized, as well as the need to complement and rationalize current World Bank lending in the health sector. It was considered that lending for health projects in countries which have not yet adopted formal family planning policies would give the World Bank more opportunities for dialogue on population issues and for supporting family planning services, where desired, through the health care system. The Bank's expanded activities were considered essentially complementary to those of WHO (World Bank, 1980).

In the 1980s assistance for the population, health and nutrition (PHN) sector was still marginal, though in 1987 it started to rise substantially. Efforts in the PHN sector were focused on projects dealing with population and basic health services, and on the use of community-based workers in a fashion more in line with the UNICEF approach. The Bank's population-related goals, its prime mover in health services development, are articulated clearly through the notion that the integration of family planning into the health services underscores the need to expand health system coverage in rural areas (Baum and Tolbert 1985).

Structural adjustment and social sector reforms

In the 1980s health and health-related issues tended to be undermined by the general policies, which were more in line with the neoliberal agenda that introduced policy-based lending in the form of structural adjustment loans linked with conditions concerning policy changes. According to Woodward, the basis of structural adjustment can be divided into the three central principles of reducing the role of the state relative to that of the private sector, 'getting the prices right' and opening the economy (Woodward, 1992) (Box 3.2). Concern over the human costs of the structural adjustment policies emerged in the mid-1980s. The impacts on women and children, in particular, have been stressed (Cornia *et al.*, 1987; Costello *et al.*, 1994; Sparr, 1994; Logie and Woodroffe, 1993; Lancet, 1994a; Lugalla, 1995; Kanji and Jazdowska, 1993; Evans, 1995). The concern over the impact of structural adjustment on health has been at the centre of the debate on health and social development ever since.

UNICEF has had an important role in developing efforts to mitigate the suffering through documentation, empirical studies and the initiation and formulation of the dominant social mitigation approach (Cornia *et al.*, 1987; Jolly, 1991a and 1991b; Gayi, 1995). Alternative strategies such as Structural Adjustment with a Human Face do not represent major departures from World Bank policies on the general level, however, and many of the issues dealt with under the rubric of structural adjustment relate more to questions usually debated as development issues (Helleneier, 1994). The actual impact of the alternative strategies may also be smaller than is usually acknowledged, as according to Gibbon most of the proposals in the Structural Adjustment with a Human Face strategy were borrowed from the World Bank's own *World Development Report* in 1980 (Gibbon, 1992).

Since 1987, the World Bank Operational Guidelines have required analysis of the impact of adjustment programmes on the poor and proposals for

Box 3.2 The principles of structural adjustment according to Woodward (1992)

The current approach to structural adjustment is based firmly on the orthodox neoclassical view of economics. Its basis can be divided into three central principles:

1. Reducing the role of the state relative to that of the private sector. This is based on the view that private sector commercial operations are generally more efficient than those of the public sector, and that private markets result in a more efficient allocation of resources than public provision. The reduction of the role of the state under structural adjustment takes three main forms:

- Restricting the level of governmental expenditure as a share of national income;
- Shifting production and the provision of the services from the public to the private sector; and
- Relaxing or removing regulations affecting transactions in private markets (including labour and financial markets, as well as those for goods).

2. 'Getting the prices right'. This is based on the view that economic efficiency in the economy as a whole can be maximized by allowing prices and incomes to respond freely to market forces (or setting them at the levels which could be reached in a free market). This applies mainly to:

- Key overall prices in the economy, particularly the exchange rate, interest rates, and real wage rates;
- Other prices which are fixed by the government rather than being determined on the market, particularly agricultural producer prices and state-owned enterprise prices; and
- Other structural adjustment policies affecting prices and incomes such as tax reform, the removal or reduction of subsidies and/or price controls, and the introduction of (or increases in) user charges for health, education and other public services.

3. Opening the economy to foreign trade and investment. This is based on the view that free access to imports and the discipline of foreign competition improves the efficiency of domestic production; and that foreign investment helps to relieve the scarcity of capital and encourages the transfer of technology into the economy.

The three basic principles are supplemented by institutional strengthening and capacity-building designed to overcome the limitations in the adjusting country's administrative capacity. This may include, for example:

- Changes in institutional structures (for example, the closure or merging of ministries, streamlining of administrative procedures, etc.);
- Reform of supervisory structures affecting the private sector, and increasing the state's ability to implement them effectively, where these are seen as necessary to the effective operation of the market – for example in banking supervision, staff training; and increased or more efficient use of office technology.

measures to alleviate the negative effects (Ribe and Carvalho, 1990). In many countries a range of compensatory measures to mitigate the social costs of adjustment have been introduced. According to Vivian, the answer to the dilemma of the need to increase social support while reducing overall expenditure is targeting in two ways: allocation of the existing social expenditure, firstly, in order to enhance efficiency and equity (in basic health services and education, for example) and, secondly, to create specific programmes to reach the poor and those directly affected by adjustment (Vivian, 1995). The social programmes mitigating adjustment impacts have been criticized both in terms of their potential to mitigate the effects of structural adjustment and also for their impact on the more long-term restructuring process in the social sector (Kanji *et al.*, 1992; UNRISD, 1995; Vivian, 1995; Macintosh, 1995; Gayi, 1995).

Social sector reforms, safety nets, pension and social insurance policies are an emerging area for World Bank activity in many countries, with subsequent criticism of the policy prescriptions (Paul and Paul, 1995; Singh, 1996; Beattie and McGillivray, 1995; UNRISD, 1995). One of the fundamental concerns over the social safety net approaches promoted is that rather than seeing social services as one part of the normal primary functions of a modern state, the new view is that social institutions should come into play only when the alternatives – basically, the family and the market – break down. While this fits in well with neoliberal attempts to roll back the state, it is doubtful whether it is the best way to help the poor. Rights tend to empower the receivers, gifts the givers, and by isolating them from the rest of the community residualism serves to perpetuate social divisions (UNRISD, 1995).

Health sector reforms

The World Bank's increased involvement in the health sector coincided with criticism of its policies during structural adjustment and the move towards sectoral reforms, and the publication *Financing Health Services in Developing Countries – an Agenda for Reform* (World Bank, 1987) reaffirms both the policies of structural adjustment and the need to focus more closely on the social and human resource aspects. According to Bloom (1991), the report is heavily influenced by the neoliberal agenda, and the health service which would emerge from the principles promoted in the report would be similar to that of the United States – a combination of privately run and financed curative services complemented by public health programmes targeted at certain defined classes of patients (Bloom, 1991).

Since 1987 the World Bank's share in financing, coordination and research in the area of health and health reform has been extended, culminating in *Investing on Health,* the World Development Report published in 1993, which

Box 3.3 Disability Adjusted Life Years (DALYs)

The Disability Adjusted Life Years (DALYs) were introduced in the 1993 World Development Report as a means of measuring the global burden of disease as well as improving the effectiveness of health interventions and the allocation of resources in the health sector. The DALY is a composite measure of health status, combining the impacts of the time lived with a disability together with the time lost due to premature mortality. In this measure the standard expected years of life lost from different illnesses and conditions have been calculated for different age groups, sexes and geographical regions. Disabilities have been assessed and categorized in different classes ranging from death to perfect health. In the combination of these two measures future years of life-lost have been discounted. In addition, the highest value for life-lost was given to the middle-aged groups. Where evaluation, assessment or judgement were needed, expert opinions have been obtained (World Bank, 1993a; Murray, 1994; Murray and Lopez, 1994). DALYs have been part of the research into the Global Burden of Disease, initiated in 1992 by the World Bank and conducted in collaboration with the WHO. However, there have since been differences between the two organizations with respect to the use of DALYs in health policy decision making and their applicability in the assessment of health: WHO has taken a more cautious approach, considering them potentially useful, but requiring more research (Murray and Lopez, 1997).

As measures the DALYs are comparable to QUALYs and other measures which include weights for time spent in less-than-perfect health. As composite measures involving judgements and expert opinions DALYs entail value judgments. These, as well as the context in which the DALYs were framed and developed, may not be explicit when composite measures are used. The practical considerations affecting the use of DALYs in resource allocation for health perhaps entail the most problems. DALYs may give inadequate or even biased grounds for decision making in the health sector. They may, through their focus on disease and the outcome, reinforce strategies for health which provide clear-cut and measurable single outcomes and lead to prioritization on the basis of diseases. Not only is the determination of 'priority diseases' misleading with regard to allocative efficiency, but it also ignores the multi-sectorality of health determinants (Prost and Jancloes, 1993). The broader public health interventions do not turn to DALYs as easily, not to mention the difficulty of reducing issues such as poverty or social exclusion to this measure. The DALYs are also poor answers for health care systems responsive to the felt needs of the communities.

According to Barker and Green the problems of DALYs are rarely brought forward. These include: the limitations of a single-outcome measure; the disproportionate enhancement of the medical model of health; a narrow focus on vertical approaches to health, as it is difficult to compare multi-input/multi-output programmes; the incorporation of value judgements on the distribution of resources; and the privileging of the expert power in the priority-setting process in health policies and in choices about resource allocation. They also draw attention to the role of DALYs in relation to equity and social justice, and argue that the DALYs approach, like other approaches which attempt to target resources so as to maximize the benefits gained, is likely to help those who can most benefit, over and above those who are in greatest need. In addition, they question whether the DALYs are worth the bother in countries with few resources and insufficient reliable data. While there is a necessity to improve the understanding between needs and resources available, it is important that DALYs are not accepted as substitute without adjusting them to the judgments and priorities of local communities and to the service of these communities (Green and Barker, 1996).

has been seen as a World Bank move to take the lead in health policies (*Lancet,* 1993a). Whereas this report may be considered as the final legitimization of the World Bank's entry to the field of health, other actions associated with it may be viewed as means to establish relationships with other organizations in the field. *Investing in Health* also launched the Disability Adjusted Life Years (DALYs). While WHO has taken part in the development of DALYs, the World Bank has been much more eager to promote their use and application in policy making (Box 3.3). A specific report on health policies and strategies in Africa – *Better Health for Africa* – was published in 1994. The World Bank coordinated donor meetings on the issue, and the UNICEF executive director and WHO regional director signed the foreword to the publication (World Bank, 1994b). The economic situation in large parts of Africa makes it quite probable that it will be the blueprint for health system development in many African countries. Guidelines for health sector reform prepared by the World Bank are planned for publication as a companion volume to *Investing in Health* (World Bank, 1994a).

The emerging areas of interest in the World Bank's work in the health field have been specified as managed-care arrangements in both developing and industrial countries, the efficacy of differing systems of health care, and pharmaceutical policies with an emphasis on promoting access to and quality of essential drugs (World Bank, 1994a). According to the World Bank's own view, substantial additional resources have been devoted to health sector reform activities in 1994 because borrowers and donors alike look to the World Bank for leadership in this field (World Bank 1995a). Health care reforms have been chosen as the central theme of future World Bank activities in the field of health (Claeson, 1996).

It is clear that the extent of its health financing, aid coordination and policy work gives the World Bank a key role in influencing the health policies implemented in many developing countries. In 1996 IBRD lending on health, population and nutrition, not including social sector or public sector management, was US$1,495.2 million and IDA lending US$ 858.2 million (World Bank, 1996b). The World Bank advocates a threefold approach, relying on the promotion of economic growth and basic education, the redirecting of public spending towards the most cost-effective public health interventions and clinical services, and the encouragement of greater diversity and competition in the financing and delivery of health services (World Bank, 1995b). In its 1995 Annual Report, the World Bank announced its commitment to the expansion of lending to the social sector and its intention to give more systematic attention to safety nets and social impacts in the design of structural adjustment programmes. It also plans to increase its social spending by 50 per cent over the next three years (World Bank, 1995a). Special emphasis is also to be placed on women's reproductive health and nutritional supplements (World Bank, 1994c).

Conflicting pressures and aims

The World Bank policies on health also face conflicting pressures. There are many who would like to see the World Bank adhere to its more 'constitutional obligations' in promoting private foreign investment. In 1994 a report outlining reform proposals for the Bretton Woods system, the influential Volcker Commission, argued for a decisive shift in the balance of World Bank activities, with the focus on investment in private sector development and the enhancement of private capital flows (Oxfam, 1995a). This has in fact been reflected in the recent emphasis on private sector in the World Bank agenda. Although support for health and social sector funding can be found in the Articles of Agreement (see Box 3.1), there are grounds for concern as to which purposes will eventually be prioritized in World Bank policies, and whether these purposes will always be compatible. The World Bank has acknowledged, for example, that policy-based loans, advice and other assistance by the Bank play a key role in opening markets and increasing trade for businesses in the United States (World Bank, 1996c).

The World Bank's engagement in promoting private foreign investments provides a rationale for it to promote choices in health care policies which would open up investment opportunities for the health care industry. Already the World Bank's Vice-president Choksi has given the green light to managed care, considering it the biggest hope for developing countries (Smith, 1996). The World Bank's formal policy on tobacco takes a fairly straightforward position against tobacco production, processing and marketing (World Bank, 1993a), although the role, implementation and actual consequences of the formal policy are still open questions. This is especially so with respect to the issue of the marketing of tobacco, the tobacco trade and policies enhancing the liberalization of that trade.

According to its Articles of Agreement, the World Bank is committed to act on economic grounds. While this may be a reasonable stand when lending on projects, the issue becomes more problematic when more complex issues are involved. A specific dilemma may be tracked to the publishing of an internal memorandum speculating on different options on environmental pollution and health. While it cannot be considered as reflecting any policy line in the World Bank, it does show clearly the problems of decision making on merely economic grounds. In this memo the World Bank's Chief Economist Larry Summers reflected on whether, according to the approved basis for decision making in the organization, the World Bank should give greater encouragement to the migration of dirty industries to the Third World. He gave three reasons for such a policy:

> (1) The measurement of the costs of health-impairing pollution depends on the foregone earnings from increased morbidity and mortality. From this point of view a given amount of health-impairing pollution should be done in the country with the lowest cost, which is the country with the lowest wages. (2) The costs of pollution are likely to be nonlinear, as the initial increments of pollution probably have very low cost. The underpopulated countries in Africa are vastly underpolluted; their air quality is probably vastly inefficiently low compared to Los Angeles and Mexico City. (3) The demand for a clean environment for aesthetic and health reasons is likely to have very high income elasticity. (Anon, 1992).

Some parallels emerge from the World Bank's continual extension of its activities in the two areas of health and the environment. In the 1980s it faced criticism over the social and environmental consequences of several large development projects (Rich, 1989; Payer, 1982). Environmental reforms were strongly promoted by the USA, and, for example, the Nordic governments asked for more emphasis on social issues (Brown, 1992; Nordic, 1991). The World Bank's net transfers of resources turned out to be negative in 1987, and it has been claimed that the pressure to find new 'bankable' projects was the reason for increasing involvement in the environment and for creating the Global Environmental Fund (GEF) (Rich, 1994). Criticism of the social costs of adjustment also gained ground in the late 1980s, and from then onwards interest in health and social sector reforms, and in investment in human resources, started to flourish in the World Bank. World Development Reports on both issues were published in the 1990s, with a similar framework which involved handling the issues through economics and promoting market-based solutions to the problems (World Bank, 1992a, 1993a). Furthermore, in the World Development Report for 1993, the GEF is used as an example of an institutional arrangement for a global fund pooling donor assistance for research on health (World Bank, 1993a). While the World Bank is taking the lead and becoming increasingly involved in issues which it has been criticized for neglecting previously, many environmental and public health activists now share similar concerns about the damaging results of this increasing involvement (Sachs, 1991; Werner, 1994).

Cooperation

Among specific governments and actors, the United States has had an important role in the operations of the World Bank. In seeking to understand the Bank's decisions on loans to countries such as Peru, Chile, Argentina and Vietnam in the 1960s and 1970s, the attitude of the US government emerges as a prime explanatory variable (Ayres, 1983). According to Gwin, the US policy inconsistencies and dwindling support have strained relations between it and other member countries. Any weakening of the World Bank would run counter to US interests, generally well served at a remarkably low cost by Bank policies and operations (Gwin, 1994). In the light of the promotion by the US of a weighted voting system, ostensibly as a means to minimize the ability of the Third World majority to politicize World Bank activities, it has been observed that certain shortsighted US policies within the Bank demonstrate that weighted voting does not remedy politicization, but instead merely facilitates politicization by the USA (Brown, 1992). Dwindling US support is expected to herald the increasing role of Japan and the European countries in the 1990s. There have been continuing problems of governance at the top management level, however, where the limitations of the Board as a governing instrument are structural in character (Mosley et al., 1991). In addition to the clear-cut foreign policy emphases, the different national and regional traditions of the employees and consultants of the World Bank may influence policy prescriptions. According to Deacon and Hulse, current World Bank social policies in the post-communist countries are divided between the European and the American emphases within the World Bank, with a European camp committed to a greater degree of social security and an American camp which prefers individualism with a safety net (Deacon and Hulse, 1997).

In the mid-1980s other United Nations agencies, including WHO, UNICEF and the ILO, called for more attention to the social aspects of structural adjustment (Jolly, 1988). The nature of the cooperation between the different United Nations agencies since then has not been very clear. The major input of World Bank funding in the sector, and the polite nature of the communications on the projects and policies, make it hard to tell from published material whether the policies have accorded with the aims of WHO and UNICEF, or whether their only choice was to join the moving train of World Bank-funded policies and projects as coordinators, implementers, technical experts and co-partners. At the 1995 Social Summit in Copenhagen special emphasis was placed on the coordination of assistance for social development between the United Nations organizations and the Bretton Woods institutions (Copenhagen Declaration, 1995). While the World Bank is willing to cooperate it does not wish to be coordinated under the United Nations umbrella (Khor, 1995a; Jolly, 1995).

Special efforts are being made to promote the involvement of NGOs in World Bank collaboration (Paul and Israel, 1991; World Bank, 1994a; World Bank, 1995a). During the 1980s and 1990s NGO criticism has been widespread, especially concerning the environmental issues and structural adjustment, and World Bank policies and projects are still coming under attack[1] (Anon, 1994a; Anon, 1994b; Rich, 1994; Barnes, *et al.,* 1994; Rich, 1995; Lokayan, 1994; Costello *et al.,* 1994; OXFAM, 1995b). The World Bank problems with NGOs and local groups are reflected in its tendency to consider projects which local people have merely protested against as participatory, and its lack of transparency and failure to encourage participation (Salmen and Eaves, 1991; Rich, 1995). In the area of population policies the Bank has looked to NGOs as a promising alternative mechanism for channelling Bank investments, because of the highly differentiated nature of the client population and the organizational context within which public family planning services are offered (World Bank, 1994d). In the 1990s and especially in the Wolfensohn era the World Bank has increased dialogue with the NGOs as well as seeking for more inclusive policies, which may be expected to lead to some divisions amongst the NGOs, with some remaining critical while others become more cooperative.

Concerns and constraints

As a development institution, the World Bank has been criticized severely for more than a decade for the nature of its projects and their failure to reach the poor, for development policies promoted through funding, and for the social and environmental consequences of specific projects (Payer, 1982; Eklöf, 1993; Rich, 1989; Rich, 1994; OXFAM, 1995a; OXFAM, 1995b; Caufield, 1996). The World Bank has been blamed for continuing projects which ignore environmental and social issues, and special concern has been raised over projects involving resettlement schemes: millions of people have been forced to resettle as a result of World Bank projects in the 1990s (Rich, 1994; Eklöf, 1993; OXFAM, 1995a). According to the Bank's own review of 146 projects carried out between 1986 and 1993, nearly two million people were found to be in various stages of resettlement (World Bank, 1994a).

[1] Examples can be found in the Internet pages of Friends of the Earth, Third World Network and Global Policy Forum, or from various issues of the *Ecologist* and *Third World Resurgence.*

Another line of criticism has focused on the content and effects of structural adjustment policies and the policy-based lending with loan conditionalities aiming at policy changes (Mosley *et al.*, 1991; Sparr, 1994; Loewenson, 1993; Logie and Woodroffe, 1993; Costello *et al.*, 1994; OXFAM, 1995b). The World Bank has been and still is the target of global campaigns and networks whose aim is to change the Bank's policies and structures (Anon, 1994a; Anon, 1994b; Rich, 1995; Barnes *et al.*, 1994). In addition, the World Bank has not escaped the calls for reform and efficiency addressed to the United Nations organizations. Some specific measures suggested relate to the controlling of administrative costs and propose decentralization, changing the staff mix and curbing nonoperational costs by privatizing or contracting out certain parts of the nonoperational programme activities (Mistry 1995).

The World Bank World Development Report on poverty and increased funding on social sector and health has won approval (Mosley *et al.*, 1991; de Vries, 1996). The actual contents of this initiative, however, as well as its policy consequences, have been criticized (Ugalde and Jackson, 1995; Laurell and Lopez-Arellano, 1996). According to Ugalde and Jackson the World Bank's well-documented history of secrecy, lack of legal and political accountability, emphasis on free-market strategies, and its record as an institution which actually fosters wealth transfer from South to North, does not bode well for those who wish for improvements in Third World public health. The recommendations presented in *Investing in Health* correspond closely to neoliberal economic principles and promote the World Bank's own ideology, minimizing the role of governments in public health interventions and health care delivery. The report places most responsibility for health on individuals, minimizes corporate responsibilities and health risks caused by industries, and contributes indirectly to the unleashing of market forces in order to maximize profits for Western multinational corporations such as pharmaceuticals and agribusinesses (Ugalde and Jackson, 1995). Laurell and Lopez-Arellano have concluded that *Investing in Health* is primarily a blueprint for a new health policy within the context of structural adjustment and, while it includes a broad range of arguments, its implicit premises are neoliberal (Laurell and Lopez-Arellano, 1996). Werner has argued that the World Bank has turned health into investment, taking a dehumanizingly mechanistic marketplace view of both health and health care. Despite all its rhetoric about alleviation of poverty, strengthening of households, and more equitable and efficient health care, the central function of the World Bank remains the same: to draw the rulers and the governments of the weaker states into a global economy dominated by large multinational corporations (Werner, 1995; Werner *et al.*, 1997). In addition, the World Bank lending policy on AIDS has been seen as strongly informed by the neoliberal discourse, where neoliberal economic principles have been foremost in the allocation of resources for AIDS over other health needs, backed by large amounts of financing by the Bank. The neoliberal discourse has also led to an increased emphasis on non-state health care financing and service delivery as viable alternatives to nonexistent or weakened government institutions. (Lee and Zwi, 1996)

If the World Bank prescriptions on health have been criticized chiefly on the basis of the contents of the strategy, other critical insights have highlighted the role of health and social sector reforms and their linkages to broader policies and aims. Shiva has emphasized the antisocial nature of World Bank lending, claiming that the organization's commitment to privatization of the social sectors is basically a prescription to take away from the poor all rights and entitlements to health, education and survival itself (Shiva 1994a). Hutchful has drawn attention to the poverty alleviation strategy of the World Bank, which relies heavily on the restructuring of public expenditure, rather than on new funding. Fresh funding for programmes has been limited, and very little of it has come from the Bank's own resources. There is also evidence that 'poverty reduction' is being used to justify the same old policies that used to be rationalized on other grounds. In the structural adjustment programmes the argument about poverty alleviation is now being stood on its head: instead of the perception that macroeconomic reform has intensified problems of poverty, poverty alleviation now becomes a rationale for adjustment (Hutchful, 1994). Loewenson has argued on somewhat similar lines in pointing out that Ministries of Health in Africa are not being asked to shape policies for the health sector, but rather to define ways of making the health sector accommodate the economic measures contained in the structural adjustment programme (Loewenson, 1993).

Gibbon has analysed the changes in World Bank policies and voiced similar criticism. The World Bank entered the 1980s in a position of considerable weakness and with doubts about its future, and while the next twelve years saw few positive results of its development initiatives, its political manoeuvrings have been highly successful. By 1992 some common trends in the World Bank's tactics had been clarified. The organization recognized that its best chance of survival was expansion and worked to a game plan of launching bids for expert status with regard to current issues, manufacturing consensus around its interpretation of them, blaming others for its own mistakes in the area, proposing market solutions with mitigatory or compensatory elements, using plans for mitigation or compensation as a basis for attracting new funding, and using the outcome to promote cross-conditionality which strengthened its own hegemony. While the World Bank has been the gainer in this process, the issues themselves have suffered theoretical and practical trivialization (Gibbon, 1993). Amongst the NGOs, some have had enough of an institution which continues to treat substantive criticism as an image problem to be countered with mass media advertising or promotional techniques rather than as an incentive to change (George and Sabelli, 1995).

The World Bank's extensive and growing research and publication programme has been criticized as intellectually inclined towards support for the Bank's operational priorities, and sometimes misleading in its efforts to justify operational positions which have later been proven wrong, often as a result of independent research work carried out externally. A case in point concerned work on the social dimensions of adjustment, of which the World Bank was forced to take note as a result of the findings by external researchers and pressure applied by donors and the United Nations system. External researchers cannot replicate much of the Bank's research work in order to confirm or refute its findings, however, because of the organization's access to privileged information and its possession of perhaps the most comprehensive data banks on all aspects of development that exist in the world today (Mistry, 1995). According to George and Sabelli, the problem was also present in the World Development Report 1993, where a section on structural adjustment and health refers mostly to publications directly connected with the World Bank; the only one not linked to the Bank was added to the list later and completely ignored by the text (George and Sabelli, 1994).

Challenges and future prospects

The role of the different units may not have the same weight when policies are determined in practice, and the emphasis on issues may not be similar in all departments. In practice, discrepancies and counteractive action by different World Bank departments and in terms of endorsed policy aims in different sectors have been documented (Chowdhury, 1995a; Brunet-Jailly, 1993). The World Bank has had an Operations Evaluation Department (OED) since the 1970s. Its expressed function is to carry out independent audits for completed projects and to prepare recommendations to ensure that errors are not repeated. It has been observed that though many of the most critical indictments of the Bank's performance can be found in OED studies, the department is one of the most marginalized and impotent parts of the Bank – viewed by many bank staff as professional purgatory, a dumping ground for those who cannot be fired or who are exiled from operations where the real action of moving money takes place (Rich, 1994). These problems are especially important in the field of health and health systems development, which may become all too easily compromised by actions in other sectors or merely by the exhaustion of funds due to major development projects in the poorest countries.

The structures and functions of the World Bank as an institution have been compared to those of a medieval church with a mission of orthodox economics (George and Sabelli 1994). There are also indications that there may not be enough professional capacity or prioritization to handle in depth the issues concerning health and social policies, and to understand the national contexts in which the policies are to be conducted. In view of the World Bank's role in health, the number of staff with other backgrounds than economics and finance is still limited. According to George and Sabelli, only in 1992 were the eligibility criteria for the World Bank Young Professionals Programme extended beyond economics and finance to include other fields of expertise (George and Sabelli, 1994). Due to the increased lending on population health and nutrition the average time spent by the World Bank staff on projects in this field in the early 1990s was close to the average time devoted to other projects (World Bank, 1992b). It may be expected that the time available is inadequate, especially with respect to more complex health care reform projects. From the multilateral perspective, however, it should be considered whether the additional staffing needs to be in the World Bank, and to what extent expertise can be gained through consultation.

In an internal assessment (Wapenhans report) of 1,800 current World Bank projects in 131 countries, involving loans totaling US$138 billion it was reported that over 35 per cent of projects completed in 1991 were deemed failures (Childers and Urquhart, 1994). World Bank policies on health in Mali, and on health sector financing in India, have been criticized heavily for their ill-informed, ill-conceived and simplistic approaches (Brunet-Jailly, 1993; Banerji, 1993). In Kenya the government – under heavy pressure from the World Bank – had to accept a strategy generating less revenue and greater inequities rather than the alternative strategies considered. It was also noted that if the policy first recommended by the Bank had been implemented, it would have benefited middle-income and high-income groups rather than the poor majority of the country (Dahlgren, 1990). Evidence from the core policy prescriptions has led to doubts over their actual impacts, too. In China the empirical evidence from the Chinese provinces has been contradicting the World Bank's health financing policy package of user charges, privatization, decentralization and health insurance in terms of leading to an escalation of health expenditures and a shift from preventive medicine to curative medicine and to tertiary curative care (Bogg et al., 1996).

The World Bank's organizational structure may not be the most suitable for its increasing involvement in policy-based funding in the health and social sector. When the World Bank started to lend funds for population projects, several problems were identified: the cost consciousness of the organization in terms of input of staff time in relation to the amount of the loan; the need to provide funding in local currency; and slow disbursement compared to the quick-disbursing infrastructure projects (Wolfson, 1983). It has also been noted that the World Bank's separation from implementation, its specialist supervision system, the capital intensity of its operations, and in general its centralized organization put it at a comparative disadvantage in implementation support for projects that are either socially or institutionally complex

(COWIconsult, 1991). The centralized decision-making structures and the policy of restricting information even within the World Bank have also been causing concern lately: there have been calls to increase the transparency of and access to information, and to democratize and decentralize decision making in the organization (Daly, 1994; Rich, 1994; George and Sabelli, 1994).

According to Clements, the World Bank is not well structured to promote the interests of the poor. The World Bank does not implement projects in the field but transmits funds through a variety of channels to other institutions that spend them. When monies are lent, it is not the funded entity that is responsible for repayments, but the government that requested the project. One of the most frequently voiced criticisms of the World Bank has been its undue emphasis on moving money. The quantities of money processed by the World Bank's officers and their physical distance from project sites have guaranteed minimal levels of supervision. While money-moving behaviour and ignorance of local subtleties may not have been optimal for capital intensive projects sponsored by the World Bank, they have been particularly unfortunate for poverty alleviation projects (Clements, 1993). The fast increase in lending on new areas in the health and social sectors in the late 1980s and 1990s may also be seen as asking for trouble: in contrast with infrastructure, the broad policy implications and institutional complexity of the issues may not receive due attention, resulting in more failures which must be paid for from the public budget at the expense of the poor.

The World Bank's influence on health is clearly not limited to its work in the health sector, as has been shown in the case of structural adjustment. On the larger scale, the World Bank's role and advocacy at the global level should not be ignored. According to Kothari, the tributes being paid to the Bretton Woods institutions for both 'stabilizing' and 'structurally reforming' the global economy are being voiced precisely at a time when their mission seems to be to undermine the very institutions through which the postwar enterprise of development was undertaken (Kothari, 1995). The Bretton Woods institutions have been keen promoters of the global liberalization of trade. According to UNRISD, the rise of market forces has strengthened greatly the hand of international investor and creditor countries, and of the multilateral financial institutions – the IMF and the World Bank. Correspondingly, it has weakened the positions of countries heavily dependent on foreign capital or aid. The dominant actors in economic integration are transnational corporations (TNCs). The world's 37,000 parent transnational corporations and their 200,000 affiliates now control over 75 per cent of world trade in commodities, manufactured goods and services (UNRISD, 1995).

It is this broader role of the World Bank in relation to health and social well-being that needs more consideration. Internal divisions in policy emphases and prescriptions have been observed within the organization's social policies in the

1990s (Deacon and Hulse 1997). There are also indications that hitherto controversial issues such as debt forgiveness and rescheduling in certain countries, the necessary role of government, and the recognition of social capital in terms of institutional capacity – are being considered within the organization. In the global context, however, and with regard to the overall policies of the organization, there is a danger that while the increased focus on health, women, environment and social issues may give the organization a more 'human face', its broader policies will remain incompatible with the long-term goals of health and social well-being.

Private sector financing has been a focus for the World Bank in lending in the 1990s. In the context of health system development the World Bank plans to address poverty while at the same time promoting private investment, aims which are not readily compatible: any strategy which emphasizes private sector actors and thus competition can easily lead to escalation in costs and compromises in equity. Problems should be expected if, for example, health-care activities were to be financed more through the IFC and MIGA, in accord with the current emphasis on the private sector within the World Bank. From the health and equity point of view, it should be questioned also whether the encouragement of private sector investments by public sector funds is the most appropriate way to use these funds (Hildyard, 1996). Thus the main source of concern over World Bank strategies is the emphasis on private sector financing and the liberalization of trade, and the extent to which health and social policies may be neglected, compromised or distorted by this emphasis.

In spite of its stated good intentions, the practical effect of the World Bank's policy prescriptions, as well as the continuous criticism by NGOs of the social and environmental impacts of World Bank projects, still cast a shadow over the health activities of the organization as a whole. In addition, there are concerns over how the basis and framework of World Bank policies have changed in the 1990s Wolfensohn era. These are reflected well in the observations by Brent Blackwelder, president of Friends of the Earth, as cited by Caufield: 'he won't change the World Bank's basic philosophy on lending. With Wolfensohn, we are still up against a stone wall, but it is a much smarter stone wall' (Caufield, 1996).

The World Bank's focus has been shifting to knowledge-based activities and policy advice: in health care this has meant extending its activities into WHO's territory to the extent that the World Bank is sometimes seen as having taken the lead in this field. It needs to be discussed whether the World Bank is the right organization to have such a major role in the definition of policies on health and social sector development? While its interest in the social, environmental and health impacts of development projects and policies is to be welcomed, this issue should be kept distinct from the extension of its power to those spheres of life and development where decisions made purely on economic grounds may be not only of limited value but also counteractive in nature.

4

United Nations Children's Fund (UNICEF)

The United Nations International Children's Emergency Fund (UNICEF), later named United Nations Children's Fund, was established in 1946, during the first General Assembly of the United Nations, as a temporary body to meet the emergency needs of children in postwar Europe (UN resolution 57/1) (United Nations, 1994a). In the late 1940s, UNICEF oriented its work more towards the needs of Third World children (Lafond, 1994; Black, 1996). In 1953 a United Nations resolution (802/VIII) placed the Fund on a permanent footing and broadened its mandate to giving assistance, particularly to Third World countries, in the development of permanent child health and welfare services (United Nations, 1994a). The emphasis over the following 30 years was on the 'silent emergency', caused by economic crises and food shortages that threatened children in the Third World (Engberg-Pedersen *et al.*, 1992).

In 1959 the Declaration of the Rights of the Child was adopted by the General Assembly of the United Nations, and particular responsibility was placed on UNICEF to implement these rights (Union of International Associations, 1992). In 1989 the Convention on the Rights of the Child was adopted, and gained unprecedentedly quick support from most countries. Although the Commission on Human Rights was responsible for that process administratively and technically, UNICEF's role in mobilizing support was important. The World Summit for Children, an initiative largely resulting from UNICEF's active efforts, also took place in 1990 (Black, 1996).

By specializing in the needs of children, and not in a particular technical area, UNICEF's work cuts across many sectoral and policy issues. Nevertheless, it is still perhaps best recognized for its work in the health sector (Lafond, 1994).

Organization

UNICEF reports to the Economic and Social Council of the United Nations

(ECOSOC). UNICEF is governed by a 36-member Executive Board, elected by ECOSOC for three-year terms, rotating annually. In electing the members, the geographical distribution and representation of the major donors and recipients are considered. The Executive Board is responsible for providing intergovernmental support to and supervision of the activities of the Fund (United Nations, 1994a). The Executive Director is appointed by the United Nations Secretary General in consultation with the Executive Board (Union of International Associations, 1992).

The basic operational structure of UNICEF includes three levels: the headquarters level located at six centres; six regional offices; and country offices in developing countries. The organizational structure of UNICEF is decentralized, as compared with other UN organizations, with relatively more emphasis being placed on country offices and less on the regional offices (Engberg-Pedersen *et al.*, 1992). UNICEF has a network of 200 offices in 117 countries, and more than 80 per cent of the organization's staff members serve in field locations (*UNICEF Today,* 1994). Major operational decisions are left to the discretion of country representatives, and they also direct all UNICEF operations at field level, answering directly to the Executive Director (Lafond, 1994). In addition, UNICEF has its NGO-based 33 National Committees in the industrial countries (*UNICEF Today,* 1994). As a result of an ongoing reform process, more power is being transferred from the headquarters to the regional offices.

Finances

As a United Nations fund, UNICEF relies on voluntary contributions rather than assessed UN contributions (in contrast with the UN itself, and with the regular budget of WHO and other specialized agencies). The annual income of UNICEF has been about US$1,000 million in recent years. In 1994 two thirds of UNICEF's total income was contributed by national governments, of which 81 per cent was provided by the top ten donors from North America, Europe and Japan. One third of the total income came from nongovernmental sources such as the National Committees. About 10 per cent of the total income was raised by selling greeting cards and other products (UNICEF, 1995a).

The UNICEF income is allotted to two major categories: General Resources (also called 'voluntary contributions'), which are not earmarked, and Supplementary and Emergency Funds, intended for specific purposes. In 1995 General Resources comprised about 54 per cent and Supplementary and Emergency Funds 46 per cent of the total budget (UNICEF, 1996a).

In 1994 the programme expenditure was US$801 million (UNICEF, 1995a). Activities involving child health have made up the largest programme.

The relative size of the child health programme grew in the 1980s, and in the early 1990s accounted for more than 30 per cent of programme expenditure (Engberg-Pedersen *et al.*, 1992). Since then the proportion has been decreased to 25–26 per cent (UNICEF, 1995a; UNICEF, 1996a). Two components of the GOBI (Growth monitoring – Oral rehydration – Breast feeding – Immunization) approach, namely oral rehydration and immunization, accounted for about half of UNICEF's expenditure on child health activities (Taylor and Jolly, 1988). According to Lafond (1994) nearly 80 per cent of the earmarked Supplementary and Emergency funds are allocated to health programmes, increasing the direct influence of the major donors from Europe and North America. The other programme expenditures are: (1) education and early childhood development; (2) water supply and sanitation; (3) community development, women's programmes and children in especially difficult circumstances (each of which accounts for about one tenth of the programme expenditure); (4) child nutrition (4 per cent); (5) planning, advocacy and programme support (15 per cent); and (6) emergency relief. The proportion of emergency relief has varied widely, from about 8 per cent to about 20 per cent (Engberg-Pedersen *et al.*, 1992). In recent years the proportion of expenditure on emergency relief was exceptionally high: 25–28 per cent (UNICEF, 1994, 1995a, 1996a). In financial terms, activities involving water and sanitation and child nutrition have been declining in their relative volume (Engberg-Pedersen *et al.*, 1992). In 1993 UNICEF used 38 per cent of its income on purchasing supplies, and about 8 per cent of the total on vaccines and 6 per cent on drugs (UNICEF 1995b).

Accountability

UNICEF's accountability involves four major groups: (1) the body which approves the country programmes and allocates resources (the Executive Board); (2) the bodies which provide resources to UNICEF (the sponsors); (3) the governments of Third World countries as its primary partners; and (4) the target group of children and women (Engberg-Pedersen *et al.*, 1992).

As a fund the basis of whose income consists of voluntary contributions, the direct accountability to the donors in terms of accounting, cost-effectiveness and target-achievement is most tangibly felt. UNICEF's situation is thus similar to that of many other organizations, in that the influence of the major funders is considerable (Lafond, 1994). The influence of donors on health programmes can be especially strong, since a substantial proportion of the funds comes from earmarked Supplementary Emergency Funds.

From the donors' point of view, the multiple sources of income, the decentralized structure of UNICEF and the fact that its programme activities are integrated with those of its partners, limit the transparency of its activities. There have been claims that at the country programming level accounting for the strategies chosen, the development of the programmes and the effectiveness of UNICEF support has been limited (Engberg-Pedersen *et al.*, 1992). A disclosure of serious fraud and misuse of resources in the Kenyan country office in 1995 showed that better operations and internal inspections to control expenditure at the country level are needed. Very recently accountability has been strengthened by organizational reforms (UNICEF, 1996b).

Policy

Alma Ata

In the area of health policy UNICEF was one of the first international agencies to shift from sectoral health concerns to a comprehensive approach called 'planning for the needs of children' (Wisner, 1988a). In 1960, UNICEF commissioned a special survey into the needs of children, in which the specialized UN agencies WHO, FAO, UNESCO and ILO participated. The subsequent report on Children of the Developing Countries set out the case for considering the needs of children within the context of national development plans (Black, 1996).

At the end of the 1970s, during the process that led to the Alma Ata Conference Declaration, the WHO/UNICEF Joint Committee on Health Policy worked on an outline of the comprehensive primary health concept. In the 1980s, however, the focus of UNICEF's approach to health shifted to specific primary health care interventions and from the broad development concerns towards those of children's issues. The turn of UNICEF towards the selective primary health care approach shortly after the Alma Ata Conference caused irritation in WHO's leadership (Walt, 1993; Unger and Killingsworth, 1986).

From Children's Revolution to the World Summit for Children

In its 1982–3 report on *The State of the World's Children* the outlines of a 'children's revolution' equivalent to the GOBI approach were presented (Grant, 1982). A year later GOBI was enlarged to GOBI-FFF (Grant, 1983), in order to include elements of family spacing, female education and food supplementation. Later in the decade UNICEF narrowed its focus even further, increasing the emphasis on immunization alone in the form of the 'Universal Child Immunization by 1990' (UCI 90) campaign (Lafond, 1994). Despite its deep involvement in the primary health care concept at Alma Ata,

UNICEF's health policy from 1982 onwards reflects a selective primary health care approach (Unger and Killingsworth, 1986), and in the 1980s and 1990s the organization's health policy can be characterized as increasingly target-oriented.

The IYC in 1979 paved the way for the Convention on the Rights of the Child in 1989, and for the World Summit for Children in 1990. UNICEF was the initiator of the Summit (Black, 1996). Drawing on the experience gained from the universal campaign for immunization, specific targets were designed for the World Summit for Children (Parker and Jespersen, 1994). The Summit was attended by political leaders, and the 'World Declaration on the Survival, Protection and Development of Children' with a Plan of Action including 20 specific targets, was agreed upon (Grant, 1991). Subsequently, UNICEF was charged by the United Nations General Assembly with specific responsibility for follow-up and monitoring of the implementation of the Action Plan (UNICEF, 1995b). During the early 1990s UNICEF's organizational structure became dominated by these goals (Black, 1996). The field officers were instructed to advocate and monitor all Summit goals, but to be selective in the choice of goals for inclusion in the UNICEF country programme. They were further advised to select a small group of 'flagship' goals that have a strong likelihood of succeeding and that can lead the way towards the achievement of other goals (Engberg-Pedersen et al., 1992).

Adjustment with a human face

In the period 1980–5 some 20–30 developing countries per year initiated stabilization or adjustment programmes with IMF assistance. On average, each year during the period 1980-6, there were 47 countries with IMF programmes and 48 had received adjustment lending from the World Bank (Jolly, 1991b). In 1982 UNICEF decided to undertake a study on 'the impact of world recession on children' in conjunction with the Institute of Development Studies at Sussex University. The study concluded that, although the evidence was far from being adequate, it pointed to a worsening situation among children and women, especially among poorer groups and in poorer countries (Jolly and Cornia, 1984).

UNICEF started discussions with the IMF and the World Bank in 1982, and in 1984 made a proposal in which eight possible lines of action by the IMF were presented, in ascending order of difficulty and challenge. The first proposal involved relatively easy changes such as asking country missions to analyse and consider the likely impact of their recommendations on child nutrition and health (and then, at least, to avoid opposing government policies and actions to protect child nutrition and health). It was also proposed that the missions, if possible, consciously seek ways consistent with other adjustment objectives to protect and improve nutrition and health levels of under-five children in the poorest sections of each country. The other recommendations explored a more ambitious range of interventions: to be responsive to proposals for targeting government expenditures, investments, imports and credit toward priority sectors and groups; to show positive concern for structural adjustment within social sectors, to increase resource flows to the poorest countries; and to develop stabilization and adjustment programmes adapted to the needs of children and other vulnerable groups in the particular circumstances in the poorest countries (Jolly, 1991b).

In 1984 it was agreed by UNICEF and the IMF that any UNICEF involvement should be at country level, directly with the government concerned. If the government wished to incorporate child concerns into its adjustment policy, the government itself should make representations to the IMF, drawing on UNICEF expertise. The UNICEF role in bringing attention to the negative consequences of adjustment policies for children did not, however, end here, and the issue was brought up in several interagency meetings. UNICEF also had an important role in creating interagency linkages to tackle the problems. Until the proposals made to the IMF, UNICEF involvement in macroeconomic issues had been decidedly marginal. In 1985, however, UNICEF's professional involvement in the policy issues related to adjustment was welcomed by the Executive Board (Jolly, 1991b).

In 1987 the report entitled *Adjustment with a Human Face*, Volume I, based on in-depth country studies of the effects of structural adjustment policies, was published (Cornia *et al.*, 1987b). The report concluded that in many areas in the developing countries of Latin America, Africa and the Middle East, levels of health, nutrition and education had worsened during the 1980s. The alternatives suggested by the report for health policy draw largely on UNICEF's GOBI approach and emphasize the provision of essential drugs (offering as an example the Tanzanian experiment with kits ready packed in Denmark by UNICEF). The three Fs of the GOBI-FFF were dealt with in the sections on education and nutrition.

According to Jolly (1991b), the following points important in UNICEF's contribution to adjustment policies: the evidence was empirical; a clear analytical framework was presented; and the conclusions for action were specific and practical. Jolly further emphasizes that UNICEF never claimed that adjustment policies were the cause of deterioration in the human situation, or that some adjustment would not be necessary in most cases (Jolly, 1991b).

The Bamako Initiative (see below) can even be seen as a UNICEF tool for adjusting the Third World countries to the diminishing role of the state linked with the structural adjustment programmes.

The Bamako Initiative

Recession and economic adjustment policies in many less developed countries in Africa have led to resource shortages in government health systems. Increasingly it has become difficult for these countries to pay for health care. Expenditure on imported drugs made up a substantial part, often up to 40 per cent of governments' overall health budgets. During the 1980s, these countries increasingly asked foreign donors to pay for their drug bills. There were also fewer resources available for all primary health services (Kanji, 1989).

The Bamako Initiative (BI), based on experience of two small projects (Unger *et al.*, 1990; *Lancet*, 1988), was announced by UNICEF in September 1987 in Bamako, Mali, at a meeting of African Ministers of Health sponsored by WHO and UNICEF. The basic concept of the BI was to strengthen primary health care by financing it through selling drugs. The original BI proposed that UNICEF, working with WHO, the World Bank and the African Development Bank as well as other bilateral agencies, would provide funds to the least developed countries in sub-Saharan Africa for the following: initial funding of development costs for basic equipment required for primary level health services; a limited number of basic drugs during the period of the programme and support costs during the programme period. The provision of drugs would be dependent on the levying of drug charges in amounts sufficient to cover operational costs, including salaries and the replenishment of drugs and supplies for the Maternal and Child Health/Primary Health Care (MCH/PHC) programme. The MCH/PHC is described as UNICEF's GOBI-FFF strategy with the addition that Community Health Committees should be operating for 75 per cent of the population. The role of these committees would be to manage the revolving drug funds (Kanji, 1989).

Although the US$180 million requested from donors by UNICEF has not been forthcoming, some 15 countries in sub-Saharan Africa were implementing Bamako-type projects in 1990 (Unger *et al.*, 1990). Since its initial launching the Bamako initiative has taken on different forms. The clearest features seems to be some form of community financing at the primary health care level, most often in the form of user fees based on consultation. Various other cost-recovery systems have arisen, involving, for example, a fee for drugs prescribed, prepayment and user charges based on separate fees for consultation and drugs, or with rates based on 'standard therapeutic protocols' (Jarrett and Ofosu-Amaah, 1992; McPake *et al.*, 1992).

EVALUATIONS AND CRITICISM OF THE BAMAKO INITIATIVE

Criticism of the ideology behind the BI has included doubts concerning the equity and access aspects, and concerns about problems associated with integrating BI activities into the rest of primary health system. Worries about an overemphasis on drugs relative to other components of the health delivery system, the danger of encouraging the inappropriate use of drugs, and dependency on UNICEF for the supply of drugs have also been expressed. There have also been fears that the initiative may emphasize the curative aspects of health care at the expense of preventive health care. It has further been feared that it will not be possible to obtain enough money from the revolving drug funds. Management skills at local level have also been doubted (McPake *et al.*, 1993; Hanson and McPake, 1993; *Lancet,* 1988).

Early UNICEF evaluations in five African countries report that relative improvements in affordability and quality appear to have resulted from Bamako Initiative activities (Jarrett and Ofosu-Amaah, 1992). The World Bank has given credit to the collecting of a high percentage of the operating costs in some pioneering sites taking part in the scheme (World Bank, 1993a). The evaluation team headed by McPake also found clear improvements in accessibility and relative affordability in some countries studied, although problems in absolute affordability remained in all countries. The exemption mechanisms were found to be extremely limited, ineffective in practice or nonexistent (McPake *et al.*, 1992). The UNICEF view, based on initial observations, was that community charity would provide some protection to those unable to pay (Jarrett and Ofosu-Amaah, 1992). The evaluation team concluded that retention of revenue is a necessary condition for improvements in relative affordability (McPake *et al.* 1992), but as to date the money collected in the form of fees has not necessarily flowed back into health care (Baza *et al.*, 1993; McPake *et al.*, 1992).

In the five countries studied by the evaluation team, overprescribing was found in systems where income was related to drug sales, and overdiagnosticizing when income was dependent on the number of diagnoses. In some countries it would have been possible to buy from local drug manufacturers, but their products were not used in the projects. The pilot projects have used drugs supplied through UNICEF's Packing and Assembly Centre (UNIPAC). It still remains to be seen – when development committees take over the funds – what difficulties may arise from devaluation of currencies and the attendant problems in buying drugs from industrialized countries. Initially it was assumed that the time needed to attain self-reliance would be short, but it was later admitted that in some countries self-reliance might not be achieved in the near future. The Initiatives have not yet reached national level (McPake *et al.*, 1992).

UNICEF failed to consult WHO on the policy content of the Bamako Initiative, and on its implications for WHO's essential drugs policy, before announcing the initiative. Although WHO joined the initiative, this became an additional issue straining the relationship between WHO and UNICEF.

The Bamako Initiative also imposed additional strain on the relationship between WHO headquarters and its African regional office. WHO's Drug Action Programme (DAP) had by and large circumvented the regional office in its essential drugs policy (Walt and Harnmeijer 1992). Now the regional office was ready to proceed with the Initiative, while headquarters dragged its feet.

The Bamako Initiative was a significant step towards the creation of different cost recovery systems. It has been claimed that, with the Bamako Initiative, UNICEF aligned itself with the World Bank, and further that this is not surprising, as World Bank and donor support is crucial to UNICEF (Kanji, 1989; Hardon and Kanji, 1992). As regards its future role in experimenting and formulating policies on health care financing, UNICEF maintains that it will need to play a more prominent part in guiding health financing policies (UNICEF, 1996a).

Health policies in the 1990s and onwards

In January 1996 the Executive Board approved UNICEF's first mission statement, which clearly established that UNICEF is guided by the Convention on the Rights of the Child. As universal ratification and implementation of the Convention requires that every child has access to the basic services and support necessary for survival, according to the present Executive Director, Carol Bellamy, UNICEF will pay increasing attention to the 10 per cent not yet immunized, to the malnourished half, and to the 70/1,000 who will die before the age of five (Bellamy, 1996a).

In September 1995 UNICEF's Executive Board approved a new health strategy framework for the organization's work. In its health policy UNICEF encourages privatization of health services if it improves quality equity and cost-efficiency; the establishment of community financing mechanisms; measures to ensure that the poorest people benefit from quality care; and the removal of financial, cultural and geographic barriers (UNICEF, 1995c). The stated preconditions for privatization are difficult to meet. Furthermore, under privatization and community financing measures, access of the poorest to quality care could imply a two-tiered system. These policies come close to those of the World Bank, and are evaluated in more detail in the section on health care reforms. The strengthening of outreach services will build on immunization efforts, and the emphasis on a result-oriented approach with specific time-bound targets and outcomes, and continuing monitoring. In health promotion the emphasis is on informing and advocating, although healthy public policies are also mentioned (UNICEF, 1995c).

Concerns and constraints

UNICEF as organization

UNICEF's efforts on behalf of Third World children in highlighting the crises exacerbated by structural adjustment policies have been widely appreciated. Meanwhile, UNICEF has continued to campaign on several other critical issues, such as the use of child labour and landmines. In the course of this work, UNICEF has been particularly effective in building alliances across a variety of organizations.

UNICEF is also good at advocating its own work (Basta, 1989), and many of its initiatives and slogans are widely known. For example, the Child Survival and Development Revolution (CSDR) rhetoric has been recognized as an effective tool for UNICEF's work (Taylor and Jolly, 1988). The universal child immunization programme has provided several political leaders with photo opportunities – such as introducing polio vaccine into the mouth of a baby in front of the TV cameras – for personal identification with the children's cause (Black, 1996). For most of its 50 years, the organization has also used film stars and other public figures as its Goodwill Ambassadors and Special Representatives to represent UNICEF and the needs of the children in the international community. The Unicef Ambassadors, who currently number five, are also on the organization's Executive Board (Bellamy, 1996b).

A report by UNICEF's own evaluation office on the organization's external relations, however, found that UNICEF suffered from *ad hoc* management, in terms of both finances and human and time resources (Basta 1989). There are reasons to believe that these weaknesses in management may also apply to some extent to UNICEF's other activities. For example, UNICEF has acknowledged that in the Child Survival and Development Revolution initiative, a great weakness was the pressure to get something/anything started fast. Insufficient attention was paid to long-range objectives, and predictably some of the immunization coverage achieved declined (Taylor and Jolly, 1988).

In UNICEF's policy formulation during recent decades, the personal role of the late Executive Director, James Grant, has often been significant (Black, 1996). According to Maggie Black, the evolution from the comprehensive PHC approach to the selective GOBI approach was largely a result of Jim Grant visiting a friend working for USAID in Haiti. He became persuaded that the lacking political will to put existing life-saving technologies in place was the major obstacle to achieving health. Grant challenged a meeting of leading international health and nutrition experts held at the UNICEF headquarters to come up with a short list of interventions that were suitable for widespread promotion at a time of severe recession. The resultant 'Child Survival and Development Revolution' with GOBI as the backbone solution was launched as a promotional statement addressed to the world – not in a closely argued policy paper put to the Executive Board, nor as a distillation of UNICEF programme experience (Black, 1996).

Another example of major policy formulation is the rise of the Bamako Initiative. Grant launched the Initiative at a meeting of African health ministers without proper preparation and prior consultation either with UNICEF's own Executive Board nor with WHO, and although UNICEF's Executive Board accepted the Initiative afterwards, donors at the Executive Board meeting were rather reluctant to fund it (*Lancet,* 1988; Walt and Harnmeijer, 1992). Furthermore in the case of UNICEF's position and action concerning the effects of structural adjustment policies, the Executive Board was consulted after the initial steps – including discussions with the World Bank and IMF – had started. It seems apparent that, at least in these cases, the role of the Executive Board has not been very important in the formulation of policy directions; instead, it seems to have been asked to approve the directions taken. Changes in the organization since these events, however, may have changed the situation. The Executive Board was made smaller, and its meetings more frequent: currently, the Board meets four times yearly. Furthermore, the organization has a new Executive Director.

Policy approaches

UNICEF has long practised a 'country programming approach' that covers a wide range of activities in addition to health (Taylor and Jolly, 1988). In the country programming, UNICEF's programmes are integrated into national plans. According to Basta (1989) of UNICEF's evaluation office, the quality of the country programming process has been well received by Third World governments. While the quality of the reports has been confirmed by external evaluations, some concern has been raised that the governments have not always been sufficiently involved in the country programming activities, and that sometimes the programming may have been used to promote UNICEF's programmes and to build alliances, even at the expense of not making long-term plans based on each country's situation. There is also a risk that integration of UNICEF's programmes into national institutions may lead to distortion of their priorities. (Engberg-Pedersen *et al.*, 1992; COWIconsult, 1991)

Over the past decade UNICEF has placed increasing emphasis on support for public service delivery, the aim being the rapid achievement of global goals. This work has often been done through vertical structures and, in the course of implementation, parallel structures have often been created for service delivery. Support for implementation has been the primary concern, and has aimed at ensuring the effective management of UNICEF-supported programme operations. Emphasis on capacity building has so far been limited (Engberg-Pedersen *et al.*, 1992; COWIconsult, 1991). With its history as a supply organization, UNICEF is still the biggest of the organizations providing items such as drugs, vaccines and medical equipment at favourable prices to Third World countries (World Bank, 1993a).

Despite cuts in health budgets and other health activities in many developing countries, the coverage of GOBI components (immunizations, ORT) increased markedly in the period 1981–6 in Third World countries (Taylor and Jolly, 1988). Recently, however, there have been reports of a decline in immunization coverage and an increase in infant mortality (WHO, 1995a), especially in sub-Saharan Africa. Sustaining the hard-won enthusiasm of the donors and thereby the results of UNICEF's programmes may prove increasingly difficult. For vaccination programmes it may be especially difficult, since the target of 80 per cent vaccination coverage has already been achieved, and funds for 'only' sustaining the results may be more difficult to obtain. As cited above, there are some indications that UNICEF may in the future strive, not only for 80 per cent or 90 per cent coverage, but even for 100 per cent.

As a fund, dependent on voluntary contributions from donors, UNICEF has to formulate its policy in a clear and attractive manner. This emphasizes the need for clear monitorable goals and rapid achievements, and the need to stay out of political controversies. As described above, UNICEF's answer to the deteriorating situation of children during structural adjustment was largely its own GOBI-FFF; and to the financial crises of primary health care, the answer was drugs given by donors and packed by UNIPAC.

Increased demands for accountability made by donors have also been cited by UNICEF officials as a reason for the shift towards more selective interventions and narrower goal setting (Lafond, 1994). Global programmatic thrusts may in some countries have the effect of diverting UNICEF attention from areas where other types of intellectual and programmatic input could have had a more profound effect (Basta, 1989; Engberg-Pedersen *et al.*, 1992; COWIconsult, 1991). It has been claimed, for example, that in order to make a success story of the immunization programmes, UNICEF has had to put greater emphasis on them than required by a simple consideration of the needs of the recipient country. In recipient countries, advocacy and resources made available by UNICEF have also resulted in increased attention to UNICEF's approaches, and sometimes in less attention to other health approaches that are urgently needed (Engberg-Pedersen *et al.*, 1992; Lafond, 1994; COWIconsult, 1991).

UNICEF has been a strong supporter of social marketing approaches since the mid-1980s. Social marketing implies using mass media to market medical products and ideas. The approach has been criticized for its one-way communication, in which the ability to learn from local knowledge and skills is nonexistent. Social marketing has been claimed to involve winning the hearts and minds of people in order to persuade them to accept a pre-designed health care package. According to this criticism, the messages are inevitably simplified and are targeted at individuals, leaving no room for mediating structures or for local-level social groups. Social marketing information also implies that the answers to problems lie in individual behaviour and decisions; it focuses on products rather than processes. Concern has been expressed about a risk of accelerating the dependence of national governments on external donors, the pharmaceutical industry, UNICEF and PHC services. Approaching the problems of diarrhoea and dehydration with ready-made packages of oral rehydration solutions instead of exploiting existing local means for rehydration is an example of the sort of activity criticized in UNICEF's social marketing approach (Wisner, 1987; Wisner, 1988a; Werner et al., 1997).

Criticism of the sustainability of selective PHC approaches is presented in Chapter 8. The general criticism applies well to UNICEF, since GOBI, GOBI-FFF, CSDR and the Bamako Initiative have defined the basic needs from above, and participation is needed mainly to make the delivery of the goods and services possible. These are marketed by means of social marketing; ORS has been sold in ready-made packages; drug kits for Bamako are packed in Denmark. In addition to its role in the implementation of projects, UNICEF has played an important role in the procuring of vaccines and pharmaceuticals (Beardsley, 1995).

Empowerment has so far been stronger in the form of advocacy and alliance building than in direct empowerment of women and children to address and solve their own problems through organization, access to resources and participation in decision making (Engberg-Pedersen et al., 1992). In the Bamako Initiative, for example, participation aspects were often limited to financing and the management of funds (McPake et al., 1992). According to Wisner (1988a), the target groups have sometimes not had any role other than to accept the supplies offered and to receive the 'message', and he has further claimed that there is a foreshadowing of GOBI as the substitute for even a minimal safety net (Wisner, 1988b).

Partners

UNICEF and WHO have collaborated closely and continue to share several initiatives. It has been claimed that UNICEF's policy has drawn closer to that of the World Bank (Unger and Killingsworth, 1986), and that increasingly its activities have been coordinated with the Bank's (Hardon and Kanji, 1992). According to UNICEF, through the Bamako Initiative the organization has become an active partner in the World Bank's policy dialogue with governments. The World Bank has also praised UNICEF for its 'on-the-ground presence' and 'in-depth involvement' in Bank-funded projects (UNICEF, 1993a).

Although UNICEF's health strategy, approved in 1995, formally confirms the leadership role of WHO in international health policy making, it also states that while earlier common health goals were set principally in the WHA, the goals and targets of the UNICEF-initiated World Summit for Children have come to play an important role not only in UNICEF's own health policy making, but also in the policies of other actors (UNICEF 1995c).

The formal health policy forum between UNICEF and WHO, the UNICEF/WHO Joint Committee on Health Policy (JCHP), established in 1948 – and the organizer of the Alma Ata conference – has not in recent years been a site of important health policy discussions. Rather, it has evolved into a body for following up targets set at the World Summit for Children.

Collaboration between UNICEF and UNFPA was virtually nonexistent (Mendehlson *et al.*, 1993) until recent years, when there have been indications of increasing cooperation. In the Executive Board meetings of their respective organizations at the beginning of 1997, UNICEF and WHO decided to reform the JCHP into a committee that would include UNFPA, to be known as the WHO/UNICEF/UNFPA Coordinating Committee on Health. Unfortunately, there is a risk that major health policy discussions will remain beyond the scope of this committee, too.

A strong presence in both donor and recipient countries has brought enhanced visibility for UNICEF and for the cause of Third World children. UNICEF has been a favoured partner of recipient governments because of its general effectiveness in providing supplies and equipment, facilitating financial assistance, and providing programme advice in often neglected areas (Engberg-Pedersen *et al.*, 1992). The great strength of UNICEF lies in its vesting authority in the country office rather than in regional offices or headquarters. The country office is able respond to local needs with speed and agility (Mburu, 1989). Most country operations are managed directly from the country office, and programme officers in many cases have a flexible programme management authority (COWIconsult, 1991). UNICEF is also known for employing skilled staff from the recipient countries rather than relying more on expatriate experts (Lafond, 1994). The drawback has sometimes been that while the best national skills have been employed in UNICEF programmes, the lack of skilled staff in other programmes has added to the distortion of national priorities (Engberg-Pedersen *et al.*, 1992).

The organization has engaged in various initiatives, often in collaboration with other intergovernmental agencies and NGOs. Many of the campaigns have been intersectoral, concerning issues such as the desirability of breast feeding, the prevalence of child labour, the effects of structural adjustment on children or the horrors caused by war, and especially landmines. According to the four-country study by COWIconsult (1991), country programmes have an impressive record of successful new intervention concepts developed through UNICEF seed money and later adapted by a number of other donors. The evaluators maintain that a concentration of efforts would be likely to produce even better results.

In the 1970s development policies were considered principally as interstate activity and there was a strong emphasis on cooperation at governmental level. During the 1980s, however, the situation changed and increasingly government action and efficiency in developing countries were questioned. This led to a redefinition of the role of governments as the recipients of international cooperation and as the major actors in development policies. More emphasis was placed on nongovernmental actors, NGOs and grassroots activities, although more frequently in speeches than in action. As UNICEF tends to act more like an NGO, this trend also enlarged its role in international health policies.

From the late 1980s onward, both in the field and at headquarters, UNICEF began to give more NGOs a weightier voice and a larger role in its programmatic and advocacy work (Black, 1996). Already at the beginning of that decade UNICEF was collaborating with a number of NGOs in promoting the adoption of an international code to limit the marketing of babyfoods in developing countries (Walt, 1993). UNICEF uses NGOs effectively in implementing its projects, while many NGOs are also important funders. Overall, UNICEF has cooperated actively and effectively with different types of partners, and also intersectorally.

Challenges and future prospects

According to Taylor and Jolly (1988) the most urgent questions have to do with achieving the longterm sustainability of accelerated programmes as they evolve. These include:

1 Sustainable primary health care infrastructure, maintaining intersectoral cooperation, sustained motivation and commitment of policy makers and workers at different levels, and financial sustainability.

2 The role of national mobilization in generating new awareness of health needs and the potential to build new alliances.

3 How to relate objective priority setting by experts to community felt needs.

4 How to improve understanding of correlative risks and influence child survival.

5 How to ensure that programme acceleration leads to the broadening of action and extension into other health and development activities.

6 How priorities should be set, and where. For international agencies the priority setting is done where the headquarters are based.

7 Finally, how to reach those in greatest need: one suggested answer was a more cost-effective approach with means of identifying those in greatest need and at most risk.

A pull in two different strategic directions in the 1990s was identified in the evaluation report by Engberg-Pedersen *et al.* (1992). On one hand there are demands to expand UNICEF's support for the achievement of specific global goals and targets. This is an extension of the focus that prevailed in the 1980s and can be seen in the quantitative formulation of most of the goals of the World Summit for Children (WSC). On the other hand, the Convention on the Rights of Children, the WSC declaration and several Executive Board resolutions have broadened the agenda for UNICEF activities to include child development and protection, system development in PHC, and empowerment of the target groups, especially women. The two types of programme objectives are viewed as complementing each other, and advocacy has focused on both, whereas the programme operations have focused on selected elements of basic need fulfilment (Engberg-Pedersen *et al.*, 1992).

Recently there has been a large turnover of staff in UNICEF's health-related sections. The number of staff was decreased significantly. The earlier three health-related units were merged together and have been placed under the leadership of the former drug expert of the World Bank (personal communication with UNICEF headquarters, 1997). These changes have caused concern, but according to its Executive Director UNICEF continues to see health as one of the most important sectors of UNICEF's mission (Bellamy, 1996a).

Clearly UNICEF will continue to be an important organization championing the comprehensive well-being of children. In line with its commitment to the Convention on the Rights of Children it will continue advocacy work for a broad spectrum of issues. In practical health-related activities, however, this commitment may continue to concentrate on the 'flagship goal' approach, aiming at 100 per cent coverage of a few elements of health care, most notable immunizations. Its other main emphasis is likely to be on the promotion of activities like the Bamako Initiative, where the role of pharmaceuticals has been important. Judging from the background of the new Chief of the Health Section and UNICEF's history as an important procurer of drugs through its own supplies division, the role of pharmaceuticals in UNICEF's future health policy approaches is unlikely to diminish.

5

The United Nations Development Programme (UNDP)

The United Nations Development Programme (UNDP) was set up in 1965 to replace two existing organizations, the Expanded Programme of Technical Assistance and the United Nations Special Fund, as the central funding and coordinating organization for United Nations technical assistance to developing countries (Ahlberg and Lovbraek, 1985).

The UNDP is a fund and is therefore financed by voluntary donations. All development projects are based on grants and are made within a framework of Indicative Planning Figures (IPFs) designed to finance five-year country programmes. The country programming cycle was to form the basis for a tripartite system in which the government was responsible for the programming of the United Nation's resources, the UNDP was in charge of approval and financing, and the United Nations specialized agencies executed the projects. This narrow and weak funding base, with annually pledged voluntary contributions in national currencies, has undermined its role as the United Nations' central funding organization for technical cooperation (Nordic, 1991).

Organization

Within the UNDP, the Executive Board is responsible for the provision of intergovernmental support to and supervision of the organization. The governing council was transformed into a smaller Executive Board in the reform process of the 1990s. Developing countries have had a formal majority in the organization, according to the one nation, one vote rule customary to United Nations bodies. In reality, however, the wishes of the donors have prevailed; they are footing the bill after all (Nordic, 1991). The Executive Board has 36 members, eight from African states, seven from Asian states, four from Eastern European states, five from Latin American and Caribbean states and twelve from Western European and other states. Elections to these seats are for a period of three years (United Nations, 1994a).

UNDP country programmes cover a period of three to five years and are prepared within an IPF. Individual projects are approved at a later stage by the Administrator of the UNDP. Current approval trends reflect the fact that approximately 40 per cent of the projects funded by the UNDP are executed by governments, the remainder being implemented by agencies and organizations within the United Nations system, regional economic institutions and regional development banks (United Nations, 1994a). The UNDP has also changed its policy over the last decade so that local NGOs are receiving allocations in the IPFs that used to be reserved exclusively for governments (Gordenker and Weiss, 1995). The IPF formula is used to decide how to share the core resources among programme countries. It takes into account the country's population and *per capita* gross national product (GNP). Additional criteria favour recipients that face the greatest geographical disadvantages, such as landlocked countries or countries in economic difficulties and suffering from deteriorating terms of trade (UNDP, 1993a). At the beginning of the 1990s, the UNDP was involved in nearly 6,000 technical assistance projects, employed 9,000 international experts and 30,000 local staff members and maintained 12, 000 trainees abroad. (Nordic 1991)

Finances

The financial resources of the UNDP are derived primarily from voluntary contributions by governments of participating states. Recipient governments are normally expected to pay the local costs of implementing projects in areas under their jurisdiction. In addition to the core programmes, the UNDP manages special purpose funds, and it is also active in cofinancing arrangements (United Nations, 1994a).

In the early 1990s the total UNDP income was over US$1.4 billion. The share of health (not including population) in the field programmes was about 6 per cent (UNDP, 1993a). The UNDP's share of technical assistance in the UN system was reduced from 65 per cent in 1968 to 38 per cent in 1980. The inability of the UNDP to act as a coordinating agency has been reflected in the donor policies and their tendency towards technical assistance funding to the regular and extrabudgetary programmes of specialized agencies. In the late 1980s, the OECD countries provided 95 per cent of the funds, with Nordic countries giving 30 per cent and the USA less than 12 per cent (Nordic, 1991). In 1993 Denmark, Sweden and Norway were among the major donors, together contributing more than US$200 million – more than the largest donors, Japan and the USA, together.

The UNDP, the UNFPA and the World Food Programme have often occupied the same premises and shared a common head in the person of a Resident Representative (Ahlberg and Lovbraek, 1985). A major part of the extrabudgetary programmes of the specialized agencies was funded by the UNDP in the late 1960s, but financial constraints forced this figure down to about 10 per cent in the case of WHO in the late 1970s. Nevertheless, the major WHO extrabudgetary programmes are co-sponsored by the UNDP and the World Bank (Nordic, 1991). The average UNDP project size has been small, costing only US$1.5 million of which the UNDP has contributed US$0.7 million. In 1989 the cost of UNDP programmes was US$1,010 million and their average duration was 4.5 years. This means that every year 1,300 projects were finished and 1,300 new ones started (Nordic, 1991).

Accountability

In principle the UNDP should be accountable to both partners in development efforts, and they are represented on its Executive Board. In practice, this may be hampered by the funding mechanism of voluntary contributions.

Policy

According to the Jackson report in the late 1960s, the UNDP was to be the core organization for United Nations development efforts, because of its large share in funding and large country-level network. A central and coordinating role was therefore proposed for the UNDP in relation to the activities of the specialized agencies. Strong objections from the specialized agencies ensured that the recommendations were never fully implemented. Nevertheless, the concept of the country programme developed in the 1970s (Ahlberg and Lovbraek, 1985).

Because of country programming and its country-based nature, the UNDP has, among the United Nations organizations, the largest share of staff members located in field offices. In the 1980s the UNDP became more involved in emergency operations, though these are not a central item on its own agenda. The United Nations Office for Emergency Operations in Africa was established under the UNDP Administrator Bradford Morse, and this new organization has used the UNDP field offices in collecting data. The emergency activities have created overlapping with the work of UNICEF (Ahlberg and Lovbraek, 1985: Pietilä, 1985; COWIconsult, 1991). The UNDP has also been active in disaster preparedness and longer-term development programmes aimed at refugee reintegration and rehabilitation, thus working in a 'relief to development continuum' (Askwith, 1994).

In the 1980s the UNDP was the organization called upon to perform support functions for other United Nations organizations, because of its large proportion of staff in the field offices. In the late 1980s and in the 1990s the UNDP has been taking the human resource leadership in development policies, a role formally suggested for it. Under this agreement, the UNDP would be the lead agency in the 'soft' human resources sector and leave the hard technical assistance and the economic sector to the banks and bilateral lenders (COWIconsult, 1991; Nordic, 1991). The UNDP's role in coordinating aid has been organized through round-table discussions corresponding to the consultative group meetings organized by the World Bank. The UNDP's potential and scope for acting as the coordinating agency in international development cooperation are hampered, however, by its limited capacity for analytical work at country level and by its marginalized role as a funding agency in international development work (COWIconsult, 1991; Nordic, 1991). Despite its aim to be the leading agency in the human resources sector, the fields of health, education and employment still receive less of UNDP's budget than the 'harder' areas of industry, science and technology, and transport, trade and development (UNDP, 1995a).

In the 1990s the UNDP has presented its analytical work in the Human Development Reports, which, as far as health issues are concerned, have emphasized diverse viewpoints, some shared with several of the other agencies (World Bank, UNICEF and WHO). The reports have involved international scholars with established reputations in the fields of development and social issues as consultants. They have taken up initiatives such as the 20/20 Initiative, the Tobin Tax and Human Security, bringing new ideas forward for further and broader discussion within the framework of development policies. In general the UNDP reports have had a basic needs emphasis, with some resemblance to World Bank reports in the 1970s and 1990s but with more stress on social rights, redistribution and public action in achieving these (UNDP, 1994). The first report, released in 1990, introduced the human development index (HDI) as a measure to be used in development policies and comparisons between countries (UNDP, 1990–4).

The UNDP has a broad mandate, and the number of staff dealing specifically with health is limited. At least so far, the UNDP's role in the field of health may be described as supportive. Because of the small amount of health-related funding and expertise in the organization, it naturally needs to cooperate with other organizations. In the field of health, therefore, the UNDP has formed its role mainly in cosponsored programmes, emergency-related actions and the funding of health-related projects and activities. The UNDP shares common actions and initiatives with WHO, UNICEF and the World

Bank. In the case of AIDS policies, the broader human development priorities of the UNDP and more narrow biomedical priorities of the WHO resulted in a conflict, but it has been acknowledged that UNDP advocacy has influenced global AIDS policymaking as regards, for instance, the recognition of the vulnerability of young women (Bailey, 1994). In addition to its work on AIDS, UNDP action on health has focused more on maternal mortality (UNDP, 1995a).

The UNDP interagency role has changed from that of its original mandate. According to the Nordic United Nations study, the role of the UNDP as the central funding and coordinating agency has been reduced substantially and marginalized in the field of development cooperation. The absence of coordination in the United Nations system has actually led to competition between the UNDP and the specialized agencies in executing projects, thus exploiting rather than mitigating the weaknesses of the recipient country's coordination capacities (Nordic, 1991).

The agency has reformed its structures and activities to reflect the trends and priorities of the 1990s. In 1994 the UNPD Executive Board endorsed a plan called 'Initiatives for Change'. According to the plan the UNDP's main goals are (1) to help the United Nations to become a powerful and cohesive force for sustainable human development; (2) to strengthen international cooperation for sustainable human development and serve as a major substantive resource on how to achieve it; and (3) to concentrate its own resources on a series of objectives central to sustainable development, focusing on poverty elimination, the creation of jobs and sustainable livelihoods, the advancement of women, and the protection and regeneration of the environment (UNDP, 1995a).

It has been claimed that the administrative backstopping of projects executed by agencies not present at country level is a burden on the UNDP's field staff. This has applied especially to UNDP's relationship with the World Bank and the FAO. The UNDP's relative strengths in the multilateral donor community have been defined as its ability to cooperate closely with central government institutions and to focus on capacity building within these institutions. The flexibility and diversity of the UNDP in financing and its strong country representation have been recognized. In addition, its detachment from the actual implementation of projects has been considered a strength, as these should be taken over by the public and private institutions in the recipient countries (COWIconsult, 1991).

The UNDP's relationships with the World Bank and the IMF have sometimes been strained, not least because the UNDP, by the very nature of its business, is believed to be more sympathetic to the developing countries' aspirations than either the World Bank or the IMF. Nevertheless, in the late 1980s cooperation between the UNDP and the World Bank was said to be excellent, and both organizations seemed to be taking a more positive approach to each other's activities than in the past (Williams, 1987). In the 1990s, however, several disagreements between the World Bank and the UNDP on Global Environmental Facility issues have been reported (Chatterjee, 1993).

Concerns and constraints

The clearest constraining factor affecting the UNDP has been its declining budget. According to Williams, agency rivalry over funds is only one factor. The UNDP philosophy is that it should rely on the recipient government's decisions about its economic and social priorities in deciding on the allocation of the technical assistance funds to individual countries. This means that it is not tempted to give weight to external interests in the way bilateral donors do. Donor governments have admitted that, although they have confidence in the UNDP as a channel for their multilateral assistance funds, they nevertheless do not like to see the resources they provide lost in the general pool of multilateral funds, where donors can have little say in how the money is used and get little credit for their contribution (Williams, 1987). During the 1980s, funding from OECD countries to the UNDP diminished in relative terms, while funding to the World Bank increased.

There have been calls to revitalize and reaffirm the role of the UNDP as the major and potentially most effective instrument of multilateral development cooperation, and to reverse the relative decline in the role of the United Nations development organizations in order to avoid the surrender of responsibility for global development issues to financial institutions (Nordic, 1991). Many developing countries have regarded the UNDP as a welcome partner in technical cooperation, and in some countries it has been viewed as the most important and relevant UN body. UNDP technical assistance is usually considered to be well targeted and to have comparative advantages over bilateral technical assistance: it can take a multisectoral approach, is supported by the specialized agencies, and is capable of mobilizing experts worldwide (Nordic, 1991). In 1995 an increasing amount of developing countries have also shown support for the UNDP in terms of new support and increase in annual pledges for some (UNDP, 1995b).

On the other hand, it has been claimed that UNDP country programming is an inadequate instrument to guide field operations. The large number of small projects has led allegedly to 'projectitis', a term that refers to the large number of projects characterizing the UNDP's country-level operations and to the preoccupation of its staff with project cycle management: the identification, preparation, approval, administrative backstopping and monitoring of countless small projects. Combined with UNDP's unavoidable tasks of representation and information exchange, this runs the risk of producing a vicious circle of dequalification of UNDP field staff (COWIconsult, 1991). Some critics would also like to merge UNDP with the World Bank and thus put the UNDP under the Bank's control. It has been claimed that this view has gained support even among UNDP executives, and many World Bank senior staff would accept it. While the UNDP is seen as a one-stop-shop for the Nordic countries, the Bank is considered as able to do the job with only minimal extra staffing (Righter, 1995).

The roles of the UNDP and World Bank in development work are complex. According to Childers and Urquhart, despite the emphasis on co-operation and coordination, they have been very limited in practice. As the UNDP has been marginalized in terms of both funding and policy initiatives, the role played by the World Bank in these areas has grown. Starting in the mid-1970s, donors tapered off their contributions to UNDP and began authorizing a huge expansion of World Bank technical assistance – much of which developing countries have to borrow at commercial interest rates (Childers and Urquhart, 1994).

The UNDP's broad mandate and relatively small share of persons with expertise in health indicate a limited capacity as far as substantive issues at country level are concerned. UNDP involvement in health has been through cosponsored programmes, emergency action and the funding of research. The Human Development Reports have been considered a welcome contribution to the policy dialogue in general, even though the HDI has been dismissed also as just another redundant composite development indicator (McGillivray, 1991). The HDI emphasizes measurable entities and thus may be seen as an example of expert measure building on national averages and statistics, which often are of limited quality and reliability. Nevertheless, the Human Development Reports should be given credit for highlighting equity issues, social development and new and often still controversial ideas.

Challenges and future prospects

The future challenges are closely linked to the UNDP's process of reform and to changes in the role and nature of technical cooperation. According to Singer, attention is now focused on enhancing the role of the UNDP Resident Representatives in such a way as to make them equivalent to United Nations coordinators or even United Nations ambassadors, in an effort to restore the role of the UNDP. Similarly there is a parallel effort to place the technical assistance activities of United Nations agencies into a country-programming framework devised and negotiated by the UNDP. To give the UNDP or United Nations representative the enhanced role aimed at, proposals may be made that the United Nations coordinator and possibly also representatives of specialized agencies should take part in the discussion of stabilization and structural adjustment programmes (Singer, 1995).

The UNDP has carried out evaluation work on technical assistance and also critical analysis of the potential and problems associated with it. According to Fukuda-Parr the problems associated with technical cooperation have been under discussion, and the problems related to the expatriate expert component, (costliness, substitution rather than capacity transfer, the demoralizing effect on natural counterparts) have been acknowledged (Fukuda-Parr, 1995). The UNDP has also been active in trying to develop and employ new mechanisms and approaches for sustainable human development (Banuri *et al.*, 1994; Parnell *et al.*, 1996). As the aims of international development efforts evolve, some of the UNDP's relative strengths in human resources development may be found in exactly those areas perceived as sources of ineffectiveness in the donor countries – the number of personnel, the size of projects, the nature of decision making and the mode of granting aid. The emphasis on NGOs and cooperation with them necessarily implies a smaller average size of projects, and work in the social areas is known to require more personnel than is needed in the traditional spheres of technical cooperation. Furthermore, large development projects have often been a major cause of criticism, and increasing emphasis has been laid on the role of the nature of decision making in development cooperation.

The UNDP has also developed its analytical and advocacy work on global issues, an aspect most clearly expressed in the Human Development Reports. Though the *Human Development Report, 1994* may be criticized for creating threatening images, the proposals include several insights of importance. Among these, one may cite the definition of sustainable human development, emphasizing the importance of tackling current inequities as a prerequisite for sustainable development, and the proposals for global taxes, including a tax on international currency transactions (the Tobin Tax) (UNDP, 1994). The *Human Development Report, 1996* highlights poverty issues and human development, taking a distance from the human resources development approach in arguing that while human resources development aims at improving human resources for economic purposes (for example, through education and health care), the human development approach sees education, health and human security as aims in themselves. The same Report also introduces a broader human capability index as a measure for poverty, as well as possible measures for 'equity in access to health care' (UNDP, 1996).

In 1994 the UNDP administrator James Gustave Speth summarized criticisms of the UNDP in three categories: first, its weak substantive capacity, as a 'mailbox' and processing agency; second, its lack of a clear mission and focus, spreading its resources too thinly; and third, that its coordination role is not accepted fully by the United Nations system as a whole, and its central funding role has not been achieved. In response, three clear priority areas for the UNDP mission were identified: first, to strengthen international cooperation for sustainable human development and to serve as a major substantive resource on how to achieve it, second, to help the United Nations family become a unified and powerful force for sustainable human development; and third, and most important, to focus the UNDP strengths and assets to make the maximum contribution to sustainable human development in the countries it serves, with special reference to poverty elimination, job creation, environmental regeneration, the advancement of women and the four Es of employment, environment, empowerment and equity (Speth, 1994). In the 1990s the UNDP has also fostered analysis of the consistency between economic policies, social development and environmental protection and regeneration, including the health implications of economic policies (see for example, Anand and Chen, 1996).

The major challenge for the new UNDP may relate not only to the reassessment of technical cooperation, the content of its policies and the efficiency of its action, but also to the organization's role among international agencies and the securing or increasing of the level of its funding. Its voluntary funding base necessitates donor preference in the choice of an organization through which to channel multilateral assistance. In the definition of policies on human development its relationships with the Bretton Woods institutions need to be reassessed. In this process, the strengthening of the UNDP's involvement and of its position as the coordinating agency will be of major importance .

6

The United Nations Population Fund (UNFPA)

In 1967 a small Trust Fund for Population Activities was created by the Secretary General of the United Nations. Two years later the fund, renamed United Nations Fund for Population Activities (UNFPA), was moved to the United Nations Development Programme (UNDP) (Finkle and McIntosh, 1994). Later UNFPA became the United Nations Population Fund. The mandate of UNFPA is:

1 To build the knowledge and the capacity to respond to needs in population and family planning;

2 To promote awareness in both industrialized and developing countries of population problems;

3 To assist developing countries, at their request, in dealing with their population problems in the forms and means best suited to individual countries' needs; and

4 To assume a leading role in the United Nations system in promoting population programmes, and coordinating projects supported by UNFPA (UNFPA, 1997a).

In 1996 the Executive Board of UNFPA endorsed a mission statement identifying the three main areas of work as (1) to help ensure universal access to reproductive health, including family planning and sexual health, to all couples and individuals on or before the year 2015; (2) to support population and development strategies that enable capacity building in population programming; (3) to promote awareness of population and development issues and to advocate the mobilization of the resources and political will necessary to accomplish its areas of work. It is also noted in the mission statement that UNFPA is guided by and promotes, the principles of the International Conference on Population and Development (ICPD). In particular UNFPA affirms its commitment to reproductive rights, gender equality and male

responsibility, and to the autonomy and empowerment of women everywhere
(UNFPA, 1996a).

Organization

UNFPA is a subsidiary organ of the United Nations General Assembly. Its
governing body is the Executive Board of the UNDP, to which it reports on
administrative, financial and programme matters. UNFPA receives policy
guidance from the United Nations Economic and Social Council (ECOSOC)
(Goss and Gilroy, 1991). The executive board has 36 members representing
their governments. Membership is rotating and observes the 'one person, one
vote' principle. Geographical distribution is taken into account in the election
of the board. The Executive Director is appointed by the Secretary General of
the United Nations.

UNFPA has its headquarters in New York, with about a third of the total
UNFPA staff (801 in 1992). It has field offices in 95 countries, headed by the
UNDP Resident Representative. In 59 country offices UNFPA also has a
Country Director, subordinate to the UNDP Resident Representative. In the
beginning of the 1990s there were in all only 555 staff to cover the 95 offices
(Mendehlson et al., 1993).

Finances

Like other UN funds, UNFPA relies on voluntary contributions from governments. The major part of this income is contributed to the general budget,
which is not earmarked. In addition to general funds, UNFPA administers
funds on behalf of the donor government for an agreed project or group of
projects. The major funders of UNFPA in 1994 in order of size were Japan, the
United States, the Netherlands, Germany, Norway, Denmark, Sweden, the
United Kingdom, Canada and Finland (UNFPA, 1994). Many European
governments channel most of their population assistance through UNFPA
(Green, 1996). Once the major funder of UNFPA, the USA ceased contributing in 1985, returning only in 1993. There has been a significant increase in
the number of Third World countries among the contributors. While the pre-
cise amounts given have been nominal, their contributions have served a symbolic purpose in demonstrating support for the Fund's activities (Lee, 1994).

UNFPA – along with USAID and the World Bank – is one of the three
largest funders of population assistance. The share of UNFPA was approximately $US206 million in 1992 (UNFPA, 1994). About a quarter of all
population assistance flows through UNFPA (Green, 1996). Its disbursements

– by geographical region and by major function – are presented in the Box 6.1. The work of UNFPA has concentrated almost exhaustively on Third World countries. The major recipients in monetary terms in 1994 were India, Vietnam, China and Bangladesh (UNFPA, 1994).

Box 6.1

UNFPA assistance by geographical region in 1995 (%)

Asia and the Pacific	31
Africa	32
Arab States and Europe	11
Latin America and the Caribbean	14
Interregional & Global	12

UNFPA assistance by major function in 1995 (%)

Reproductive health/ Family planning	52
Communication and education	18
Formation and evaluation of population policies	8
Basic data collection	5
Population dynamics	4
Multisector activities	6
Special programmes	8

Source: UNFPA 1997a

New criteria for priority setting of resource allocations to countries include indicators such as the proportion of deliveries attended by trained health personnel, contraceptive prevalence, access to basic health services, infant and maternal mortality rates, and indicators for the female education level (UNFPA, 1996b). As compared with the previous criteria, the new ones put more emphasis on the access to primary health care and to education. It is expected that with the new criteria UNFPA's assistance will concentrate more on the poorest countries, and especially on countries in sub-Saharan Africa.

Accountability

The accountability of UNFPA involves the following major parties: (1) the Executive Board; (2) major funders; (3) recipient governments; and (4) the target groups (women and men of reproductive age).

UNFPA's dependence on voluntary contributions means that, along with the Executive Board, the major donors have their say in its policies, programmes and projects. UNFPA assistance is always given in cooperation with the receiving government, and thus UNFPA is also directly accountable to the government receiving assistance. It has been noted, therefore, that UNFPA has to maintain a delicate balance between the wishes of its donors and recipients, as represented on its Executive Board (Finkle and McIntosh, 1994). The involvement of the assisted populations has been limited largely to their being targets in demand creation, study objects in the knowledge–attitudes–practices studies, and recipients of the programme services (Mendehlson *et al.*, 1993). The wishes of the recipient government and of the target groups may also clash.

Policy

The mandate of UNFPA allows a broad spectrum of population-related activities, but the main emphasis traditionally has been on funding family planning programmes (Hartmann, 1987). UNFPA has had a programming target (MCH/FP) of 50 per cent for country programmes. Projects in Asia tend to emphasize family planning in their objectives, strategies and results, whereas in Africa and Latin America there has been more emphasis on the maternal and child health component (Mendehlson *et al.,* 1993).

Population programming at country level generally has had two aspects: demand creation and supply development. Most of the projects covered by the evaluation of UNFPA commissioned by the German, Canadian and Finnish development agencies had been formulated with no attempt to include women's components and no awareness of the need to direct employment or training towards women. In general, the needs and concerns of women were not taken into account adequately, and the participation of women in all phases of projects and their access to project benefits were not equal to those of men (Mendehlson *et al.,* 1993).

Usually, UNFPA country programmes have not provided for many of the broader issues of sexual and reproductive health, which have been enunciated in the ICPD programme of Action (UNFPA, 1995b). Since the Cairo conference on population and development in 1994, UNFPA has sought to broaden the scope of its actions, and, for example, has provided training in gender issues to its staff.

UNFPA has also had an important role in organizing the United Nations population conferences (Sadik, 1994). UNFPA funds nearly all population activities implemented by other United Nations organizations and thus plays a major role in setting their work plans in the population sector (Green, 1996).

The creation of UNFPA was linked to the reluctance of both WHO and UNICEF to become more actively involved in the politically sensitive population area (Lee *et al.*, 1996). Initially, UNFPA was not intended to be an executive agency, but simply a funding body. It was also expected to act as a coordinator of activities carried out by the specialized agencies, particularly WHO, ILO, UNESCO, FAO and UNICEF. The idea was that the availability of special funds earmarked for population activities would act as an incentive for the specialized agencies to encourage and assist developing nations to limit their population growth. At least through the 1970s the performance of the specialized UN agencies was a disappointment from the UNFPA point of view: their primary loyalties remained true to their core missions: primary health care and maternal and child health at WHO and UNICEF, basic education at UNESCO. As a consequence Executive Director Salas diverted increasing sums to the direct support of population work by governments and private organizations in Third World countries (Finkle and McIntosh, 1994).

During the 1990s UNFPA has increased its role as an executing agency for its programmes. While in 1989 about 5 per cent of programme expenditure was spent on projects executed by UNFPA itself, in 1994 the corresponding figure was 41.5 per cent. The role of governments as executing agencies has remained more or less constant during the 1990s, accounting for about 24 per cent of programme expenditure in 1994. The role of the United Nations and WHO has diminished. In 1994 about 5 per cent of the programme expenditure went on projects executed by WHO, whereas in 1989 the corresponding figure was 17 per cent (UNFPA, 1990; UNFPA, 1994). In 1994 about 15 per cent of programme expenditure was spent on programmes executed by the NGOs (UNFPA, 1994). Both the ICPD Programme of Action and the evaluation by the development agencies encourage private sector involvement (Mendehlson *et al.*, 1993). More recently, UNFPA has established an NGO Advisory Panel to advise its Executive Director on better interaction with the NGOs and the private sector (UNFPA, 1995b).

Concerns and constraints

According to Vaughan *et al.* (1995), generally UNFPA is seen as a leader in its field, with limited technical capability and implementation capacity but an effective procurement service. It has been valued for its achievements in setting up and maintaining networks at regional level. Today UNFPA is seen by some as a cross between the UNDP and UNICEF: that is, as a funding body with an advocacy role (Vaughan *et al.* 1995).

While others have judged that UNFPA is the *de facto* coordinating agency in the field of population in some countries (Mendehlson *et al.*, 1993), others have brought up that UNFPA has had a limited role in countries, and other donors, such as the World Bank and USAID, have been much more prominent (Lee, 1994). Some argue that UNFPA has contributed substantially to advancing awareness of and support for population activities worldwide, but others believe that it has played a minimal role within the countries concerned (Lee, 1994).

Ensuring universal access to reproductive health services has been defined as one of UNFPA's three main areas of work. In the Cairo document reproductive health has been defined with terms resembling those of the WHO's definition of health (as has also been described in the chapter on Population policies and reproductive health) and within the UN system, WHO has been defined a the lead agency for reproductive health (Green, 1996). According to UNFPA, it looks to WHO to provide an overall framework to define policies, identify research priorities, and give technical guidance for the full spectrum of reproductive health services (UNFPA, 1995c). Thus WHO is given the formal lead in reproductive health matters, but at the same time UNFPA funds the major part of WHO's collaboration with countries in this field (Kessler, 1994) and has therefore its say in the work of WHO. The overlapping functions of WHO and UNFPA in this field may pose a potential clash between the two organizations (Lee *et al.*,1996).

According to the UNFPA evaluation, many decisions concerning regional and interregional programmes were made at headquarters, with little input from the field level and with little information to the field level. It was also suggested that UNFPA was spread too thin over too many countries and in too many programming sectors, and that the country management was left with limited backup. The evaluation also concluded that there were improvements to be made both in the monitoring and operational capacities. (Mendehlson *et al.*, 1992).

In recent years UNFPA has sought to decentralize its operations by, for example, giving the country representatives more authority (Green, 1996). UNFPA has also expanded training opportunities for staff and established country support teams for tasks such as providing technical assistance in programme and project development and appraisal (UNFPA 1997b). UNFPA also aims to improve the procurement of contraceptives by establishing a global contraceptive commodity programme (UNFPA, 1995c).

We have seen UNFPA needs to balance between the donors, recipient governments and target groups. The evaluation report financed by some major donors maintained that the process of project initiation can be influenced negatively by government biases or conservatism, leading to gaps or less than optimal programming. The report suggests that UNFPA should be more forceful in negotiating with the recipient governments what it feels to be an optimal programming mix from UNFPA's point of view (Mendehlson *et al.*,

1993). Former Executive Director Salas is reported to have reminded his staff constantly of the sovereignty of the states concerned, and to have urged them to consider seriously all viable requests from governments once they had developed their own population policies and priorities. Responding to such requests, UNFPA allocated substantial sums to projects 'beyond family planning'. For their part its richest donors periodically reminded UNFPA that its first priority should be family planning (Finkle and McIntosh, 1994). The conflict, it would seem, persists.

Although UNFPA is in theory committed to the principle of voluntarism, Hartmann (1987) has claimed that in effect UNFPA does not do what people want, but what governments want. These two wills can be at odds, especially when governments are committed to fertility reduction by means of coercive population control policies. The example of UNFPA assistance to China, presented in Box 6.2 (p. 78), serves to illustrate the controversy. It should be remembered, however, that similar problems have been found in other countries, especially in India, though this does not mean that they are in any way caused by UNFPA. It is nevertheless interesting to examine how UNFPA has reacted to the problems that have been raised for public debate.

It has been noted that despite the abrupt cessation in 1985 of US financial support for UNFPA, the Fund and the United States continued to engage in dialogue. Because both sides anticipate that the United States will once again become a major contributor to UNFPA, the United States has retained more influence than would otherwise have been expected (Finkle and McIntosh, 1994). An expression of this influence was the fact that although UNFPA did not receive US funds after 1984, it adopted a neutral stance on abortion issues, apparently because it desired to see US funds restored (Crane, 1994). In 1995, UNFPA asked its Executive Board for guidance on UNFPA's role, if any, in assuring the quality and monitoring of abortion services in circumstances where abortion was not against the law. UNFPA furthermore stated that it did not promote abortion as a method of family planning and stated that its support in this area would be directed at the prevention of abortion, the management of complications arising from abortion, and post-abortion counselling and family planning (UNFPA 1995b).

Challenges and future prospects

Since the Cairo conference, UNFPA has worked to reinterpret its mandate, in order to move from its previous focus on maternal and child health and family planning to a broader concept of reproductive health (Vaughan *et al.*, 1995), and from the predominantly demographic focus towards one of putting the well-being of individual women and men at the centre of sustainable development.

Box 6.2   UNFPA support to China, and the controversy that has arisen from that country's population policies

China was the second largest recipient of UNFPA assistance in the 1980s (Crane and Finkle, 1989), and the country is still among the largest recipients (UNFPA 1994). While the population assistance to China given by UNFPA is only about 1 per cent of the total expenditure of China's population programme, it can be viewed as giving international approval to the Chinese population policy (Crane and Finkle, 1989). The director of the National Research Institute for Family Planning in Beijing, Xiao Bilian, has expressed his gratitude for the UNFPA assistance provided through the UNDP/UNFPA/WHO/World Bank Special Programme for Research, Development and Research Training for Human Reproduction (HRP) for its strengthening effects on the Chinese institutions (Khanna et al., 1992).

The coercion built into the population policy practised in China (Mosher, 1983; Aird, 1990) and in India (Gwatkin, 1979) had received publicity, and yet in 1983 the first annual United Nations Population Award was given to the Minister in Charge of China's State Family Planning Commission and to Indian Prime Minister Indira Gandhi. The decision on the awards was made by an international committee, convened by UNFPA (Crane and Finkle, 1989). US funding for UNFPA was terminated in 1985 as a result of its refusal to stop funding the Chinese population programme (Grimes, 1994). While the USA's decision was based on internal politics and the rise of the New Right, with its close links to the anti-abortion movements (Crane and Finkle, 1989), the stands taken by UNFPA in defending China's population policies are interesting. As late as 1986 Executive Director Salas was still saying that China's birth control practices were coercive by Western, but not by Chinese standards (Aird, 1990). Salas also asserted in 1986 that 'the relationship of individual freedom of choice to the needs of society is a matter for each country to decide' (Crane and Finkle, 1989). As a response to a television documentary shown in 1995 on some extreme features of China's population policy, UNFPA stated that it did not support China's one-child policy, but that it is the prerogative of any sovereign nation to formulate its own laws and policies. UNFPA further stated that it has been in constant dialogue with China on matters pertaining to human rights, (UNFPA, 1995a). After so many years of population assistance, the statement sounds hollow, and may not promise major changes in the stands to be taken by UNFPA.

This perspective reflects the shift expressed in the ICPD (UNFPA, 1995c). Combining the original primary aim of UNFPA – assisting efforts to reduce the speed of population growth – and the new emphasis on the well-being of individual people can be easy in areas such as meeting the need for high quality family planning services. But as donor pressures for more effective reduction of population growth rates is unlikely to diminish, and since meeting the unmet need may not bring about a speedy reduction of population growth (see also Chapter 11), UNFPA may at times find it difficult to balance the demands deriving from these two focuses. The expectations of the donor community, the recipient government and the target population may not always be the same, or not at least in the terms of priorities. It therefore remains to be seen how UNFPA succeeds in coping with potentially conflicting demands.

The emphasis on individual well-being rather than on demographic goals and on development as intrinsically linked with population issues, is also challenging the division of labour between multilateral organizations, especially between WHO and UNFPA, and between UNFPA and UNDP (Lee *et al.*, 1996). It should also be noted that the World Bank has been very active in the field of population since the 1960s, and its power in formulating population policies at country level should not be underestimated. UNFPA is also faced with the challenge of building up its capacities in management and technical assistance further. If UNFPA is to widen its mandate to include broader issues of reproductive health and to include human rights and gender awareness in its approaches, the challenge is even greater.

7

Other Actors in
International Health Policies

International health policies are not defined only by international organizations such as WHO, the World Bank and UNICEF. The interests of nation states have formed one of the building blocks of the realistic international relations theories. However, it would be wrong to assume that international health policies reflect only the self-interest of nation states. This assumption has been challenged during recent years, especially in relation to international organizations and their role.

There are more international organizations and actors in the field of health policy than can be described here. Neither have we dealt with the national level. The scope of international actors is wide and seems to grow wider. In this section some of the other makers of international health policies are described briefly in order to give a perspective of their policies, relevance and actions. In addition, we explore some concerns and constraints in relation to their activities and their policy-making role. We have also dealt very briefly with less precisely defined actors such as the private sector, health-care industries, research bodies and religious institutions.

International organizations under the aegis
of the United Nations

Under the United Nations Charter, the Economic and Social Council (ECOSOC) is the principal body coordinating the economic and social work of the United Nations and its specialized agencies and institutions. The Council is also the central body for discussing international economic and social issues and for formulating policy recommendations. The Commission on Social Development is a functional commission of ECOSOC, established to advise the council on social policies. It focuses on policies designed to promote social progress, setting goals, programme priorities and targets for social research in areas affecting social and economic development. The United Nations Conference on Trade and Development is the principal organ of the General Assembly in the field of trade and development. UNCTAD's work also involves two other bodies, the Commission on International Investment and Transnational Corporations and the Commission on Science and Technology for Development. (United Nations, 1995).

United Nations specialized agencies

If WHO has the mandate and main responsibility, other United Nations special agencies have indirect roles in health and health policy formulation. The International Labour Organization (ILO), the Food and Agriculture Organization (FAO) and the United Nations Educational, Scientific and Cultural Organization (UNESCO) all have an interest in the field.

The FAO deals with issues related to food and production, including products from farms, forests and fisheries. The WHO and FAO are jointly responsible for the Codex Alimentarius process and normative rule-setting functions in agriculture and food-related spheres. The Committee on World Food Security in FAO is the responsible intergovernmental body in its field within the United Nations system. It has a monitoring, evaluating and consulting role.

The ILO is unique among world organizations in that workers' and employers' representatives have an equal voice with those of governments in formulating its policies. The International Labour Conference is composed of delegates from each member country and one of its most important functions is the adoption of conventions and recommendations which set international labour standards in such areas as freedom of association, wages, hours and conditions of work, social insurance, industrial safety and labour inspection. The ILO conventions create binding obligations to put their provisions into effect, while recommendations provide guidance for national policy, legislation and practice (United Nations, 1995). International labour standards not only serve as guidelines for legislation by member states, but when ratified can also offer a kind of international guarantee against backsliding (Otting, 1994). In addition, the ILO also assists member countries in such fields as occupational safety and health and social security systems, which is of relevance for health system development in countries where health financing is linked to employment-based social insurance schemes.

UNESCO's broad mandate on educational, science, culture and communication has links with many aspects of health policies. One of the broadest is to achieve basic education for all, and one of most concrete has been its work in education for the prevention of AIDS (United Nations, 1995).

United Nations Funds and Programmes

In addition to the UNDP, UNFPA and UNICEF, several other United Nations Funds and Programmes are involved in health-related activities. In the field of environment and health the United Nations Environmental Program (UNEP) maintains the International Register of Potentially Toxic Chemicals (IRPTC) and has exerted background influence on the Basel Convention of the Control of Transboundary Movements of Hazardous Wastes and their Disposal (1989). The World Food Programme (WFP) works on hunger and poverty, providing relief assistance and food aid to poor people in developing countries. The World Food Council is the highest-level body in the United Nations dealing with food issues. United Nations High Commissioner for Refugees (UNHCR), the United Nations Development Fund for Women (UNIFEM) and the United Nations International Drug Control Programme (UNDCP) all work on health-linked issues. The United Nations Research Institute for Social Development (UNRISD) is an autonomous agency that engages in multidisciplinary research on the social dimensions (including health) of contemporary problems (United Nations, 1995).

CONCERNS AND CONSTRAINTS

The United Nations system and other specialized agencies have been criticized in the 1980s over similar issues – and come under similar reform pressures – as those described for the WHO and the UNDP. The 'politicization' criticism led to the withdrawal of the United States and the United Kingdom from UNESCO (the United Kingdom decided to rejoin UNESCO in 1997). In addition, the World Bank and international actors such as the OECD and the European Union have had impact not only on the making of health policy, but also on the definition of agricultural policies, education and labour affairs with implications for the FAO, UNESCO and the ILO. The World Bank has gained a predominant role in educational policy making (King, 1991), with subsequent criticism over the market emphasis of the prescriptions made (Puiggros, 1997). The ILO challenge is currently focused on the policies related to unemployment and cost-containment in medical benefits and pension systems, areas in which the OECD and the World Bank have been active (Otting, 1994). In the 1990s there have been concerns over the position of UNCTAD and the shift towards the WTO in international trade policies.

In contrast with the United Nations reforms imposed mostly from the industrialized Northern countries, the South Centre has also formulated views on the issue. It has expressed concern over the emphasis of United Nations reform and asserted the need for a strong and democratic United Nations, with enhanced capacities within UNCTAD and other United Nations agencies to counteract the current shift towards the international financial institutions in global policy making. The South Centre also draws attention to the lower salary levels within United Nations as compared with the European Union or the World Bank, and points out the necessity of providing a sound professional core within the United Nations, where the number of professionals is severely limited in comparison with their tasks in many UN organizations (South Centre, 1996).

The collaboration between specialized agencies on different issues seems to be less problematic than that between UN specialized agencies and international financing institutions, or between UN specialized agencies and other United Nations organizations. WHO shares common forums with the FAO in Codex Alimentarius and with the ILO and UNEP in the International Forum on Chemical Safety. There have been concerns over the confusion of mandates between United Nations organizations working in the health field, but less research on the actual coordination and interaction between the specialized agencies and other United Nations programmes and institutions. It may be expected that global issues – climate change, liberalization of trade, travel and more specific international agreements on environmental issues – will enhance the need for increasing interagency collaboration in future.

International financing and trade institutions

The International Monetary Fund (IMF)

The IMF was established at the same meeting as the World Bank in Bretton Woods in 1944 and came into official existence in December 1945. The IMF's sphere of action is based on its Articles of Agreement, where its aims are defined (Box 7.1). The power within the IMF lies in the quotas, or membership fees, paid by the IMF's 181 member countries, which also defines the country voting power.

The IMF role in international policies was primarily that of overseeing the international monetary system and promoting exchange stability and relations among its member countries. It also gives short-term and medium-term credits to all its member countries to assist in balance of payments problems. The mandate of the IMF was clear and easily defined until the convertibility of dollar to gold ended and the era of fixed exchange rates formally terminated. This left the IMF with a very indistinct mandate; where the major industrialized countries have been able to determine effectively what global monetary arrangements are to be (Browne, 1996). The Bretton Woods organizations have converged in their policies; with the stabilization and structural adjustment programmes, and IMF involvement in medium-term assistance via its Structural Adjustment Facility (SAF) and Enhanced Structural Adjustment

---

Box 7.1 Aims of the International Monetary Fund
(IMF, 1997)

1   To promote international monetary cooperation through a permanent institution which provides the machinery for consultation and collaboration on international monetary problems.

2   To facilitate the expansion and balanced growth of international trade, and to contribute thereby to the promotion and maintenance of high levels of employment and real income and to the development of the productive resources of all members as primary objectives of economic policy.

3   To promote exchange stability, to maintain orderly exchange arrangements among members, and to avoid competitive exchange depreciation.

4   To assist in the establishment of a multilateral system of payments in respect of current transactions between members and in the elimination of foreign exchange restrictions which hamper the growth of world trade.

5   To give confidence to members by making the general resources of the Fund temporarily available to them under adequate safeguards, thus providing them with opportunity to correct maladjustments in their balance of payments without resorting to measures destructive of national or international prosperity.

6   In accordance with the above, to shorten the duration and lessen the degree of disequilibrium in the international balances of payments of members.

Facility (ESAF), the roles of the IMF and the World Bank have become blurred. The IMF's assistance is conditional and the policy changes required of assisted countries have been debated broadly in relation to adjustment and stabilization operations and their time-frames (see Chapter 3, Box 3.2).

The IMF has not been involved in health directly, but its policy analysis and advice do have implications for public sector organization and health policies. Against the background of the IMF's mandate and in the context of a country's overall macroeconomic framework, the IMF in practice advises on social policies in their broader context, especially but not only in its dealings with indebted and poor developing countries. For example, the IMF has recently assessed the social impacts of European Monetary Union (IMF, 1997).

CONCERNS AND CONSTRAINTS

Criticism of the IMF has been broad-ranging, from lack of transparency and power sharing, through the practices and policy contents of IMF advice, to the failure to act according to its original mandate (Browne, 1996; Sen, 1996; Budhoo, 1990; Singer, 1995). Concern over power sharing arises from the influence of major industrial countries in the IMF, with specific reference to the United States. Criticism over the practices and policy contents of IMF advice have been linked to the rigidity and short time frame of the advice given, the quality and nature of the advice in terms of economic theories and emphases; neglect of the social, distributional and environmental impacts of economic policies; and the ideological contents reflected in an overemphasis on privatization and the interests of the major industrial countries. In contrast with criticism of the IMF's high-handed dictation of policies, others have considered the organization's role as negligible and described IMF conditionality as something of a toothless tiger (see, for example, Killick, 1995). Structural criticism of the IMF and its mandate has drawn attention to its failure to prevent or mitigate the debt crisis: instead, it is seen as having compounded the crisis through its inappropriate actions (UNDP, 1992).

The question in relation to IMF and health policies is clearly that of linking the impact of economic policies, taxation and public sector organization with health. In this process the IMF and its policy advice has been seen more as part of the problem than as a helping hand for governments to deliver social and health policies with an equity emphasis. Since the 1980s there have been subtle changes within the organization towards a poverty-oriented emphasis. In principle, the IMF could go down this road via policy advice and the conditions it sets at the country level; by emphasizing debt-reduction; and by extending its original task at the global level – in searching for mechanisms to prevent capital flight and exchange rate speculations, or developing financing mechanisms that address global issues. The crucial element in this is on what conditions and in which framework changes in action and aims for collaboration would be made.

The World Trade Organization (WTO)

The World Trade Organization was established in 1995 as an embodiment of the results of the Uruguay Round and as the successor to the General Agreement on Tariffs and Trade (GATT), from which it differs in many aspects. It is a permanent institution with its own secretariat; WTO commitments are full and permanent; and WTO rules also cover trade in services and trade-related aspects of intellectual property. The agreements which constitute the WTO are almost all multilateral and thus involve commitments for the entire membership (WTO, 1995).

The WTO has been defined as the legal and institutional foundation of the multilateral trading system, which provides the principal contractual obligations determining how governments frame and implement domestic trade legislation and regulation. It is also the platform for trade negotiations. The

WTO structure is based on the Ministerial Conference as the highest authority: meeting at least every two years, it can take decisions on all matters under any of the multilateral trade agreements. The day-to-day work falls to a number of subsidiary bodies but principally to the General Council, which delegates responsibility to three other major bodies, namely the Councils for Trade in Goods, Trade in Services and Trade-Related Aspects of Intellectual Property. The WTO Secretariat has around 450 staff and a budget of about US$83 million, with individual contributions calculated on the basis of shares in the total trade conducted by WTO members (WTO, 1997).

One of the stated aspects of the WTO mandate has been to cooperate with the IMF, the World Bank and other multilateral institutions to achieve greater coherence in global economic policy making, with a separate Ministerial Declaration adopted at the Marrakesh Ministerial Meeting in April 1994. This Declaration also recognized the importance of economic liberalization and structural adjustment programmes in spite of their often significant transitional social costs (WTO, 1995; WTO, 1997). The Preamble of the Agreements establishing the WTO guides members to conduct their trade and economic relations with a view to 'raising standards of living, ensuring full employment and a large and steadily growing volume of real income and effective demand' (WTO, 1997). It is assumed that economic liberalization and structural adjustment will be compatible, if not elementary in achieving these aims.

The WTO role in international health policies is one of defining the framework for trade policies which will have further implications for health. The WTO policies will also have a more direct health relevance in terms of Multilateral Agreements on trade in Goods and Services and on Trade-Related Aspects of Intellectual Property (Kinnon, 1995; see also Chapter 10). These would include issues of food production, trade and safety, as well as health-related standard setting and the provision and financing of health and health-related services. In the case of food safety, the reference standards in the Agreement will be those established by the Codex Alimentarius Commission relating to food additives, veterinary drug and pesticide residues, contaminants, methods of analysis and sampling and codes and guidelines of hygienic practice. Should a member choose to apply a national standard stricter than the corresponding international one, it would need adequate supporting scientific evidence in the case of trade dispute (Kinnon, 1995). The implications of the Agreement on Trade on Services remain so far limited as regards health, but may open up more dilemmas with the increasing contractual basis of service provision in the public sector and the extension of the WTO sectoral focus. Depending on the fate of the currently negotiated Multilateral Agreement on Investment (MAI), substantially broader implications could be felt with respect to health services (OECD letter, 1996; OECD, 1997a).

CONCERNS AND CONSTRAINTS

According to the WTO documents the organization may be described as a system of rules dedicated to open, fair and undistorted competition (WTO, 1995). Different views exist, however, about the fairness of the system in terms of social justice and human equity as between bigger and smaller actors on the global level. Criticism of the WTO has been focused not only on its emphasis on trade liberalization, but also on the lack of transparency: on the presence and interests of multinational enterprises; and on the abilities of strong industrial nations to influence agenda setting and negotiations in the WTO (Stichele, 1994; Khor, 1997; Anon, 1997). According to Stichele, the decision-making process in the WTO does not conform to democratic principles of transparency, accountability and equity. Many discussions and decisions are reached informally between the ambassadors of a few countries; and informal agreements between the European Union and the United States, sometimes in consultation with Japan and Canada, can be decisive if brought into the WTO process (Stichele, 1996).

There have been attempts to include more social and environmental clauses in the WTO, in order to enhance the consideration of environmental and public health issues in multilateral agreements – although this has led to concern that in this process the context of decision making changes into one in which trade interests predominate at the cost of environmental or public health interests. There has been even greater concern, especially amongst the developing countries, that these clauses will be used as new trade barriers. These concerns are evident in the arguments of those who maintain that WTO is serving predominantly the interests of strong countries and blocs such as the United States and the European Union, and that the social and environmental clauses are protectionist trade practices serving the interests of the strong and wealthy (Khor, 1997). It is argued that instead these issues should be dealt with in UNCTAD and other United Nations institutions which are well situated to facilitate such cooperation (Stichele, 1994).

WTO agreements have been of concern especially with respect to policies on the control of tobacco and on the pharmaceutical trade (see Chapter 10). More trade disputes over public health precautions and trade barriers may be expected. There is a danger of dilution of standards and mechanisms for protecting public health, and from trade policies cushioned as health considerations but favouring industries in developed countries.

Other intergovernmental institutions

Regional Development Banks

The main regional development banks (RDBs) include African, Inter-American, Asian and European Development Banks, which cover approximately 25 per cent of international lending to add to the World Bank's 60 per cent (Mistry, 1995). These banks resemble the World Bank in organizational structure and governing principles (see Chapter 3). Research work and information collection is more limited in the RDBs, however, and they have fewer specialist personnel in broader fields of action. All RDBs except the European Development Bank have a soft loan window comparable to IDA. According to Culpeper, while the World Bank has received substantial attention, the RDBs are little understood, even in their own geographic areas (Culpeper, 1997).

The RDBs are necessarily aligned to their regions, but they also differ from the World Bank in the sense that they are not part of the United Nations System. They have a reputation for performing better in smaller projects and those involving a good understanding of the local culture and policy making. In principle RDBs compete for the same capital and development aid sources as the World Bank and conflicts sometimes arise. The Inter-American Development Bank was established close to the Cuban crisis and the Asian Development Bank during the Vietnam war (Culpeper, 1996), which may not be accidental, in view of the close relations between the United States and the World Bank in the 1960s. During the era of policy-based lending in the 1990s, however, the lending practices and policies of RDBs do not seem to differ to a major extent from the World Bank's practices and policy prescriptions (Tussie, 1995; Kappagoda, 1995).

Some observers expect RDBs to be involved more in health and social issues in future, and many of the banks have stated as much. The European Development Bank, however, focuses on the private sector, and therefore has a more limited role in direct social sector activities. This may also explain the more active role of the World Bank in Eastern Europe. The Inter-American Development Bank has devoted a higher proportion of its total lending to the social sectors than the African or Asian Development Banks or the World Bank. It is also estimated to have a higher social priority ratio. Lending to the social sector has gained ground during the 1990s and almost doubled between 1991 and 1992, and for the Eighth Replenishment its lending on social needs, equity, and poverty reduction account for 40 per cent of total volume and 50 per cent of the total number of operations (Tussie, 1995). The Asian Development Bank has also started to gear its lending practices and actions more towards social sector lending. According to Kappagoda, the incorporation of this social dimension in Asian Development Bank operations will require considerable effort on the part of staff to fall in line with the new orientation (Kappagoda, 1995). There also seems to be an interest in finding a role for businesses in HIV prevention in Asia under the umbrella of this RDB (Kimball and Thant, 1996). The African Development Bank has earmarked funds for education and health and has produced a health policy paper in late 1980s, but in its projects and policies it has tended to follow the

World Bank prescriptions, with limited research work of its own (English and Mule, 1996).

CONCERNS AND CONSTRAINTS

The RDBs can be expected to increase their lending for health and social sector reforms, as well as orienting their lending more towards the private sector. This means that in practice they will share the World Bank's fundamental conflict between the aims of supporting private markets and private sector on one hand, and addressing poverty and human security on the other. It may also be expected that many of the concerns and constraints related to these banks will be similar to those associated with the World Bank, as they tend to follow its emphases and practices. The regional scale and geographical and cultural closeness may make a difference, however: some regional banks, or subregional banks, such as the Caribbean Development Bank, have won reputations for providing smaller loans for projects (Culpeper, 1997). As the major industrial-ized countries have shares in the RDBs, their regional status does not imply regional power sharing only, although the balance of shareholders will be more representative of the region, with generally more than half of the voting power shared by regional members (Culpeper, 1997).

Limited research capacities make RDBs vulnerable in terms of complex social sector projects and policy questions. They also share problems similar to the World Bank's with respect to the professional background of their workforce. Health policies within the RDBs largely seem to follow the World Bank lines. As the RDBs do not belong to the United Nations system, collaboration with or coordination by United Nations agencies may not be sought as a policy choice. There could be considerable scope for advice and consultation with the specialized agencies, however, at the project or programme identification levels if the RDBs are to embark on increased social sector lending.

The Organization for Economic Cooperation and Development (OECD)

The Organization for Economic Cooperation and Development (OECD) is an international organization with 29 member countries from North America, Europe and the Asia-Pacific area in 1997. Collectively, OECD countries produce more than half of the world's goods and services and its members include most of the world's largest economies. The original focus of the OECD was the building of of its own member economies, but this has broadened into interaction between the member countries and the important non-member countries. The Organization may take decisions which are binding on all member countries and enter into agreements with members, non-member states and international organizations. In contrast with the international financial institutions, power in the OECD is shared on the 'one member one vote' principle, but financing is determined according to the size of each country and its economy. The OECD comprises two main structures: the Council is comprised of ambassadors from all member states who guide and approve the work of the organization. The Committees are comprised of specialist representatives of member countries and work for particular subject areas, such as education, environment, trade or investment. Committee discussions which use the research and guidance of the Secretariat are generally confidential (Box 7.2).

Box 7.2. The aims of the OECD according to its constitution
(OECD 1997)

The aims of the OECD, according to the first article in its constitution are (1) to achieve the highest possible sustainable economic growth and a rising standard of living in member countries, while maintaining financial stability, and thus to contribute to the development of the world economy; (2) to contribute to sound economic expansion in member as well as non-member countries in the process of economic development; and (3) to contribute to the expansion of world trade on a multilateral non-discriminatory basis, in accordance with international obligations. In the pursuit of these aims there is a commitment to reduce or abolish obstacles to the exchange of goods and services and current payments, and to extend the liberalization of capital movements; and an agreement to cooperate closely and where appropriate to take coordinated action.

The OECD has given guidance on a broad set of issues related to health and public sector management, providing policy analysis on diverse issues as well as comparative research and country-level studies. The OECD Development Assistance Committee (DAC) evaluates and assesses development policies and practice. The Public Sector Management Programme (PUMA), has continued to evaluate public sector performance as well as to suggest changes towards contracting of services, privatization or semi-privatization, and the use of more market steering in public service management. The OECD work on health has been most prominent in terms of health systems development, where the OECD has gathered information and compiled comparative research with specific reference to cost containment and the implementation of health care reform policies (OECD, 1992a, 1994, 1995). In the development of health policies the OECD has been described as a facilitator, whose influence comes from the power of the analyses which it sponsors and from the influence of the individuals and institutions in the networks which it supports (Moran and Wood, 1996). In the 1990s the OECD has launched policy agendas both for social policies and for health. The recent social policy agenda emphasizes the need to move from 'passive' income support to more activating support mechanisms such as community work, education and unpaid trial employment; increasing the role of nongovernmental actors; increasing the flexibility and risk-taking of the workers; the principle of capitalization of income security as short-term choice; and integrated policies in the prevention of social and health problems (OECD, 1996a).

The OECD role as a forum for intergovernmental negotiations has implications not only for the OECD countries, but on a much larger scale: with respect to multilateral investments, for example. The OECD forum for issues of development cooperation, the DAC, has emphasized the role of population policies and private sector development (OECD 1992b). The DAC has also evaluated the effects of aid tying, with an estimated 15 per cent increase in costs, and the OECD Helsinki agreement restricts the use of tied aid credits to countries below a certain income threshold and to projects which could not get commercial finance (Reality of Aid, 1996).

CONCERNS AND CONSTRAINTS

The OECD is an organization of the affluent countries of the world, and its basic aim is to increase affluence. Increasingly, the OECD has also taken on the role of monitoring, supervising and guiding broad spheres of development both within its member countries and in their development cooperation. There is variation in OECD policies, however: the PUMA and social policy initiatives fit the public choice approach well, while the other OECD policies lean towards neoliberalism. In the health sector the OECD has diverted major attention towards the aim of cost containment, with the emphasis on diminishing health care costs through competitive and more market-oriented policies. However OECD reports concerning the practice of implemented health care reforms have filled an important gap in comparative information on health system development in the OECD countries. A recent OECD document on new trends in health care policy also discusses the need to extend medical care policies towards a more comprehensive approach of health provision, where 'purchasers' are responsible for improving the overall status of their populations with a more effective involvement in broader policy issues such as education, housing and social policy (OECD, 1995).

On the international scene the policy advice, monitoring and guidance functions of the OECD have gained ground as a reference point and as external evaluations used in policy discussions and priority setting within and between countries. The OECD 'best practices' often offer more than mere representation of information, thus coming close to 'OECD guidelines' in practice. As with the comparative analysis on health services, the OECD provision of information on development policies by member states, and its collection of data and information on their activities, has provided a basis for the comparison of development cooperation policies between OECD countries. Policy problems in the OECD are linked to the nature of its work, which tends to focus on statistics and numbers in a framework of necessary developments and trends, which may be used in the policy dialogue within the member countries without stating the political and value-based assumptions and choices inherent in the advice and policy analysis given. Many of the OECD documents, however, are clear policy documents with value-based policy recommendations involving broad implications for the scope, basis and practice of public policies.

European Union (EU)

The European Union has developed from a principally trade-related regional union, but since the Maastricht Treaty has been evolving towards closer relations and union between the member states. The process of policy convergence within Europe is expected to accelerate with the maturing of plans for a European Monetary Union. The EU is primarily a regional actor, but also has policy impacts at a more global level in terms of policy coordination by the member states with special reference to trade agreements, the European Commission's representation in international institutions and through development aid programmes, programmes in transitional countries and development financing through the European Development Fund.

Even though the subsidiarity principle[1] in EU has limited its policies on health, the Union is involved in health policies through research funding and support and collaboration in the development of health systems and public health policies. The most significant provision in the field of health was introduced in the 1991 European Treaty on European Union, which gives the Union a new competence in public health by identifying three areas for action: disease prevention and research; health information and education; and the incorporation of health protection requirements in the EU's other policies (Abel-Smith *et al.*, 1995). Although the harmonization of laws and the regulation of member states were specifically excluded in the European Treaty,

[1] The subsidiarity principle has been defined in the European Union Treaty and states that the Community shall act within the limits of the powers conferred upon it by the Treaty and the objectives assigned to it therein. In areas which do not fall within its exclusive competence the Community shall take action, in accordance with the principle of subsidiarity, only if and in so far as the objectives of the proposed action cannot be sufficiently achieved by the Member States and can therefore, by reason of the scale or effect of the proposed action, be better achieved by the community. Any action by the community shall not go beyond what is necessary to achieve the objectives of this Treaty.

the EU does in practice set standards in such areas as drinking water quality, food additives and the movement of the professional workforce. The Maastricht Treaty requires also that EU policies towards developing countries should 'take into account' development cooperation objectives, with the Commission holding responsibility for ensuring consistency in the external activities of the EU (Reality of Aid, 1996). In addition, the EU is a substantial actor in financial support and cooperation in Eastern Europe (OECD, 1996b). The EU is also slowly encroaching on areas and issues which overlap with the work of the European Regional Office of WHO. Limits for this subregional relationship are set, however, by the participation of many countries in Europe that remain outside the EU.

CONCERNS AND CONSTRAINTS

The crucial areas of health policy interest emerge not only in relation to the incremental involvement of the EU in health services organization through interpretation of the subsidiarity principle, but also more directly through policies in areas such as the pharmaceutical industry and agriculture. A major question is whether the policies of the EU will reach beyond the context of trade interests. The EU, for example, still subsidizes tobacco production (Joossens and Raw, 1996). The dividing line between pharmaceutical and health policies is important, and there is a danger that policies may neglect public health and safety issues when dealt with in a framework of trade and industrial policy or the promotion of European industries at the international level. The context also matters where policies on food, alcohol and chemical safety are concerned.

In the field of development policies similar issues in relation to coherence emerge. The issue is not only the aim of the EU to increase coherence in development policies amongst member states and with other EU policies, but also on what conditions more coherence is sought. The EU commitment to poverty alleviation has been undermined by trade and agriculture policies which may be devastating for people's livelihoods in the South (CIIR, 1996). In spite of the Maastricht emphasis on measures to counteract disadvantage and poverty, the Commission still seems to be placing too much reliance on the idea that poverty reduction will follow when the political and economic context is 'right'. There has been a changing tune in EU development co-operation, with more emphasis on European 'self-interest' and trade and foreign policy interests, which seem to be turning EU commitment away from the least-developed countries (Reality of Aid, 1995).

National level actors and international cooperation

Often international policies have been perceived as the result of rational action by nation states aiming at self-interested results. In this book we have focused more on international actors and organizations than on national actors. In addition, we have excluded the national level as such from the focus of the book, although it needs to be taken into consideration when analysing or assessing health policies in practice. Different national actors, however, influence international policies. In order to avoid the whole set of issues usually dealt with under the title of international relations, we have here focused mainly on those national actors, most relevant to the development of health policies in the international context of multilateral cooperation and development aid. There is a need to consider to what extent the general framework and prerequisites of health policies at a global level are influenced by the trade policies and public sector management policies sought by Ministries of Finance. In addition, in the formulation of international policies on health the Ministries of Health and Foreign Affairs may have different views and emphases.

In the 1980s and 1990s international policies with respect to the multilateral institutions have been dominated by organizational streamlining and reform within these organizations. The United States has been the most vocal and powerful policy maker and a recent representation of this can be seen in the change of the Secretary General of the United Nations. The initiatives for United Nations reform in the 1980s and 1990s have been based on streamlining and effectiveness. It has been argued that the changes sought in the UN system parallel neoliberal reforms at the state level: positivist efforts to 'fix' the system and make it more technically efficient. It has been hoped that in this way, UN development activities will be integrated with the institutional framework of the global political economy (Lee, 1995). The most recent initiative has been the Nordic reform, suggesting increasing integration of four UN development agencies (UNDP, UNICEF, UNFPA, WFP) and a predominantly normative role for the specialized agencies (Nordic UN Reform, 1996). In addition to donor groups, individual donors have also generated initiatives in order to draw attention to specific issues: an example is the Swedish International Development Cooperation Agency (SIDA), with its equity initiative in WHO (WHO, 1996c). In the mid-1990s, there is now a momentum for change in which the focus on organizational reforms could give way to more emphasis on the actual substantial policies, policy prescriptions and practices within the United Nations organizations.

Development cooperation and international policies on health

Development cooperation agencies are most often situated within Ministries of Foreign Affairs where decisions on multilateral aid are also made, whereas country representation and collaboration with United Nations specialized agencies (WHO, UNESCO, FAO) are based on collaboration with the relevant ministries. In spite of the international health policies agreed by Ministries of

Health from each country in the WHA, the development agencies may divert their support to programmes, projects and policies in bilateral and multilateral aid which may not be in line with the policies agreed by Ministries of Health at the international level. In many donor countries there is much to be improved in the coherence of agreed international policies on health and the policies actually supported through different aid channels and multilateral actors.

The agreed international target is a 0.7 per cent share of GDP to development aid. It has been achieved by few countries, but the size of the economy of some donor countries clearly increases their role in international development cooperation. In 1994 the Scandinavian countries of Norway, Denmark and Sweden allocated around 1 per cent of their GNP for development aid, whereas in volume Japan, United States and France were at the top of the list despite respective allocations of 0.29 per cent, 0.15 per cent and 0.64 per cent. In general, the relative share of health in aid decreased from 5.7 per cent in 1987–9 to 4.1 per cent in 1993 (Reality of Aid, 1996). The United States and the European Union may be defined as major blocs in development cooperation, with Japan making an increasing impact. In addition, a group of like-minded countries – often understood as the Nordic countries, Canada and the Netherlands – may be defined. The like-minded countries have been seen as more committed to development cooperation and especially to the social, environmental and gender impacts of this activity.

There are different policy lines and bases amongst the aid agencies: USAID, for example, has a stated preference for the private sector. According to Hewitt and Killick, the major donor countries tend to be in congruence with the Bretton Woods policies, although some have been more ambiguous in their policies (Hewitt and Killick, 1996). The promotion of 'right' or 'necessary' economic policies needs to be considered in the broader context: it should be asked to what extent this is related to the practical survival of aid projects and programmes, and to what extent it is linked with general international policies towards greater economic liberalization.

TRENDS IN INTERNATIONAL COOPERATION AND DONOR POLICIES

Development aid funds have been decreasing in the 1990s, along with the rethinking of the purpose and practice of aid. The aid flows remain small when compared with either debt repayments back to the developed countries or the private investment flows to southern countries, although private investment flows may not be seen as substitutes for aid as they are concentrated on a few countries and are in general not oriented to actions which bear the greatest relevance for health or the cause of the poorest. This has in practice meant stagnating or diminishing funds for public sector activities in many of the poorest countries. In the 1990s economic cooperation and support to countries in transition has created a new bloc of aid recipients on the map of global economic cooperation. In addition, the share and relevance of different donor countries is evolving: again, the increasing role of Japan in the field is an example. Within the health sector there is increasing emphasis on reform within the national and regional development agencies. There remains a debate about the extent to which specialized health agencies, like WHO, or the health budget of bilaterals should be used to promote health development through support to other sectors. Some development agencies favour the promotion of specific strategies – such as community financing or user charges – in their policy and institutional agenda. Opinions differ about the desirability of introducing changes based on the experience of industrialized countries – particularly in relation to managed-market reforms (Cassels, 1996).

There is also a clear trend for the increasing support of nongovernmental actors in the development field. The best-known are the international NGOs, but there is also a trend within the donor governments to allocate more resources both to northern nongovernmental organizations and to local or international nongovernmental organizations used in the implementation of development projects. The NGO share in international development cooperation has been increasing: in 1990 their contribution was equivalent to 13 per cent of the net disbursements of official aid and 2.5 per cent of the total resource flows to developing countries (UNDP, 1993b). The major official donor to NGOs working in development has been USAID, and the United States was the first country to channel official development assistance through NGOs. In 1986 USAID contributions to NGOs exceeded in absolute terms the total contributions of all other OECD countries in the DAC, making the United States easily the largest source of financing for NGO efforts in inter-national assistance (Korten, 1991). The large international organizations are also substantial actors in the development field, with a scope of the same magnitude as several multilateral actors. This is especially clear in international relief and welfare organizations, where the traditional actors of Red Cross and Crescent are supplemented by an increasing number of international organizations. The role of private institutions and private sector support has been increasing in development financing and has been a stated aim for example in the DAC policy recommendations (OECD, 1992b). Support to the private sector is also linked with donor policies in development banks and other funds oriented more directly towards private sector support.

CONCERNS AND CONSTRAINTS

The divergence of global substance-oriented policies in the United Nations specialized agencies, on one hand, and on the other hand the economic interests, foreign policy issues and development cooperation emphases of donor countries may give rise to inconsistency if not outright contradiction. Often-stated support for the reduction of poverty and for basic needs has not been reflected strongly in policy emphases or in the allocation of development aid. In multilateral aid there has been a shift from the United Nations funds towards international financing institutions. There has been little questioning of the policy choices made, however, or the policy preferences stated in this move. Donor 'shopping' amongst international organizations on the grounds of comparative advantage may also distort the relations between the multilateral institutions and lead towards 'fashion' and 'marketing' approaches which may not be in the best interest of these organizations or of their stated aims in international cooperation.

In the 1990s more donor coordination has been called for in different spheres and in the form of different initiatives. One of the reasons may be found in the situation of those countries with a substantial share of external financing and aid in the health sector, and a good number of donor countries, agencies and NGOs implementing their own agendas. The burden of inadequate coordination is carried by the recipients and may be reflected in a plethora of conditions and objectives, and the relative neglect of some countries as bilaterals flock around others (Reality of Aid, 1996).

The term 'aid' has been questioned since a larger share of the funds actually returns to the donor countries through salaries, contracts and the sale of equipment. While this has been a traditional problem of bilateral aid, pressures on multilateral aid have also increased. According to Reality of Aid, the donors are placing much more emphasis on pursuing their own policy priorities within multilateral agencies. In addition, budget cuts may be politically easier to implement in multilateral aid. Finally, and linked to the question of shrinking resources, donors are frequently defending multilateral contributions on the basis of returns to the domestic economy from multilateral procurement. As funding for the multilateral banks and institutions declines, these institutions look to bilateral donors to support the design and appraisal phases of projects, with the understanding that donor funds will be tied to consultants from the donor country. This then gives consultants from the bilateral donor an increased opportunity to win contracts in the resulting project (Reality of Aid, 1996).

International nongovernmental organizations, institutions and networks

Nongovernmental organizations and networks

NGOs are by definition a large group of different actors. The labels 'nonprofit' and 'nongovernmental' say more about what organizations are not than about what they are, and they thus form a kind of residual category (Brown and Korten, 1991). Thus the label NGO is often used of very different organizations, ranging from local community-based organizations to large international organizations, funds, institutions and corporations with very different aims, structures and levels of action. Even though it is not usually explicitly stated, the NGOs are often expected to work on a non-profit basis and to be more value-bound in their work. It is also useful to consider the differences between NGOs which often work on behalf of others and social movements or 'people's movements', which are more political by nature, often focusing on social struggle and advocacy work.

In addition to NGOs, many use also the notions of INGOs (international NGOs), BINGOs/BONGOs (business-oriented NGOs) and GONGOs (government-oriented/funded NGOs) in order to tell more about the nature of the NGOs. The role of NGOs in international health policies is manifold, but may be generalized as three overlapping spheres: (1) advocacy, lobbying and vigilance (policy and rights); (2) provision of services on specific areas of research, counselling and technical support (knowledge and resources); (3) providing global 'poverty' services in terms of relief, welfare and service provision in health care and population policies (services and charity). While the first two roles of NGOs are more interesting in terms of health policy development, the magnitude of the third role has been growing in health issues as the share of NGOs in channelling welfare and relief funds at the international level has increased.

In the field of development cooperation, the promotion of NGOs has flourished among the development agencies to the extent that it has been claimed that the approach of voluntary organizations to Third World poverty is now the new orthodoxy, and that the voluntary agencies are now in a position to shape, even to dictate, the rich world's contribution to tackling poverty in the Third World (Gill, 1988). The funds allocated through NGOs have risen substantially over recent decades, and between 1970 and 1990 grants by Northern NGOs to projects and programmes in developing countries rose from just over US$1 billion to US$5billion (UNDP, 1993b). In the 1990s the role of funding through NGOs has been promoted and will be increasing. At the 1995 Social Summit Al Gore stated that USAID would allocate 40 per cent of its aid through NGOs over the next five years (Gore, 1995).

The policy implications of NGOs in terms of advocacy, lobbying and vigilance are related to their stated aims. The International Association of Pharmaceutical Manufacturers, for example, is one of the NGOs which has official relations with WHO, and is driving forward different policy aims than, for example, Consumers International. The role of NGOs in international policies has been most prominent in their expanded participation in United Nations conferences and summits. NGOs have had a strong involvement in fields such as human rights and environmental issues. They have been less able to influence policies and processes in trade-related issues – in GATT, for example – although on specific issues there have been visible gains (for example, in the development of codes on baby milk and pharmaceutical marketing in the 1980s.) NGOs have been involved in the drafting of documents such as the United Nations Convention on the Rights of the Child; and in the ICPD conference on population and development, women's organizations and their lobbying had an impact on the final document and the language adopted (Longford, 1996). Nongovernmental actors do not necessarily need to be international to influence international actors: for example, the United States Heritage Foundation clearly influenced the United States withdrawal from UNESCO (Beigbeder, 1997).

The role of NGOs has also drawn attention to the mechanisms, experiences and policy implications of international policy-making. An analysis of NGO–Intergovernmental organization relations in the Global Programme of AIDS has highlighted the issues of representation, formal versus informal coordination, costs of network building, degree of organization and nature of expertise, as well as the different framing of the problem by different groups, where either medical, human rights or socioeconomic aspects may be emphasized (Jönsson and Söderholm, 1996). The role of NGOs as knowledge and resource bases for specific activities has received less attention, but may be seen as an aspect of growing importance in the development of future health policies. While the scope of their work may be broad, as in the Institute for Child Health, it may also be more narrowly oriented professional advice or, for example, specific diseases or determinants of diseases. As many of these activities are undertaken under non-controversial professional and expert advice, the role of these NGOs on international and national levels tends to be undermined. There are also several NGOs and institutions involved in more policy-oriented research, such as the Catholic Institute for International Relations (CIIR) and PANOS, and also some of the large international NGOs, such as OXFAM and the Save the Children Fund.

The direct provision of services in relief and welfare has been and may be expected to continue to be a central element in the work of NGOs. In some countries the charitable status required for financing support also restricts the policy work of NGOs. According to Donini (1995), the Western disengagement, the promotion of civil society and privatization ideologies, and the quantum jump in NGO operations in the Third World are different elements of the same process. In many Third World countries, NGOs are filling important short-term gaps because of the state's inability to provide essential services, particularly in the fields of health, education and welfare. Helping to fund the recovery of states as such, whether from conflict or from failed development, is not high on the international community's priority list (Donini, 1995). There has also been a development towards larger NGOs,

Box 7.3 NGOs in the context of social and health sector reform

The health sector reforms and the policies aimed at mitigation of the social costs of structural adjustment emphasize the role of nongovernmental actors. The social adjustment packages – or, as they are commonly called, 'social safety nets' usually involve both targeted social services and benefits, and various types of project-based 'social funds'. They are part of a broader programme of social sector restructuring being implemented with varying degrees of formality in much of the developing world (Vivian, 1995). It would be a failure, however, to consider voluntary organizations only in the context of developing countries. The United States has a long history of using voluntary organizations in the contracting of public services, and certain interpretations of the subsidiarity principle within the EU also favour voluntary organizations and informal care in the future organization of social policies. A crucial question concerning the role of NGOs in these processes is whether they are or should be used as a vehicle for privatization and social sector restructuring.

The safety net schemes are thought to provide an opportunity to reshape coalitions and power relations in the society. Demand-based schemes are considered particularly effective in this respect, because through them non-governmental and nonpowerful groups are given a way to participate actively in the system – a process by which they are supposed to be empowered. In this process social funds for NGO projects are seen as the means by which new groups can be attracted to pro-poor coalitions, enabling these coalitions to generate sufficient support to maintain pro-poor governments. This type of social sector reform proposal constitutes an attempt to link the neoliberal, market-based model of social provisioning to the formerly alternative approaches of participation and empowerment in a kind of neoliberal populism (Vivian, 1995).

Not surprisingly, it has also been argued that the contemporary trend toward promoting people's empowerment through the NGO sector has in fact had a disabling consequence as far as oppressed people are concerned. It not only seeks to disorient them from demanding that the state agencies deliver the goods, but it also shifts the focus from struggle politics to NGO activity (Mohanty, 1995). According to Vivian, even a cursory examination of the implemented safety-net programmes in developing countries makes it clear that the primary rationale of most such programmes is based on creating support for adjustment measures (Vivian, 1995). The offer to the indigenous NGOs to manage and mitigate the projects themselves has been seen as tempting them into silence (Gibbon, 1993). There is a major difference between improving the efficiency and equity of social sector spending, on one hand, and propping up bad economic policies with low coverage and token social action programmes on the other (Costello et al., 1994). Among NGOs there has also been concern that, in the context of the shrinking state role and uncertain funding, the pressure of NGOs to become service providers may lead to their playing a role in the privatization of state functions (May, 1995).

The second type of concern is related to the issue of what is gained by using more NGOs in the provision of health care and what impact this has on the sustainability of health sector policies. The international development agencies have valued NGOs especially for their perceived efficiency and greater ability to reach the poorest, but the efficiency of separate organizations does not necessarily increase the efficiency of health systems. According to Green and Matthias there is little evidence available to demonstrate that NGOs *as a group* score highly on the criteria of efficiency, quality, sensitivity to the needs of communities and sustainability of service delivery, although some individual NGOs may do so (Green and Matthias, 1995). Even though in practice many countries are dependent on nongovernmental providers of health services, the reasons may not lie in their efficiency capacities. Macintosh has pointed out that in general there is no necessary reason why non-profit organizations should not behave commercially, and that, contracting for services with independent organizations requires regulation, which is difficult, expensive and very demanding on the probity of the regulators (Macintosh, 1995); (see also Chapter 9).

NGOs may not be more successful than the state agencies in overcoming poverty, and there is evidence that the combination of state reorganization and the emergence of NGOs as implementers of development assistance has contributed to undermining grassroots organizations representing poor people (Arellano-Lopez and Petras, 1994). If there are inadequacies in the account-ability of the governmental agencies, there are even more constraints on making the NGOs answerable to the people (Mohanty, 1995). It has been suggested that in order to enhance local sustainability, the NGOs should work with, rather than replace, the functions of the state (Stefanini, 1995). Consider-ing the current trend towards moving funding to the nongovernmental sector and the concern over NGOs acting as privatization agents, it is important to understand the part that NGOs are expected to play in the development of health systems and especially to understand the long-term accountability, equity and sustainability aspects of the whole process. If this process means changing social rights to charity, for NGOs seeking social justice and equity it might mean giving up values in exchange for money.

which challenge in size the development budgets of individual countries and the activities of smaller United Nations organizations. A handful of 'super' NGOs are emerging in the humanitarian area. This means that eight to ten large conglomerates of international NGOs account for what may be 80 per cent of the financial value of assistance in complex emergencies (Gordenker and Weiss, 1995). In the field of population assistance, several donors channel a portion of their aid through international NGOs. Slightly less than one third of developed-country government assistance flows through NGOs, and five international NGOs accounted for nearly three quarters of the assistance flowing in this way: the International Planned Parenthood Federation, the Population Council, the Association of Voluntary Surgical Sterilization, the Program for Appropriate Technology for Health and Pathfinder International (World Bank, 1994d).

CONCERNS AND CONSTRAINTS

The problem of retrenching state and public responsibility with the increasing role of NGOs and voluntary activities needs to be addressed. While NGO contracting has not been a very widespread phenomenon in developing countries (Robinson, 1997), the trend for increasing arrangements for contractual relations together with the closer NGO relations with government agencies has invited debate within the NGOs themselves. Edwards and Hulmes have argued both for the necessity of NGOs to work constructively and creatively with sources of funding, centres of influence, and those in political authority, and against the danger of 'growing too close for comfort' – when NGOs, like Icarus before them, may plummet to the ground as the heat of the donors melts the wax in their wings (Hulme and Edwards, 1997). In countries with a high dependence on foreign aid coupled with donor privatization policies, the debate is shifting with respect to NGO versus state provision, from an issue of comparative to competitive advantage. On the other hand, the present economic globalization could also signal a parallel globalization of social welfare, with NGOs providing a channel for its realization – in other words, a move towards a selective permanent provision of welfare services to the world's underclass (Fowler, 1995) (Box 7.3).

According to Smillie, the ultimate question is how much the 'civil society' discourse and donor infatuation with NGOs has to do with democracy and human rights, and how much it has to do with finding cheaper and more efficient alternatives to faltering governmental delivery systems. To the extent that NGOs are viewed as part of the private sector, the enthusiasm for them may have less to do with new-found understanding of civil society's role in making democracy work, and more to do with the new orthodoxy in public policies. By squinting hard, NGOs can be seen and treated simply as contractors, just another private sector alternative to government in general, and to bad government in particular (Smillie, 1995). Increasing NGO involvement and reliance on their own resources can also lead to overlooking local capacities, reducing the accountability of local government to the people and undermining the foundation upon which future and long-term improvements in people's lives must be built (Collier, 1996).

The increasing role of the NGOs in the international field has been enhanced by expectations of greater effectiveness in reaching the poorest. The process of increased channelling of funds through NGOs, however, is also reflected in the work and structure of NGOs. International support is often project-specific, which causes NGOs difficulties with the organizational costs; it is usually available only for limited periods, and international donors are often interested only in supporting capital or startup costs (Gilson *et al.*, 1994). The pressure to demonstrate concrete achievements or spend money fast may even result in discouraging or repressing participation in NGO projects and programmes involving external funding (UNDP, 1993b). Some have warned against the tendency of international development agencies to see NGOs as a kind of magic bullet providing simple solutions for sustainable development (Vivian, 1994). Increasing funding possibilities may also create private interests to be channelled into nongovernmental action where lines between for-profit firms and non-profit organizations may be blurring, or private interests in terms of income or social status may lead to increasing hollowness of non-profit claims by NGOs. The performance and accountability of non-governmental organizations have come under question (Green and Matthias, 1997; Edwards and Hulme, 1995).

While NGOs are perhaps more popular than ever, there is also increasing concern over the evolving NGO role and the actors emerging now on the scene. In the international field these concerns derive especially from problems experienced by NGOs in lobbying United Nations organizations, and from the NGO forums at United Nations conferences and summits. It has been argued, for example, that the NGOs failed to make an impact in the larger policy context of the Rio Earth Summit and actually legitimized the continuation of destructive policies (Chatterjee and Finger, 1994). In the name of NGOs and civil society participation, the large and well-funded politically conservative international organizations, as well as organizations acting as mouthpieces for industries, gained power (Chatterjee and Finger, 1994; Hild-yard, 1993). At the Copenhagen Social Summit the role of NGOs was to be quite similar. As the global background of social problems – including structural adjustment policies and promotion of free trade – remained unchallenged in the final document, the frustrations amongst NGOs were channelled into an Alternative Copenhagen Declaration, which refused to accept the framework of action of the official documents (Alternative Copenhagen Declaration, 1995). While NGOs have drawn a great deal of hope and attention because of their assumed capacity to follow up, innovate, and exercise vigilance, much less thought has been given to whether they are sufficiently qualified and supported to carry out these activities. The industries and different interest organizations have more resources for lobbying than organizations working on social and humanitarian issues, and the representatives of 'civil society' are not necessarily as visible as other groups claiming to act in their interest.

Private sector

The private sector role in international health policies is rarely discussed, although it is very evident in many spheres concerning health. The private sector has major relevance in the development of pharmaceuticals as well as policies linked with the marketing, regulation and pricing of pharmaceutical products. In addition to pharmaceutical products there is a broader industry based on health-care technologies and services. The private insurance companies, private practitioners and hospitals are older private sector participants in health-care policies with for-profit managed-care chains entering the field at a fast pace. The change in managed-care provision has been moving from non-profit to for-profit organizations and spreading and merging fast with an unprecedented change in the organization of health care in the United States (Robinson, 1996; Bond and Weissman, 1997; Imersheim and Estes, 1996). In the United Kingdom, with the government and health authorities under financial pressure and drug companies and private providers looking for commercial opportunities there has been increased cooperation between the public and the private sector: this raises the question of the future role of the pharmaceutical industry in managed care and disease management (Lawrence and Williams, 1996). The practitioners of traditional medicine and other health systems have been involved in health care for a long time in many countries. In many countries, together with 'natural' health products and tonics, these traditional medicines have emerged in a more commercialized form in the 1990s.

International policies also cover products or marketing practices hazardous to health, such as tobacco, as well as regulatory measures concerning health and safety issues. The normative and regulatory functions in health policies, such as work in Codex Alimentarius or the International Programme on Chemical Safety (IPCS), are of direct relevance to international industries – as well as issues of pharmaceutical safety, price regulation or the regulation of private practice in health. There has been an increasing recognition of the need for better regulatory action in health, and the necessary role of the state in this. Similar needs may be expected to gain ground in international policies with the globalization of trade interests and the implications this holds for the rule setting and normative functions of international organizations involved in health and safety issues. In addition, advances in genetics and biotechnology are creating new ethical dilemmas and issues with respect to privacy, patenting, therapies and reproductive technologies.

CONCERNS AND CONSTRAINTS

There have been constant calls for more 'partnership' with public and private sector on national and international levels in the 1990s. However, there is less discussion on the impacts of this on policy priorities, or on the potential of such collaboration to lead to increasing public sector costs and to misallocation of public funds. It is also to be expected with the increasing role of the private sector in health care provision and with the public sector contracting, that there should be a need for stronger legislation, regulation and monitoring on the national and international levels. Yet there is also a trend towards deregulation and the use of incentives, with a shift towards a more trade-related context of regulatory action and emphasis on market access, intellectual property rights and licensing, with less consideration for health, safety and affordability issues.

The transnational nature of many of the industries with direct health relevance, such as the pharmaceutical, food and chemical industries, has implications for international policies and action on health. The transnational companies have been shown to export drugs and chemicals banned in their country of origin to the developing countries, and the tobacco manufacturers have orientated their marketing efforts towards the developing and newly industrialized countries (UNRISD, 1995). Although transnational corporations potentially could play an important role in social development, their current impact on this process is moderate at best. Transnational company officials often advance disingenuous and morally suspect arguments against corporate social responsibility. In fact, recent developments – bilateral investment treaties, multilateral trade agreements, privatization efforts, weakened national regulations regimes and the predominance of the free-market ideology – reinforce this perspective by minimizing the responsibilities of transnational corporations while expanding their rights (Kolodner, 1994). This process has also led to growing concern over global corporate power (Korten, 1995; UNRISD, 1995).

The health-related industries have grown in size and complexity in mergers and cross-investing with huge transnationals in the pharmaceutical industry, where some companies have now labelled themselves the 'life-sciences industry'. In line with this new approach, the pharmaceutical industry has invested heavily in new technologies and research in genetics and biotechnology, which may be expected to entail novel challenges to regulatory action. New communication technologies use the Internet to provide world-wide markets for health-related products, with direct access to consumer. The transnational companies in health care are well resourced and prepared to exploit these new international opportunities. Distinctions between 'good allies' and 'health-hazardous' industries are increasingly breaking down as tobacco manufacturers have been investing in health insurance companies and for-profit health maintenance organizations (Boyd *et al.*, 1995). In addition to Nestlé, the pharmaceutical companies such as Mead Johnson and Wyeth have shown they have the capacity to break the international baby-milk code in the 1990s (Wise, 1997).

Other international institutions

Other international institutions with a role in health policies include, for example, the different churches and religious institutions which have significance especially in the fields of service provision and policies on sexual and reproductive health. The Catholic Church is a major provider of health services globally and has a broad influence in the developed world, for example, in the interpretation of public responsibilities and principles such as subsidiarity in the EU. Many of the major international organizations also have links to religious institutions and so do a large number of the NGOs involved in development cooperation at the local level. This is especially so in health and welfare, traditionally the major fields of charity and missionary work. In Africa the colonial governments stood aloof from rural development and concentrated on the regulatory functions of law and order. NGOs, in the form of churches and missionary societies, were the principal providers of health and education services, especially in the hinterland (Bratton, 1989). The churches represent a particularly important element of health care in Africa, and in Ghana and Malawi the salaries of all church health staff are paid by the government. The central role of the Catholic church in the delivery of health services naturally has implications for the integration of abortion and family-planning services into primary health care (Gilson *et al.*, 1994).

The scientific and research community evidently has a major place in international policy making on health, although it is rarely pointed out in practice. In addition to the straightforward functions of providing more knowledge on health-related issues, the scientific community influences health policies in more subtle ways. For example in the production of the *World Development Report 1993* certain academic institutions played an important role. Specialists in biomedical health, public health, health services research, health policies and health economics all have academic backgrounds which provide different frameworks for policy development. It is also clear that the influences, emphases and priorities within the scientific community and related institutions will be reflected in their work. In international health research the major research institutions tend to be situated in the developed countries and in many developing countries not only research but also educational possibilities in public health, health systems development or health policies remain marginal. This means that quite often persons involved in international health tend to have educational backgrounds in American or European schools of public health. The division of global health research is reflected well in the observation that while 90 per cent of the world's potential years of life lost belong to the developing countries, only 5 per cent of global research funds are devoted to studying the developing world's health problems (Commission on Health Research for Development, 1990).

Developments in technology and science also tend to challenge health policies through their impact on treatment practices, and special reference needs to be made to developments in genetics and medical technologies which provide not only new and better avenues for health policies, but also more profound ethical and political dilemmas in terms of resource allocation, equity and the value basis of public health policies.

CONCERNS AND CONSTRAINTS

There is a wide array of policy prescriptions within the international religious institutions and development organizations affiliated to churches. The role of religious institutions in policy making on health is clearly most important for broad international religions with missionary wings, but it is not necessarily linked with Christianity. One way of reflecting the different emphases is the division of policy interests into fundamentalist-conservative, organizational-practical and radical-spiritual. The fundamentalist-conservative strain has relevance especially in relation to sexual and reproductive health and moral order within societies. The organizational and practical strain is related to service provision and the role of charity activities in the legitimation of religious organizations in the society. The radical-spiritual strain is found in such movements as liberation theology and resistance to social inequities, the undermining of human rights and dignity in development policies, and to materialism and the commercialization of life. The crucial question with respect to religious institutions and their impact on health policies is which of these strains is present in the actual policies practised by these institutions.

Within the scientific community, research funding tends to follow the general values of the society. In the 1990s the emphasis has been on life sciences and technology, and with the shift of funding towards the private sector this trend is expected to strengthen. The problem in public health policies is the need for independent research and funding for the regulatory activities requiring competence in various areas outside the private sector. It is no secret, for example, that the tobacco manufacturers have shifted their policies from advertising towards promotional targets, where universities seem to be a key target (Mayor, 1997). The pharmaceutical industry has invested heavily in genetic research, with wide future implications for health policies (Cohen,

1997). The trade-related intellectual property rights imply more limits on the broad use of the fruits of research work in the private sector (see Chapter 10). Another crucial question is the focus of research within the international organizations and the implications of research work for further policy development.

8

Health for All
and Primary Health Care Strategies

Health for All by the year 2000 has been the major formal global strategy in health and health services development. The Health for All strategy was developed during the 1970s, and launched by the World Health Assembly in 1979 (WHO 1981b) (Box 8.1). Primary health care was to be central in achieving health for all. The report and the Declaration of the International Conference on Primary Health Care (Box 8.2.), convened jointly by UNICEF and WHO, was endorsed at the same World Health Assembly (WHO, 1981b).

Box 8.1 Health for All

In 1977 the 30th World Health Assembly decided that the main social goal of governments and WHO in the coming decades should be the attainment by all the people of the world by the year 2000 of a level of health that would permit them to lead a socially and economically productive life. This goal is commonly known as 'Health for All by the year 2000' (WHO, 1984). Below is a list of reformulated (1991) global indicators for the monitoring and evaluation of progress in the implementation of the health for all strategies (WHO, 1993b).

1   The number of countries in which health for all is continuing to receive endorsement as policy at the highest level.

2. The number of countries in which mechanisms for involving people in the implementation of strategies are fully functioning or are being further developed.

3   The percentage of gross national product spent on health.

4   The percentage of the national health expenditure devoted to local services.

5   The number of countries in which resources for PHC are becoming more equitably distributed.

Box 8.1 cont.

6   The amount of international aid received or given for health.

7   The percentage of the population covered by the PHC, with at least the following:
    • safe water in the home or with reasonable access, and adequate facilities available for the disposal of excreta;
    • immunization against diphtheria, tetanus, whooping cough, measles, poliomyelitis and tuberculosis;
    • local health services, including the availability of essential drugs within one hour's walk or travel;
    • attendance by trained personnel for pregnancy and childbirth, and caring for children during at least the first year of life;
    • the percentage of women of childbearing age using family planning;
    • the percentage of each element should be given for all identifiable subgroups.

8   The percentage of newborns weighing at least 2500 grams at birth, and the percentage of children whose weight-for-age and/or weight-for-height are acceptable.

9   The infant mortality rate (IMR), maternal mortality rate (MMR) and probability of dying before the age of 5 years (q5), in all identifiable subgroups.

10 Life expectancy at birth, by sex, in all identifiable subgroups.

11 The adult literacy rate, by sex, in all identifiable subgroups.

12 The per capita GNP.

Box 8.2. Declaration of Alma Ata
(WHO 1978)

The International Conference on Primary Health Care, meeting in Alma Ata this twelfth day of September in the year Nineteen hundred and seventy-eight, expressing the need for urgent action by all governments, all health and development workers, and the world community to protect and promote the health of all the people of the world, hereby makes the following declaration

I
The Conference strongly reaffirms that health, which is a state of complete physical, mental and social wellbeing, and not merely the absence of infirmity, is a fundamental human right and that the attainment of the highest possible level of health is a most important worldwide social goal whose realization requires the action of many other social and economic sectors in addition to the health sector.

II
The existing gross inequality in the health status of the people, particularly between developed and developing countries as well as within countries, is politically, socially and economically unacceptable and is, therefore, of common concern to all countries.

III
Economic and social development, based on a New International Economic Order, is of basic importance to the fullest attainment of health for all and to the reduction of the gap between the health status of the developing and developed countries. The promotion and protection of the health of the people is essential to sustained economic and social development and contributes to a better quality of life and to world peace.

IV
The people have the right and duty to participate individually and collectively in the planning and implementation of their health care.

V
Governments have a responsibility for the health of their people which can be fulfilled only by the provision of adequate health and social measures. A main social target of governments, international organizations and the whole world community in the coming decades should be attainment by all peoples of the world by the year 2000 of a level of health that will permit them to lead a socially and economically productive life. Primary health care is the key to attaining this target as part of development in the spirit of social justice.

Box 8.2 cont.

VI

Primary health care is essential health care based on practical, scientifically sound and socially acceptable methods and technology made universally accessible to individuals and families in the community through their full participation and at a cost the community and country can afford to maintain at every stage of their development in the spirit of self-reliance and self-determination. It forms an integral part both of the country's health system, of which it is the central function and main focus, and of the overall social and economic development of the community. It is the first level of contact of individuals, the family and community with the national health system, bringing health care as close as possible to where people live and work, and constitutes the first element of a continuing care process.

VII

Primary health care:

1 Reflects and evolves from the economic conditions and sociocultural and political characteristics of the country and its communities and is based on the application of the relevant results of social, biomedical and health services research and public health experience.

2 Addresses the main health problems in the community providing promotive, preventive, curative and rehabilitative services accordingly;

3 Includes at least: education concerning prevailing health problems and the methods of preventing and controlling them; promotion of food supply and proper nutrition; an adequate supply of safe water and basic sanitation; maternal and child health care, including family planning; immunization against the major infectious diseases; prevention and control of locally endemic diseases; appropriate treatment of common diseases and injuries; and provision of essential drugs.

4 Involves, in addition to the health sector, all related sectors and aspects of national and community development, in particular agriculture, animal husbandry, food, industry, education, housing, public works, communications and other sectors; and demands the coordinated efforts of all those sectors;

5 Requires and promotes maximum community and individual self-reliance and participation in planning, organization, operation and control of primary health care, making fullest use of local, national and other available resources; and to this end develops through appropriate education the ability of communities to participate;

6 Should be sustained by an integrated, functional and mutually supportive referral system, leading to the progressive improvement of comprehensive health care for all and giving priority to those most in need;

7 Relies, at local and referral levels, on health workers, including physicians, nurses, midwives, auxiliaries and community workers as applicable, as well

---

Box 8.2 cont.

as traditional practitioners as needed, suitably trained socially and technically to work as a health team and to respond to the expressed health needs of the community.

VIII
All governments should reformulate national policies, strategies and plans of action to launch and sustain primary health care as part of a comprehensive national health system and in coordination with other sectors. To this end, it will be necessary to exercise political will, to mobilize the country's resources and to use available resources rationally.

IX
All countries should cooperate in a spirit of partnership and service to ensure primary health care for all people since the attainment of health by all people in any one country directly concerns and benefits every other country. In this context the joint WHO/UNICEF report on primary health care constitutes a solid basis for the further development and operation of primary health care throughout the world.

X
An acceptable level of health for all the people of the world by the year 2000 can be attained through a fuller and better use of the world's resources, a considerable part of which are spent on armaments and military conflicts. A genuine policy of independence, peace, detente and disarmament could and should release additional resources that could well be devoted to the acceleration of social and economic development of which primary health care, as an essential part, should be allotted its proper share.

In the field of international development cooperation, vertical disease-oriented programmes were the major form of cooperation in the 1950s and 1960s. These programmes were targeted predominantly at communicable diseases, such as malaria, yaws and schistosomiasis, but population questions and malnutrition were also attacked in this way. Belief in the emerging new technologies also paved the way for operations against the major scourges of mankind. International donors often insisted on these programmes. At this time many of the countries concerned had no widespread health infrastructure. Even though the vertical approach brought substantial advances in the control of a number of diseases, it nonetheless gradually became evident that multiple vertical programmes as a long-term approach entailed serious inefficiencies and redundancies. Some countries had more than ten separate and largely vertical programmes, while at the same time they were having to combat many health problems for which there were no programmes at all. The first moves towards an integrated approach were already being made in the 1950s and 1960s, but integration was taken up again in the 1970s and 1980s (Smith and Bryant, 1988) The experiences of several projects of NGOs and from the developing countries, with special reference to experiences in China and Cuba, provided also evidence for new policies emphasizing PHC (Segall 1983).

In addition to concern over the concrete problems associated with the implementation of the vertical approach, the policies of the Alma Ata declaration and Health for All have their background in an approach emphasizing social justice, universal access and intersectoral action. The research done by WHO also had a role in the emergence of the concept, and special attention was drawn to the report on the functions of basic health services, which showed widespread dissatisfaction. Health systems were described as failures because people were dissatisfied with their ideology and form, not because they were unsuited for malaria eradication (Newell 1988). It was argued that instead of focusing on administrative shifts from vertical to horizontal programmes in health services, the health service delivery needed to be considered as part of the whole social and economic development of a nation, and that any improvements in services needed to take into account the whole question of national structures, priorities and goals (Rifkin and Walt, 1988).

In the 1970s the international political climate was also conducive to a broad analysis and a health approach with emphasis on the New International Economic Order, also referred to in the Health for All Strategy (WHO, 1981b). The discussion of basic needs and basic human needs during the 1970s was shared with other United Nations agencies (Green, 1978). Nevertheless, the Health for All initiative and the Alma Ata Declaration were to suffer, right from the beginning, from a lack of resources and from competing viewpoints on health policies. In 1979, Walsh and Warren introduced the selective model of PHC which questioned the more comprehensive approach agreed in Alma Ata as being unattainable because of the cost and personnel required. The selective approach (Box 8.3.) would institute health care directed at preventing or treating the few diseases that are responsible for the greatest mortality and morbidity in less-developed areas and for which there are means of control in terms of the efficacy and cost of interventions (Walsh and Warren, 1979).

Box 8.3   Selective primary health care

According to Walsh and Warren (1979), until comprehensive PHC can be made available to all, services aimed at the most important diseases (selective PHC) may be the most effective means of improving the health of the greatest number of people. Selective PHC is the most cost-effective type of medical intervention. On the basis of high morbidity and mortality and of the feasibility of controlling them, a circumscribed number of diseases are selected for prevention in a clearly defined population. The principal recipients of care are children up to three years old and women in the childbearing years. The care provided is made up of measles and diphtheria-pertussis-tetanus (DPT) vaccination for children over six months old, tetanus toxoid for all women of childbearing age, encouragement of long-term breast feeding, provision of chloroquine for episodes of fever in children under three years old in areas where malaria is prevalent and, finally, oral rehydration packets and instruction. These services are provided by fixed units or mobile teams visiting once every four to six months in areas where resources are more limited. The cost of fixed units is similar to that of basic PHC, although efficiency should be much greater. Whether the system is fixed or mobile, flexibility is necessary. The care package can be modified at any time according to the patterns of mortality and morbidity in the area served. It is important, however, for the service to concentrate on a minimum number or severe problems that affect large numbers of people and for which interventions of established efficacy can be provided at low cost.

Policies

The original emphasis on PHC as expressed in Alma Ata became interpreted more as selective PHC in the context of international health policies. The selective approach soon gained substantial international support amongst the development agencies and organizations. According to Unger and Killingsworth, USAID supported the initiative actively, the World Bank was ready to place billions of dollars behind the selective PHC approach, and it also won the backing of academic institutions (Centers for Disease Control, Harvard University) and foundations such as Ford and Rockefeller. In 1982, USAID even sent telegrams to all Latin American health stations suggesting the employment of the priority intervention approach when possible (Unger and Killingsworth, 1988). A major move in PHC policies was the choice of UNICEF to promote the selective approach (Warren, 1988). These actors are not marginal in international policies on health. USAID was the largest bilateral donor among the OECD countries in official development assistance to the health sector in 1990. The World Bank and UNICEF also played larger roles in financing health sector assistance in the 1980s than previously, with increasing involvement of the World Bank in the 1990s (Michaud and Murray, 1994). While the WHO regular budget had been frozen since early 1980s, more extrabudgetary support was directed to disease or technology specific vertical programmes and research than to those with capacities to support policy level changes towards PHC (see Chapter 2).

Selective health care policies in the 1980s were clearly designed for developing countries. Nevertheless, the original policies of PHC, and especially of Health for All, were to be valid in both developed and developing countries. According to Kaprio the concept of PHC itself was perhaps the greatest obstacle in Europe, where primary care was thought of as medical care. Many European countries had reached the target in full primary medical care coverage for the population. In Europe the task was how to convert this medical care into broader, more comprehensive (and ecologically satisfying) health care (Kaprio, 1979).

According to Bryant, in spite of the broad endorsement of the Alma Ata declaration and Health for All policies, the international climate of support for Health for All has been all too often ice-cold. (Bryant, 1988) The problems at the government level of implementation were already mentioned in a joint UNICEF/WHO study in 1981, which drew attention to inconsistencies between the theory and practice of PHC in many countries (WHO/UNICEF, 1981).

Even though progress in many aspects of the Health for All policies was made during the 1980s, the gap in health between rich and poor countries and population groups within many countries has increased (WHO, 1993b; WHO, 1995a). In the 1980s problems of economic stringency were evident in health efforts in many countries. Concerns over economic support for Health for All strategies, as well as over the consequences of recession and structural adjustment policies, emerged in the late 1980s (WHO, 1987b; Cornia *et al.*, 1987). In the 1990s increasing cost-consciousness, as well as the health care reform policies, have put more emphasis on primary level care in developed countries as well (*Lancet,* 1995b; Klein, 1995).

International policies on PHC have been influenced not only by the problems in implementation and acquisition of sufficient resources in support of Health for All, but also by different approaches in PHC policies. Even though the distinctions between selective and comprehensive PHC approaches are often considered marginal in the overall context, the approach to PHC is an issue over which the policies of the international organizations have diverged, with different emphases emerging at the policy level.

WHO

Since the endorsement of Health for All and PHC policies, the WHO approach has emphasized formally the comprehensive PHC approach, including the social rights and equity aspects of primary health care in line with the Alma Ata Declaration. It has been noted, however, that in spite of the major role of WHO in the promotion of comprehensive health care, the organization itself has not changed as far as this role is concerned (Walt, 1993). The vertical programmes of WHO remained during the 1980s, and the resources used to support the aims were modest and as a whole decreasing in this period (Walt, 1993).

In the 1980s, the WHO policies also came closer to the more selective approach on some issues. For example, WHO produced its own modification of selective health care policies in the form of a risk approach. According to Backett *et al.* the risk approach aims to target health interventions at those with the highest risk and is aimed especially at maternal and child health, including family planning (Backett *et al.,* 1984). It has been described as a modification of the selective resource-allocation strategy, using markers to predict future morbidity and aimed at making the delivery of health services more efficient (Hayes 1991). The monitoring efforts and choice of indicators also had significance in terms of the interpretation and emphasis of Health for All policies. The aim was to follow the progress of Health for All by using indicators, of which twelve were chosen for the global level in 1981 and revised in the 1990s (WHO, 1981b; WHO, 1993b). (see Box 8.1). In the 1990s WHO moved further in this direction through assessment of the disease burden and the development of DALYs (Disability Adjusted Life Years) in collaboration with the World Bank (Jamison and Jardel, 1993; World Bank, 1993a).

At the same time WHO strengthened its emphasis on the development of health systems and broader policies in health. It emphasized intersectoral action on health as well as the role of the District Health Systems for Primary Health Care (Gunatilleke, 1984; WHO, 1986; WHO, 1988a). The midpoint meeting in Riga in 1988 highlighted the need for social and political action, intersectoral collaboration and the strengthening of the district health systems based on PHC (WHO 1988b). The problems involving economic support for the Health for All policies and primary health care became crucial in the late 1980s (WHO, 1987b; WHO, 1987d). According to a WHO document on economic support for the Health for All strategy, the discussions on economic support for Health for All should not be clouded by a narrow vision of financing health care or medical care by the public or private sectors (WHO, 1987b).

In developed countries the policies of intersectoral action had difficulties, as these were not easily integrated into a view of PHC with a built-in bias towards medical care. According to Baum and Sanders, countries in the First World have used PHC to describe what is more accurately termed general medical practice, whereas the rhetoric of the goal of Health for All has been used more often in relation to health promotion policies and strategies (Baum and Sanders, 1995). The European Regional Office has been very active in the Health Promotion policies and Healthy Cities project, both of which are based on intersectoral action (Box 8.4).

Box 8.4 Health Promotion, Healthy Cities and New Public Health

In 1984 a new programme in Health Promotion was established in the WHO Regional Office for Europe (Anon, 1986). The health promotion approach was further developed at the first International Conference on Health Promotion in Ottawa (1986). The Ottawa Charter advocates the use of public policy to make healthy choices the easy choices promoting supportive environments, community action, individual skills and health services reorientation. It is built on the progress made through the Declaration on Primary Health Care, the WHO Targets for Health for All document and the previous debate at the world Health Assembly on intersectoral action and health (Ottawa Charter, 1986). The health promotion approach nevertheless seems to be vulnerable to criticism similar to that levelled at the Alma Ata Declaration. According to Baum and Sanders, while the social and other environmental factors influencing health may be recognized in the policies of health promotion, most targets set relate to disease or to biological or behavioural risk factors, which parallels the rapid shift from comprehensive to selective health care (Baum and Sanders, 1995).

The Healthy Cities initiative builds to a large extent on a background similar to that of Health Promotion and may be seen as an initiative intended to lend support to city-based health promotion (Ashton et al., 1986). In 1985 the idea of a project on health in cities emerged in the WHO Regional Office for Europe (Kickbush, 1989). The first formal activity of the Healthy Cities project took place in Lisbon in 1986 (Ashton et al., 1986). Healthy Cities policies have been seen as a local application of health promotion policies (Ashton et al., 1986). The project has brought forward a broader spectrum of social and environmental concerns, resembling those of the Alma Ata Declaration but placing more emphasis on the environment and reaching the local level. The Healthy Cities project has been called a success story and a growing movement (Tsouros, 1995; Kickbush, 1989). On the other hand, according to Baum, Healthy Cities projects around the world appear to be using the language of radical social movements, with emphasis on change through conflict, but to be

---

Box 8.4 cont.

operating within a bureaucratic logic that stresses consensual, incremental change (Baum, 1993).

Healthy public policies
The term 'healthy public policy' refers to all general government policy that has an impact on health. Healthy public policy may be seen as part of the health promotion policies as defined in the Ottawa Charter (Ottawa Charter, 1986). At the WHO Adelaide conference on Health Promotion – Healthy Public Policies, four key areas were defined as priorities for healthy public policy for immediate action: support for women's health; food and nutrition; tobacco and alcohol; and creating supportive environments. Specific emphasis was put on healthy public policy in the Third World (Hetzel, 1989). While building on the same background as the initiatives on health promotion, the healthy public policy approach may reveal a greater orientation towards public health, social justice and social policies, and avoid the victim-blaming more prone to emerge in strategies focusing on individuals and lifestyles.

While concerns over the socioeconomic trends between countries and within countries have been emphasized in several WHO documents (WHO, 1987b; WHO, 1987d; WHO, 1993b), the WHO profile has remained low and consensual with respect to advocacy concerning international development policies and health. A review of economic policies and health was made together with the World Bank in 1990 (Weil *et al.,* 1990). The technical supportive approaches to the PHC and Health for All policies seem to have predominated in the 1990s. WHO is also under pressure to maintain and promote the vertical programmes. This is due to the authority given by the disease eradication programmes and the perceived efficacy and short-term measurable benefits of the vertical programmes. Nevertheless, it also indicates pressures for a return towards policies which in part led to the inauguration of the PHC approach.

UNICEF

In the area of PHC policies, UNICEF's declaration of a Children's Revolution in 1982/3 was considered a major breakthrough in the implementation of the selective PHC approach, consisting at first of oral rehydration, universal childhood immunization, promotion of breastfeeding and growth monitoring

(Warren, 1988). The UNICEF selective approach has been explained by the practical aspects in terms of promised health gains and the potential for mobilizing support from national and international sources, but it has also been emphasized that the official Alma Ata publication already acknowledged that the national programmes could start with only a limited number of the components of PHC, provided that the others are added in the course of time (Taylor and Jolly, 1988). Wisner has argued that the belief that UNICEF's present emphasis on selective health care is a precursor or 'leading edge' of comprehensive PHC is seriously mistaken and that the approach of UNICEF – diffusion of packages of technologies by means of campaigns organized from the top – is more likely to undermine the social basis for comprehensive care (Wisner, 1988a).

During most of the 1980s the UNICEF advocacy for the selective approach was public and visible in the media. The GOBI-FFF was launched in the early 1980s. UNICEF was an active partner in the development of the goals and targets for the World Summit for Children, held in 1990 and resulting in broad governmental acceptance of the explicit targets set at the Summit. Since then, UNICEF has been actively monitoring target achievement.

UNICEF's promotion of selective policies emphasizing a small number of mostly medical activities has been considered as contradictory in the light of what it has done in assembling cross-sectoral information relevant to the well-being of children, especially in its influential work on the social impact of recession and structural adjustment programmes (de Kadt, 1989). The selective PHC approach promoted by UNICEF has been closer to the health policy of the World Bank, however, than to the more comprehensive PHC policy promoted by WHO. Many of the UNICEF strategies, such as the prioritization of selective interventions with high cost efficiency, social marketing and the Bamako Initiative funding mechanisms, have enjoyed the approval of and promotion by the World Bank (World Bank, 1993a). UNICEF has not claimed that there is a need to halt structural adjustment programmes, but rather called for structural adjustment with a human face in order to seek protection for the poor and most vulnerable in times of economic adjustment (UNICEF, 1990).

World Bank

The World Bank has supported the selective – and more cost-efficient – policies in health in the 1980s (Warren, 1988). In 1982 World Bank President A. W. Clausen stated in his first health-related pronouncement that child mortality in the world could be halved through the implementation of the new 'technological breakthroughs' of oral rehydration therapy and vaccinations by means of a selective PHC-like structure (Unger and Killingsworth, 1986). In

1983 former World Bank President MacNamara and Jonas Salk met with James Grant, Executive Director of UNICEF, to suggest that immunization should be the spearhead of the UNICEF initiative, and the World Bank was also actively involved in the organization of the Task Force for Child Survival to coordinate the massive efforts to immunize children (Warren, 1988).

The selective health care approach has put a major emphasis on community health workers with short training to perform the selective interventions (Unger and Killingsworth, 1986). The cost-effectiveness of the training of community health workers has been appreciated by the World Bank, which funded and promoted schemes with community health workers in the 1980s because of their short training requirements and low cost (World Bank 1980). The World Bank promoted packages of essential clinical services or basic health services and family planning more or less belong to the same family as GOBI-FFF, though they are more integrated in that they cover different interventions and services to the district level (World Bank, 1993a; Walsh and Simonet, 1995). The common nature of these is not surprising, as the World Bank actually used Walsh, one of the two authors who first presented selective PHC, in its own report on Maternal and Child Health (MCH) (Walsh *et al.*, 1991). The World Bank's choice of packages and interventions is based essentially on the evaluation of the cost efficiency of the interventions, and becomes the criterion of highest priority in the evaluation of choices in health policies (World Bank, 1993a).

The World Bank-promoted concepts of social safety-nets, public health services and essential clinical services extended to district level have similarities with the PHC approach, but they nevertheless originate from a different framework and context. The World Bank also relates health to intersectoral action, larger development questions and donor policies. The results of these considerations, however, and the World Bank's activities in the health sector, have not been precisely the policies called for by public health activists in the spirit of the Alma Ata Declaration (Werner, 1995; Green, 1995). David Werner has claimed that the World Bank's involvement in health has meant the death of the Alma Ata Declaration. In his view, the three major components in the demise of PHC have been the introduction of selective health care policies, the introduction of changes in the financing of health services, and the entry of the World Bank into the field of health (Werner, 1994).

While equity receives attention in the stated World Bank policies (World Bank, 1987; World Bank, 1993a), the World Bank policies have also indicated a shift from the Alma Ata perspective on health as a social right to the public and private spheres of health services and to emphases on the outcomes of the different health interventions and on individual responsibilities in health (World Bank, 1987; World Bank, 1993a). The World Bank has seen community participation mostly in terms of cost sharing rather than as a social struggle for health rights and policy changes (Paul, 1987), though the latter has been emphasized recently by a former activist hired by the World Bank (Clark, 1995). While the World Bank has set an aim of universal access to the basic health care package, and has promoted the primary level in contrast to tertiary care, the context in which the changes are made renders these efforts problematic in relation to the aims of the Alma Ata Declaration (see Chapters 3 and 9).

Concerns and constraints

Constraints in the implementation

Whether or not Health for All was merely a nice thought without any realistic chances or coherent implementation plan is a question that has been debated since the Alma Ata conference. Criticism has been oriented especially towards the broad aspirations of comprehensive health care, and there have been proposals for more selective approaches and for an emphasis on cost efficiency and the feasibility of actions. The constraints on the implementation of the Alma Ata Declaration and PHC policies were already known when the policies were inaugurated. The presentation of the idea and meaning of Health for All by WHO Director General Mahler raised several issues, such as the rules of the medical establishment and industry. He also pointed out that the health professions are not alone in their conservatism as classical economics, too, is in danger of estranging itself from the aims of society by confusing economic growth with development and by constantly demanding economic proof of social benefits (Mahler, 1981).

According to Tarimo and Webster there have been six major misinterpretations of the meaning of the PHC: First, that it is only community-based health care; second, that it is the first level of contact for individuals and communities within the health system; third, that it is only for poor people in developing countries who cannot afford real doctors; fourth, that PHC is a core set of health services, often referred to as the eight or ten essential elements of PHC; fifth, that it is concerned only with the rural areas, uses simple low-tech interventions and health workers with limited knowledge and training, and it is opposed to doctors, hospitals and modern technology; and sixth, that PHC is cheap (Tarimo and Webster, 1996).

The gap between theory and practice has been of concern in the Health for All policies. According to Bryant there is no doubt that WHO has been highly successful in eliciting formal statements from all member states in support of the meaning and intent of Health for All; the troublesome questions have to do with the extent and effectiveness of both commitment and implementation of the policies (Bryant, 1988). According to Tarimo and Webster, on global solidarity in general, the PHC movement has depended almost exclusively on goodwill. The proposal of establishing a Global Advisory Council as a means of exerting pressure on various health-for-all partners to comply with their commitments has not been successful and the need for such a mechanism remains (Tarimo and Webster, 1995). De Kadt has emphasized the nebulous phraseology and doctrinaire nature of the Health for All strategy and warned that the more a fuzzy ideology born from compromise is allowed to substitute for a practical assessment of the possibilities, the less will be achieved (de Kadt, 1982). According to Peabody, the unrealistic goals of the Health for All strategy may have been counteractive: an unattainable goal is demoralizing, and the organization may be held accountable to the goals (Peabody, 1995).

Patel has argued that even several years after the initiation of the Global Strategy for Health for All, essential information on the costs of activities proposed by the strategy as well as their probable effects on health were lacking, thus hampering the transformation of the policy into a plan (Patel, 1986). In the follow-up and monitoring of the Health for All policies the lack of adequate information on even the most critical indicators from some countries made evident the striking lack of information that would enable analysis of the critical aspects of the implementation (Mahler, 1984). The monitoring and gathering of information has been of importance since. With respect to the promotion of intersectoral action, however, attention has been drawn to the institutional and political arrangements that influence the capacity to use information for management and policy making (de Kadt, 1989). The problems of health information systems in much of the developing world are not technical or intellectual but represent failures of primary care as social reality. The notion seems to have developed that the accumulation of data is a good thing in itself. It is becoming evident, however, that the cost of collecting data can impede the provision of modest health care (Opit, 1987).

Economic support

The most influential contribution on the costs of comprehensive PHC policies was made by Walsh and Warren (1979), promoting a selective approach to PHC as an interim strategy (Box 8.3). Unger and Killingsworth have summed up the reasons why the selective approach appealed to the major international donor agencies as follows:

1   The approach is capable of providing recordable results.

2   It does not hinder privatization, as selective health care is meant to fill the functional gaps left by the private sector (preventive activities), thereby tending to bypass the issue of population-oriented health service responsibility.

3 It claims to be the 'most' cost efficient approach.

4 It emphasizes prospects for the development of new high-tech commercial technologies (such as vaccines produced by genetic engineering) rather than management improvements in existing techniques.

5 It maintains the financial and institutional status quo, requiring little fund transfer from hospital care to PHC (Unger and Killingsworth, 1986).

The two evaluations of the Global Strategy for Health for All have emphasized the insufficiency of international support for the implementation of the policies (WHO, 1987c; WHO, 1993b). If the Global Health for All strategy has not received the support it should on the international level, the same problems have been encountered on the national level. In some countries there are absolute resource constraints, but in others the issues are more related to political commitment and resource allocation policies. The call for international support for Health for All policies is often perceived as a call for more resources in development cooperation. Nevertheless, in terms of resources, the impact of current terms of trade, debt servicing and global liberalization of trade is far more substantial (UNDP, 1992).

International influence on the implementation of Health for All policies extends beyond direct financial support to health sector expenditures in developing countries. There has been concern over whether the allocation of external assistance adequately addresses needs in the developing countries. It has even been argued that external health assistance is essentially unrelated to need and thus entirely political (Drager *et al.,* 1992, cited in Michaud and Murray, 1994). According to Michaud and Murray, the share of external assistance to developing countries in 1990 was less than 3 per cent of total health expenditures in the developing world, and only in a few countries did external assistance play a major financing role. At the beginning of the 1990s almost half of health assistance was spent on the development of infrastructure through grants for health services and hospitals. The other half was allocated to specific health programmes. In their view, in spite of the small overall share of external assistance, its impact could be critical in the areas of capital investment, research and strategic planning in developing countries. For example the Expanded Programme of Immunization promoted by UNICEF, WHO and several donor agencies has been seen as successful in influencing the health agendas of developing countries (Michaud and Murray, 1994). From the perspective of policy development, the influence on research and strategic planning may in fact have a substantial impact on the development of health policies in the long run. The emphasis on donor coordination and policy-based or programme-based support in the 1990s may also increase substantially the impact of external influence on national health policies.

Medical profession

Success in the implementation of policies was related to the role and support of the different actors involved. In health policies, the medical profession may certainly be seen as a major actor. Green has presented the role of medical professional conservatism, which has coincided with that of the élite interests which ensured the failure of Health for All and supported the choice of selective strategies with a framework better suited to the medical profession's interests (Green, 1994). The interests and class background of the medical profession do not coincide with the aims of PHC, public health and equity in many countries (Zaidi, 1986; Woelk, 1994; Sherraden and Wallace, 1992; Mburu, 1989; Mangelsdorf *et al.*, 1988). Professional interests based on the social class background, earning prospects and status of the profession should also be differentiated from professional interests related more to an understanding of what constitutes quality biomedical care, as these may not necessarily coincide. Concern over professional capacities has been emphasized, especially with respect to changes in medical education (Anon, 1985). WHO has been observed to be 'medical' (Walt, 1993; Peabody, 1995), and it may be doubted whether there has been commitment, even within the organization, to promoting activities which run against the interests of the medical profession.

While the emphasis on economic issues and on the effectiveness of health care indicates a decline in the power of medical professionals, the shift of power from the medical profession to the managerial or economic specialists does not necessarily increase the role and power of the community in decision making on health care priorities. According to Chase and Carr-Hill, the imposition of a cost-management rationale on the 'quality' of PHC is highly questionable. While they realize that one cannot ignore the present climate of economic adjustment programmes enforced by the World Bank and the recommended cost recovery within the health sector, they emphasize that PHC is not about selling services. To reduce community involvement in health to the level of its financial contributions, and then acknowledge the need for some token accountability to that community, undermines the whole PHC philosophy (Chase and Carr-Hill, 1994).

The criticism presented by the medical profession has often been aimed at both selective and comprehensive approaches of PHC. Mburu has noted the common reactions among Ministry of Health personnel to the PHC strategies. These reactions occur because the PHC strategy and philosophy appear to shatter the medical norm, which conflicts with the norms of modern health care service. According to Mburu, several factors are interpreted as an attack on the core of proper medical organization:

1 PHC is perceived as unhealthy in that it ignores the well-founded standards of medical care.

2 PHC makes everyone an expert in what was an exclusive domain of the highly trained in modern medicine, on one hand, and of traditional healers on the other.

3 PHC might marginalize hospitals and thus institutionalize second-rate medical practice.

4 Improper and dangerous medical treatment will be unavoidable.

5 At the broad political level, PHC is seen as a strategy to keep the poor poorer while the richer élite may gain even more disproportionately.

6 PHC may be the culmination of socialist thought, infiltrating in the guise of appropriate medical technology (Mburu, 1989).

Concerns over the strategies of PHC

STRATEGIES

The implementation and use of the selective strategies revealed the problems of the approach in practice. Walsh, one of the two authors of the original strategy, noted in 1988 that the lack of impact on health of large-scale health programmes that have provided selective interventions is probably related to inadequate recognition of the importance of community and political involvement, and of the necessary social, cultural, management and administrative underpinnings (Walsh, 1988).

Both the comprehensive and the selective approaches to PHC, but especially the latter, emphasized the role of community health workers. The experiences with community health workers have been mixed (WHO, 1989; Skeet, 1984). In an early evaluation, the lack of national planning of community health worker programmes and the inadequate support services to community health workers have been emphasized (Ofosu-Amaah, 1983). In a later WHO evaluation similar issues were addressed (WHO, 1989). According to the evaluation, the failures of community health worker programmes should not be attributed to failings of individuals or to the concept of community health workers, but to inadequacies in the planning and implementation of the programmes. Failure is inevitable when community health worker programmes are approached as piecemeal development projects and organized as vertical programmes unrelated to national and district health systems (WHO, 1989).

According to Stone, the concept of community participation entails Western values of self-reliance, equality and individualism, which may not equally characterize Third World communities or mean the same thing to their members (Stone, cited in Foster, 1987). On the other hand, while community participation has been an actively promoted part of PHC, in practice it has often been understood as participation through work, finance or change in behaviour rather than as having a say in the decision making. Samba has described a telling example of a situation where the interpretation of community participation and self-reliance in terms of sharing the costs of health facilities led to active and angry social participation when the rural community became aware that similar cost sharing was not being practised in the towns (Samba, 1981). The emphasis on prevention and behavioural changes, especially required of mothers, has also been problematized. The competing demands on women's time and its social and psychological costs of seeking care have not received the attention that they deserve in the implementation of child survival strategies (Coreil *et al.*, 1994; Leslie, 1992). Because of the social and economic heterogeneity of the population, a small subgroup is both subject to most of the disease risk and most unlikely to use the services of an intervention programme (Gadomski *et al.,* 1990). Razum has emphasized that care should be taken not to attribute low immunization coverage to the laziness and ignorance of the mothers when the main contributing factor is poor quality of services. Mothers are willing to walk even long distances to have their children immunized, provided the quality of services is adequate and treatment by health personnel is decent (Razum, 1993).

INTERVENTIONS

The major role of cost efficient health interventions was articulated clearly, especially in the selective approach, and has been at the centre of international health policies ever since. There could also be a place for a more careful evaluation of the experiences of the PHC technologies and practices promoted on such a broad scale. The reports presented may only represent sporadic cases, but some issues should perhaps receive more attention because of the potential for a more systematic failure of some of the approaches on which the 'core' of health interventions has been built in the international health policies.

Growth monitoring has been promoted as a means to reach children at high risk, but in practice the emphasis has been on the process of weighing and measuring (Nabarro and Chinnock, 1988; Gadomski *et al.,* 1990). The practice of growth monitoring has attracted criticism because of the lack of expected gains (Gerein and Ross, 1991, George *et al.,* 1993). Training health workers has been reported to be most adequate in the skills of weighing and charting, less adequate in the interpretation of growth curves, and least adequate for follow-up activities. According to Gerein, although anthropometric indicators can predict the children at risk of dying, no studies have been carried out to test whether such screening results in earlier interventions and decreased mortality (Gerein, 1988). As effective growth monitoring activities are not easily implemented in practice, it has been argued that perhaps their widespread advocacy is not a result of a careful review of policy and programme research, but more a reflection of changes in the needs and concerns of international agencies (Nabarro and Chinnock, 1988). In addition to the competing needs of the times, there have been concerns that growth monitoring could be among the factors which deter women from choosing to breastfeed for longer durations or with greater frequency (Behague, 1993). The growth of breastfed children living in favourable conditions was found in the WHO review to be less than expected when the growth chart reference was used during the latter half of the recommended exclusive breastfeeding period (WHO, 1995c). The reference growth chart, based on mostly bottle-fed infants, may have been counterproductive in terms of promoting breast-feeding. According to Walsh and Simonet, growth monitoring faded from prominence among selective health care strategies when results in the poorest countries were disappointing and other technologies, such as helminth chemo-therapy, maternal health, respiratory disease control and vitamin A supple-mentation provided more promising entries (Walsh and Simonet, 1995).

Problems associated with immunization-related policies have been discussed with regard to the diverting effects of specific campaigns in the health services organization and the difficulty of maintaining immunization targets in the long run (Banerji, 1990; Cassels and Janovsky, 1992). The disease-specific life-saving benefits of immunizations such as tetanus toxoid and pertussis are also at risk of cancellation by competing risks which make immunizations necessary, but not sufficient for child survival (Gadomski, *et al.,* 1990). Research carried out in the Expanded Programme of Immunization (EPI) has also provided unexpected evidence of the potential harm of vaccines. The best documented example is the late excess mortality in female recipients of the high-dose measles vaccine in areas with underlying high child mortality (Wright, 1995). According to Nichter the pressure put on the staff to meet the EPI targets is perceived by many community members as willingness to compromise their best interests. The vaccination of mildly ill children is taken as evidence of this. In this context, the 'missed opportunities' on the part of some staff to immunize mildly ill children may constitute a deliberate attempt to secure community confidence over time. (Nichter, 1995).

It has been noted that the decreasing diarrhoea mortality has not been accompanied by a reduction in morbidity, and that ORT is mainly efficient in the acute watery diarrhoeas (Martines *et al.*, 1993). Others have argued that the common ways in which mothers feed their children might be preferable to the use of oral rehydration solution packets in the treatment of diarrhoeas at home (Almroth and Latham, 1995). It has also been observed that ORT does not provide gains in persistent malnutrition-related diarrhoeas (Fitzroy *et al.*, 1990). At the community level, a mother may be introduced to the technique of ORT, but her ability and desire to use it will depend on the social support system. Curing a child of an episode of life-threatening dehydration and then returning the child to the home situation that led to the attack may not improve the ultimate survival chances of the child (Mosley, 1985). Werner and Sanders have linked their in-depth critique of the failure of ORT to fulfil its promise to the way policies have been concentrated in a few hands, and to the idea that a technological fix could solve an illness deeply rooted in social and economic inequities. In addition, the prioritization of product over process has lead to marketing of ORT packets rather than facilitating informed, intelligent use of local solutions. The image of a 'wonder drug' has induced false expectations and led the poorest to misspend their money on a fancy, medicalized and (for most diarrhoeas) unnecessary product. Disadvantaged people should be involved in the planning and implementation of health and development initiatives that affect them not just as an ethical imperative but as a pragmatic one (Werner *et al.*, 1997).

POLITICAL AND MORAL CONCERNS

Political and moral concerns over the strategies and their implementation arise from many viewpoints. Three interrelated themes emerge with relevance to current international health policies: (1) the way in which the policies are defined and imposed in various countries; (2) the neglect of the overall context of development policies and the limited role of health care in health and welfare; and (3) the emphasis on cost-effectiveness in health care policies, with special reference to differences between the selective and comprehensive approaches to PHC.

A political and moral critique of both PHC approaches cannot ignore the criticism of the universal imposition of development models by outside actors in line with trends in the industrialized countries rather than the felt needs or preferences of the developing countries (Zaidi, 1994; Foster, 1987). Apffel-Marglin has criticized Western medical approaches for perceiving the Western knowledge system as superior to the existing local knowledge systems. Using the example of smallpox eradication in India, she illustrates how the arrogant stands taken by the British led not only to the rejection of the project by the local people but also to the disappearance of useful traditional practices (Apffel-Marglin 1990). The intimidation, coercion and resistance which characterized the final stages of the South Asian smallpox eradication campaign are also a reminder of the need to pay attention to actual and perceived abuses when global health measures are introduced from above into regional settings (Greenough, 1995).

Professor D. Banerji strongly criticized the actions of both WHO and UNICEF when EPI was launched. He pointed out the bitter irony that UNICEF and WHO, which sponsored the famous global conference in Alma Ata, should have lent their weight to a programme that was, according to him, the very antithesis of the resulting declaration. For Banerji, the protection of children is a very desirable health action and should form an important element of PHC activities, but that this was totally different from the high-jacking of the cause of children by vested political and market interests, joining together with well-meaning but simple-minded persons in affluent countries to impose a technocentric, high-priority, target-oriented, time-bound immuniza-tion programme on a country (Banerji, 1990). EPI has emphasized the relevance of building the infrastructure, but if the aim of polio eradication by the year 2000 (set by the WHA in 1987) is to be reached, the use of more specific disease-oriented and targeted eradication efforts may be necessary (Wright, 1995).

National priorities may sometimes be undermined by the global priorities, or even by the priorities of the donor. For instance, it has been claimed that rather than emphasizing national programmes, UNICEF's country pro-grammes have sometimes emphasized the global programme for Universal Child Immunization (UCI), because immunization targets have been perceived as 'flagship' goals, useful in future advocacy (Engberg-Pedersen *et al.* 1992). Satyamala from India has also criticized the emphasis given to immunization programmes at the cost of other PHC interventions – regard-less, according to her, of the minor importance of the diseases that children were vaccinated against in under-five mortality in India (Sathyamala, 1989).

The basic framework of Health for All (HFA) is rejected by Navarro, who has claimed that the original framework of HFA is a failure in its emphasis on health care rather than other development practices as major determinants of health status. He has also claimed that the recommendations of the Alma Ata Declaration are part of the 'conventional wisdom' within the development establishment (Navarro, 1984). According to Prost and Jancloes, the selective health care strategy is both conceptually and practically misleading, as it relates cost figures to disease-control effectiveness and not to health benefits, and does not consider that the allocation of resources to one activity can have various types of benefits. On the practical side, it is almost impossible at the peripheral level to focus on a limited number of diseases. Health services are multivalent by nature. The definition of tasks should result from people's demand for care and from a comprehensive public health strategy which combines the provision of curative care, prevention, hygiene education, and interaction with other sectors that influence health. Patients have been reluctant to use the facilities available in pilot health projects set up to test the feasibility of the selective PHC strategy, mainly because they realized that these facilities could not cover the broad spectrum of their complaints and that they would have to visit another health post for complementary treatment (Prost and Jancloes, 1993).

Even though many would like to see the selective and comprehensive approaches as similar ones, with the selective approach ultimately leading to the comprehensive (Taylor and Jolly, 1988), according to others the difference is real and significant (Rifkin and Walt, 1986; Unger and Killingsworth, 1986; Newell, 1988). Rifkin and Walt have claimed that the approaches preclude each other and emphasize different expectations of the outcome of technological interventions and of the time frame involved (Rifkin and Walt, 1986). Qadeer has pointed out that while India signed the Alma Ata Declaration and pledged its implementation in 1978, the national Sixth Five Year Plan made no mention of it. On the other hand, the selective strategies were promoted and silently became a part of health sector planning. Within India's health sector, therefore, two trends are visible. One original, but frail, attempts to change the existing balance, to reach out to the majority, to build basic infrastructure, and to contextualize health within social and economic development. The other, more pragmatic, pushes selective PHC and population control strategies in the name of PHC (Qadeer, 1995).

The nature of decision making and priority setting in the policies has been an important part of the discussion of selective and comprehensive choices. Newell has pointed out the importance of the value-based nature of priority setting:

> There is no objective way of using the scientific method to choose this rather than that illness for action, to say that the death of a child is somehow worse than that of an adult, or to selectively direct public resources to one set of individuals rather than to another. These are inevitably value judgments. Only society can choose, and if a society has rights, one of them must be the right to know what the choices are, to have access to those choices in an acceptable way, and to understand the consequences and implications of the decisions. The continuing evolution of (comprehensive) PHC is the nearest thing that we have at present which reflects these rights.... Selective Primary Health Care is a threat and can be thought of as a counter-revolution. Rather than an alternative, it is a form of health services feudalism which can be destructive. Its attractions to the professionals and to funding agencies and governments looking at short term goals are very apparent. It has to be rejected, but for the right reasons (Newell, 1988).

The questioning of economic appraisal methods as the basis for priority setting in health policies has often been evident in the criticism of selective interventions. It has also been stressed that cost-efficiency is frequently in conflict with equity: the people most in need are usually most costly to reach (Smith and Bryant, 1988). The practice of health policies based on the most cost-efficient interventions also easily leads to a kind of assembly-line logic and approach to health policies, where the whole system is built on the cost-efficiency of separate and specific interventions. Green has pointed out that the cost-efficiency of different parts of a system does not necessarily increase the cost-efficiency of the whole system. As an example he quotes the non-governmental and private organizations, which technically may function efficiently, but may still be responsible for unnecessary duplication of activities, with the result that resources are wasted (Green, 1994).

The promotion of policies and priority setting in terms of cost-efficiency ratios is increasingly legitimated as a means of improving equity, often ignoring the larger context of how, by whom and why these priorities are set. According to Green and Barker the potential characteristics of economic appraisal run counter to the philosophy of PHC and in particular to its broad concept of health, its emphasis on multisectoral activities and its clear requirement for community involvement in priority setting. Even though appraisal techniques are said to be only aids to decision making, not decision making techniques, in practice, those appraisals which deliberately attempt to set out the assumptions made are often the least accessible to the non-economist planner, politician or community (Green and Barker, 1988) (Box 8.5).

Box 8.5   Priority setting

According to Green and Barker (1988) most economists involved in carrying out appraisals are aware of the difficulties in applying the results of such studies within the field of priority setting. In particular, they are aware of the following general problems which run counter to the philosophy of PHC and in particular its broad concept of health, its emphasis on multisectoral activities, and its clear requirement for community involvement in priority setting:

1   The appraisal techniques (cost-benefit and cost-efficiency) tend to reinforce a medical model of health through their emphasis on disease and their methodological difficulties in comparing multi-input/multi-output programmes; hence they are often project rather than programme oriented, and where they are programme oriented they tend to appraise vertical programmes.

2   Economic appraisal requires value judgments to be made about: national objectives; which groups, if any, are to be favoured (regional, income, disease, age); the future compared with the present; whose costs/benefits are to be included; the weighting to be given to tangible compared with intangible effects. Frequently, such value judgments are made without the active participation of communities, either because of the difficulties of doing so, or because of the mistaken belief that they are technical rather than political decisions.

3   The process of economic appraisal is open to misuse as a 'black box' technique, by providing the planning bureaucracy with the means to influence heavily, if not to determine priorities through its control mechanism, for example, through initial judgments as to which areas appraisal should focus on, and the parameters appraisal should use.

Challenges and future prospects

In the 1990s primary care has received more attention especially in developed countries. While it is probable that the change of emphasis is due to increasing cost-consciousness, it should also be acknowledged that the changes in medical education and health policies during the 1980s may only now be surfacing in many countries. Although the endorsement of the policies is usually a necessity for their implementation, it often takes time, effort and broad support to diminish the gap between rhetoric and actual shifts in policies and practice.

According to the second evaluation of the Global Strategy for Health for All (1993), the development of health systems worldwide reflects increasingly the concepts, approaches and philosophy of PHC. The health systems continue to give greater emphasis to specific diseases and conditions, however, or to some elements of care and specific types of services (mostly vertical), which may not facilitate meeting the overall needs of people at different phases of their lives on a continuing basis (WHO, 1993b). In the outlook for the future, the evaluation emphasizes the need for more effective implementation, stressing (1) the distribution of resources required for addressing priority health needs, (2) action on health promotion and protection in sectors other than health; and (3) the pursuit of equality in access to PHC, integrated with high-quality care (WHO 1993b).

While similar issues have been highlighted, other authors have been more sceptical towards the future and actual impact of the policies. According to Baum and Sanders, progress towards HFA has been extremely limited, with most of it occurring in the late 1970s and early 1980s. They emphasize increasing inequities in health and identify four trends which appear to be affecting nations across the world, detracting from rather than contributing to the aims of HFA: (1) managerialism, manifested in a goals-and-targets approach to health promotion; 2) increasing dominance of market economics and promotion of economic growth at all costs, reinforcing the inequities in health globally and within countries; (3) individualism, reinforcing the behavioural and life-style focus and undermining the more collective approach; and (4) environmental degradation. Health promoters aiming at a 'health for all' that would challenge the dominant wisdoms of individualism and market economics should advocate state involvement in areas that promise to be effective in reducing poverty; increasing equity; providing employment opportunities; and decent and appropriate housing. They argue for a return to the original philosophy of HFA: strengthening commitment to equity globally and emphasizing community-wide action rather than reducing health interventions to selected technical interventions against a limited range of diseases (Baum and Sanders, 1995). Green raised similar concerns over the current emphasis on the individual, as opposed to the more collective emphasis of Alma Ata Declaration, in health planning and recent approaches in health policies (Green, 1995).

Even though social justice and equity may not be made easily attainable through changes in health policies, the organizational or managerial changes will be of limited value without a broader approach to the problems of health, poverty, the degradation of the environment and social exclusion. In the 1990s the major challenges of the HFA and PHC policies therefore go beyond the specific targets in health status. Rather, they focus on the equality and social rights aspects of health. Though these essentially global issues are more burning in many developing countries, they are also valid in developed countries.

The HFA policies are under a process of renewal, with the aim of finalizing the strategy in the year 1998 when WHO is fifty years old. The resolution for the renewal process in May 1995 set the basic framework and started for the process (Box 8.6). The final review of the new global policy will be made by the WHO Executive Board and WHA in 1998. The renewal process also aims to build on global change and the increasing importance of international-level activities for the determinants of health (Yach, 1996). In the current global context there may be a need for caution, as there are evident pressures to reorient and streamline the HFA strategy to the current public sector and health sector realities dominated by sectoral reforms. This would mean pressures towards limited government responsibilities and increased reliance on private partnerships and actors, especially with respect to health services, thus shifting the focus from the social right of access to the health services towards support for public health measures for all.

The consultative document on renewing the HFA strategy stands on acknowledged HFA values (WHO 1995d). However, it should be noted that, according to the resolution on the new global health policy, the responsibility for health is emphasized at individual, family and community levels. This raises questions in relation to the role of governments and other actors which to a large extent define the conditions in which these responsibilities are under-taken, as well as to the potential for dilution of the social rights aspects of the Alma Ata Declaration. Recommendations to stay healthy would fit in well with the current global changes in health sectors, but do not fit the equity and solidarity requirements. While the practical realities do matter, they can not be reasons for compromising, as few policy aims could have been achieved without first asking for the impossible. Perhaps, at the core of the HFA policies, there could be a case to invert requirement for economic returns from social benefits that concerned Halfdan Mahler, and ask in turn for social and health returns from the policies aiming at economic growth.

Box 8.6
WHO response to global change: renewing the HFA strategy

The forty-eighth World Health Assembly,
Stressing the continued validity of health for all as a timeless aspirational goal, while recognizing that it may not be universally attainable by the year 2000; recognizing that political, economic, social, cultural and environmental situations are changing throughout the world; concerned by the negative trends in some of the major health determinants shown by the third monitoring of progress in implementation of strategies for health for all by the year 2000; recognizing the need to give priority attention to those most seriously deprived in terms of health or health care, whether owing to poverty, marginalization or exclusion; and recognizing also in this regard the need for intensified support of the international community; stressing the importance of a broad national and international consultation among those dedicated to health and social development in order to create a renewed commitment to health under WHO leadership; having considered the report of the Director General outlining the steps taken to implement the recommendations of the Executive Board Working Group on the WHO Response to Global Change on the updating of the health-for-all strategy, objectives and targets in response to global change; having noted with appreciation the contribution of the task force on health in development created by resolution WHA 45.24; agreeing that a new global health policy should be elaborated,

1 ENDORSES the steps already taken by the Director-General to implement the recommendations on updating the health-for-all targets in response to global change.

2 URGES Member States:
i   to take appropriate steps for consultations to raise awareness of the general public, political leaders, ministries and other partners concerned with social and economic development policy to the need to place health high on the political agenda, in order to address the serious health challenges of the coming decades and to ensure that the foundation is laid for implementation of the global health policy in countries;
ii   to forward to WHO the consensus views on health challenges and major policy orientations resulting from the national consultation to serve as a basis for the elaboration of the global health policy;
iii to adapt the global health policy, after its adoption, into national or subnational contexts for implementation, selecting approaches specific to their social and economic situation and culture;

3. CALLS ON other organizations in the United Nations system as well as intergovernmental and nongovernmental organizations active in the field of health to participate in the elaboration of the global health policy, to define their role in carrying it out and to join forces with WHO for its implementation;

Box 8.6 cont.

4. REQUESTS the Director General:

  i to take the necessary steps for renewing the health-for-all strategy together with its indicators, by developing a new holistic global health policy based on the concepts of equity and solidarity, emphasizing the individual's, the family's and the community's responsibility for health and placing health within the overall development framework;

  ii to ensure the convergence of all relevant work carried out in the subject at all levels of the Organization;

  iii to consult widely with all Member States and other partners of WHO in health development to this effect;

  iv to support Member States in the elaboration of their contribution to the global health policy, inter alia, by preparing user-friendly material to that effect, accessible to all sectors;

  v to solicit the contribution of other institutions dedicated to health and social development, such as those of the United Nations system and other international and nongovernmental organizations, to the formulation and implementation of the global health policy;

  vi to elaborate the new global health policy, based on the outcome of the consultation process, to serve as objective and guidance for the updating of global, regional and national health-for-all strategies and for the development of mechanisms to enable all concerned to fulfil their role, taking into account that essential aspects of PHC have not yet been achieved by a number of countries, especially the least developed countries;

  vii to redefine WHO's mission and the meaning of technical cooperation for WHO pursuance of that global health policy;

  viii to take the necessary measures for WHO to secure, at a special event connected to the World Health Assembly of 1998, in conjunction with the fiftieth anniversary of WHO, high level political endorsement of a health charter based on the new global health policy, in order to obtain political ownership of the policy and commitment to its implementation;

  ix to report on the plans for securing this endorsement to the Forty-ninth World Health Assembly.

9

Health Care Reforms

Health care reforms[1] tend to have an air of positive change. Health sector reform has been described as the process of improving the performance of existing systems and of assuring efficient and equitable responses to future changes. It has also been defined as sustained, purposeful change aimed at improving the efficiency, equity and effectiveness of the health sector (Berman, 1995). The issues of how, why, by whom and in what context these changes are made, and of the priorities and incompatibilities involved in the three aims of efficiency, equity and effectiveness often receive limited attention.

The background to the aims of health care reforms has three different areas: (1) the role of the government in health care provisioning and financing, given an increasing reliance on market forces and emphasis on individual choice; (2) the problems concerning health care structures and functions, with limited access to health services and scarce or declining government funds (mainly in developing countries); and (3) concern over the costs and effectiveness of medical technologies, and the measures aimed at improving the effectiveness, functioning and quality of health services in a future characterized by limited resources (mainly in developed countries). While all these areas are interlinked, the last two have more to do with problems leading to health reforms, and the first acts more as the context and the framework of the solutions offered to these problems.

In the 1980s the New Right's criticism of pluralism, the mixed economy and the welfare state gained ground, and in certain developed countries the neo-conservative or New Right views also gained support at the higher political level of government elections. Compared with other major approaches, the New Right model has had the most recent extensive and immediate impact on

[1] 'Health care reform', 'health sector reform' and 'health policy reform' are all definitions of processes of reform within the health sector and health policies. As the reform has focused mainly on the health services, we have used the term 'health care reform' in this article in general. However, in some cases we have not changed the definition which has been used in the reference.

Box 9.1 Health sector reform and public and private interests

Adapted from Macintosh (1992)

The background of many of the emerging health sector reforms may be found in the critique of 'public interest' theories of a benevolent state serving the common interests of the society, interests which can be identified and which the state is competent to identify. While this view was in favour in the 1950s and 1960s, the criticism emerged in the 1970s. It focused on the assumption of a single, identifiable public interest and highlighted the division of society into social classes and between those who own the means of production for the market and those who do not. When the role of private gains was emphasized, the critiques saw the self-interested exercise of power by the state as deriving from (rather than correcting) the unequal exercise of market power.

In the 1980s the neo-liberal theorists emphasizing individual 'private interests' became more prominent in the criticism of the 'public interest' state, and the 'private interest' or 'public choice' views came to dominate public sector reform. The 'private interest' critique considers the public not in terms of social classes but as individuals and is linked to a much more favourable view of competitive markets. The 'private interest' or 'public choice' school of economics brings the market into the state. More precisely, it extends the individualist assumptions of orthodox economic theory from those who buy and sell in markets to all those involved with the state. Politicians, voters and civil servants are all assumed to act solely in their own interest; they pursue individual gain, not public good. Rather than assuming that the politicians and government employees are corrupt, it is argued that to pursue one's own interests is an acceptable and indeed morally valuable approach to life.

The 'private interest' theories of the state emphasize (1) the economic theory of bureaucracy – the view that bureaucrats exploit their monopoly of information and services in order to expand their budgets, powers and perks, (2) the 'Leviathan state' – the view that the state always tends to grow into a monster: monopolistic, too powerful and larger than the citizens would wish and (3) rent seeking – the waste of resources resulting from individual pursuit of the income-earning opportunities created by the state regulations. The 'private interest' assumptions, not always made so explicit, have come to dominate thinking about the reform of the public sector in the late 1980s and early 1990s. While exploiting the political space opened by widespread doubts about the performance of the state, the neo-liberal desire to restrict the state has found echoes among left-wing critics emphasizing self-reliance and non-governmental action.

government decision making. 'Public interest' or 'public choice' theories have had an important role in this process. Though one need not adopt the New Right values in order to use public choice patterns of argumentation, there has been a strong correlation between using a public choice methodology and espousing New Right values, even if there is no necessary or intrinsic connection between the two (Dunleavy and O'Leary, 1987) (Box 9.1).

While universal access and equity have been among the expressed concerns in health care reforms, the emphasis on action has so far focused essentially on diminishing the cost of public financing of health services, increasing the role of nongovernmental actors and resources, and enhancing the mechanisms of markets as means to control the costs and gain changes in quality. The greater reliance on private sources in the financing of health care relates to the increasing tendency to define patients as consumers, the public health services (such as preventive interventions) as public 'goods' and the curative health services as private 'goods'. In this respect it might be correct to define the health care and health sector reforms as health reforms, in order to emphasize how the concept of health is perceived in the reforms. When health is perceived as a private good, it will be more legitimate to expect a larger private share for the curative services. Furthermore, when patients are perceived as consumers, it is also possible to expect that the market mechanisms will work in terms of improving the quality of health services through the consumer choice.

Health care reforms

As any changes in the organization and functioning of health services may be claimed as health care reform, the process is divergent and emphasizes different issues and changes in different countries, thus being dependent on the context in which the health care reform is implemented. Nevertheless, some common trends may be identified. In countries with a national health service (Russia, the United Kingdom, New Zealand) the separation of the provider and purchaser of health care has been an essential element of the reforms, the aim being to create a third-party purchaser, enabling competition between the providers. In other countries such as the United States or the Netherlands, the emphasis has been on reforming the third-party purchasing of health care. In all countries, the encouragement of competition among providers is a common aspect of the reforms. A more controversial issue has been the competition among the third-party payers (van de Ven *et al.*, 1994) (Box 9.2).

In developing countries, the health care reforms have focused on making better use of the existing resources and in increasing the nongovernmental economic share. In practice this has meant changes and reorientation in Ministries of Health, introducing user charges, privatizing of parts of health

Box 9.2 Health care reform models

In the area of health care reform policies, the most common models of organization are often referred to by different terms emphasizing or specifying different aspects of the reform policies. In most of the reform models, competition among the providers of health services is encouraged, but only in a few has competition on the financing side been encouraged.

Managed competition, managed markets and managed care
Managed competition implies a health care system using market forces within a framework of specified rules. Competition is involved in both the financing and provision sides of medical care. Employers and consumers choose from the competing health plans those with the best quality and the lowest price. The goal of managed competition is to divide providers in each community into competing economic units and to use market forces to motivate them to develop efficient delivery systems. Competition is focused on the price of the annual premium for comprehensive health care services. The 'sponsors', armed with data and expertise, advise the informed consumers on the choice of a health plan (Enthoven, 1993a). Enthoven, the architect of this approach, has emphasized managed competition as a system which is compatible with strong American cultural preferences (Enthoven 1993a). The approach has also influenced health care reform models in Europe, however, based on competition on the provider side of publicly funded services (United Kingdom) and also on the financing side (Netherlands) (van de Ven *et al.,* 1994). While managed competition represents an ideal, several elements are related to the managed care approach in the United States, though the role of the sponsors and competition is emphasized (Enthoven, 1994; Enthoven, 1993a). The problems associated with the managed competition approach in practice have been debated in connection with the health sector reform and managed care plans in the United States (Kane, 1995; Finkel, 1993; White, 1993). The theoretical and practical problems related to a similar model used in the US military forces have also been raised (Waitzkin, 1994).

In the USA, managed care has been described as constituting private sector management of privately organized health networks: health maintenance organizations or preferred provider plans. The market structures within which managed care programmes are undertaken may or may not be competitive, however, and may or may not involve a strong government role (Kane, 1995). Managed care has been among the fastest growing segments of the health care economy in United States, and it has often added large administrative costs (Finkel, 1993). It has been noted that the nature of managed care is changing rapidly from that of a field once dominated by pioneers with a sense of social mission towards greater commercialization due to the current entry of more profit-oriented businesses (Iglehart, 1994). In recent years, the insurance

Box 9.2 cont.

companies have been investing in the various managed care plans (Salmon, 1995; Watzman and Woodall, 1995). The shared ownership of managed care plans and the tobacco industry may be seen as one aspect of the corporatization of health care in the United States (Boyd et al., 1995).

Generally, the term 'managed markets' is used when elements of competition are introduced on the provider side, financed by a single purchaser or multiple purchasers without competition. Financing can be organized on a publicly funded basis through a third-party payer system (through government contracting, for example, or publicly funded national health insurance) enabling competitive elements between the providers. In countries with national health services this has necessitated contracting and separation of the providers and purchasers of health care. Several definitions have been used to emphasize the different elements in changes (Broomberg, 1994a; von Otter and Saltman, 1992). The term 'planned markets' is used when a relatively limited introduction of market mechanisms is involved within a framework of public financing and production of health services, and 'regulated markets' is used when there is greater reliance on market mechanisms and government regulations are imposed only to prevent market failures. The expression 'internal markets' is used when market mechanisms are limited to the existing public sector system (Broomberg, 1994a; von Otter and Saltman, 1992).

services (hospitals) or support services, enabling private medical care, decentralization, introducing funding mechanisms for health insurance, and different ways of contracting publicly provided services (Kutzin, 1995). The health care reforms in developing countries are implemented under conditions of economic stringency and are often fuelled either by cuts in public provisioning of health care or by a declining government overall budget without a change in the share allocated to the health sector. The World Bank has linked structural adjustment loans to public sector reforms and has developed versions of the reform model for a number of sectors including health care (MacIntosh, 1995).

According to Macintosh a number of multilateral agencies – notably the World Bank and the OECD – are currently promoting the idea of an emergent consensus on the economic and organizational aspects of social provisioning reform. In the context of reduced and 'targeted' social provision, the reform model combines the strategic and centralized direction of social policy with a system of provision that is both competitive and diverse in ownership and motivation. Central policy making is defined as public purchasing and regulation, while the policy and provider roles are separated (MacIntosh, 1995). In many countries the emphasis has been on the introduction of contracting and competitive elements in the provision of publicly funded health services, but there is also a tendency to see these changes as necessary transition stages towards a competitive integrated model, which would be close to that of managed competition (van de Ven *et al.*, 1994). This tendency to consider the public contract models in health care as one phase in a transition towards a more market-oriented health system has also been cited as a warning to those countries currently introducing market mechanisms in the public sector (Dahlgren, 1994).

Policies

World Bank

The World Bank has been active in promoting health policy reform and has certainly taken the lead over other international organizations working on the subject. While the first report on *Financing Health Services in Developing Countries – an Agenda for Reform* (1987) defines many of the basic elements in the health reform policies of the World Bank, some further elaboration and problematization of the approach may be seen in later reports. The agenda for reform is based on four recommendations (Box 9.3).

In *World Development Report 1993* (World Bank 1993a), which introduces the health policy reform under the heading 'Investing on Health', the framework is essentially the same, though the involvement and regulatory role of governments is acknowledged. Indeed, in this report the World Bank also acknowledges the need to expand the absolute amount and share of social sector funding within governmental budgets in some countries, as well as the possibility of market failure in private markets of health, with special reference to the example of insurance markets (World Bank, 1993a). Government responsibility in financing health services is limited to public health measures and to ensuring universal access to an essential package of clinical services, which is oriented towards the poor as they cannot buy such care for themselves. This arrangement is also expected to enhance equity, as the public health services will benefit all, and the limited resources of government may be targeted on the poor.

In the World Bank model the public health measures and essential clinical care together constitute a package of health care which justifies funding from general revenues, with perhaps some contribution from user fees. The essential clinical services are to be delivered within the framework of a competitive model:

Box 9.3 Four policy reforms suggested in *Financing Health Services in Developing Countries: an Agenda for Reform*

(World Bank 1987)

1 Charge users of government health facilities. Institute charges at government facilities, especially for drugs and curative care. This will increase resources available to the government health sector, allow more spending on underfunded programmes, encourage better quality and more efficiency, and increase access for the poor. Use differential fees to protect the poor. The poor should be the major beneficiaries of expanding resources and improved efficiency of the government sector.

2 Provide insurance or other risk coverage. Encourage well-designed health insurance programmes to help mobilize resources for the health sector while simultaneously protecting households from financial losses. A modest level of cost recovery is possible without insurance. But, in the long run, insurance is necessary to relieve the government budget of the high costs of expensive curative care; governments cannot raise hospital charges close to costs until insurance is widely available.

3 Use nongovernment resources effectively. Encourage the nongovernment sector (including nonprofit groups, private physicians, and other health practitioners) to provide health services for which consumers are willing to pay. This will allow the government to focus its resources on programmes that benefit whole communities rather than particular individuals.

4 Decentralize government health services. Decentralize planning, budgeting, and purchasing for government health services, particularly the services offering private benefits for which users are charged. When setting national policies and programmes, use market incentives where possible to better motivate staff and allocate resources. Allow revenues to be collected and retained as close as possible to the point of service delivery. This will improve both the collection of fees and the efficiency of service.

---

in a competitive health system, people seeking health services can choose from a diversity of providers – public, private nonprofit, and private for-profit. As developing countries move towards such competitive systems, they face a wide range of policy options that can improve the delivery of the essential clinical package (World Bank 1993a).

While efficiency and effectiveness may be defined as driving forces in the World Bank approach, equity is seen as a consequence of actions improving efficiency and effectiveness in the public sector, the promotion of economic growth, and increasing competition and diversity within the health sector.

In later World Bank documents the need for governments to encourage greater diversity and competition in the financing and delivery of health services is emphasized. The World Bank role in policy formulation is promoted as a means of having a far greater impact on improving welfare than does its lending, which plays a catalytic role. The health reform has been presented as being at the centre of World Bank policy analysis and project work in middle-income countries and an increasing number of low-income countries (World Bank, 1995b). While there may be different interpretations of the impact of World Bank health policies, the fact that implementation of public sector reforms is often linked to additional loans, with coordination of donor funding, does enable the Bank to have a profound impact on the structures and financing of health services in many countries. In practice, conditions may also apply to more specific issues in the health sector. In Uganda, for example, the World Bank's second health project loan would only be granted on condition that the government adopted a national policy promoting user fees (Okuonzi and Macrae, 1995).

The World Bank has also partnered USAID in promoting reforms in the health and population sectors (Foltz, 1994). In Kenya the World Bank and USAID exerted considerable pressure to introduce user charges, even though the World Bank model could be shown to be the least equitable and efficient compared with other choices (Dahlgren, 1990). The catalytic nature of funding will give the World Bank a substantial role in the formulation of policies and initiating changes, but may undermine the actual process of health care reform and neglect the problems arising during the implementation. The World Bank has been a keen supporter of user charges and competitive elements in health care provision, although the policies on user charges were under some reassessment for a while (*Economist,* 1995).

The World Bank is currently researching managed care arrangements in developing and industrialized countries (World Bank, 1994a). This could be a matter for concern as according to Barer and others there is no shortage of American consultants willing to advise (particularly developing) nations on how to structure their health care financing and delivery systems. Indeed these consultants see an opportunity to implement market-based principles in systems unfettered by the regulatory apparatus that characterizes their own system. While evidence to date is, predictably, dismal, this is unlikely to deter either the consultants or the huge multinational (or soon-to-be multinational) insurance/managed care corporations looking for new, perhaps initially friendlier, horizons (Barer *et al.,* 1995).

WHO

The WHO role in the process of health reform has been conflicting, and in general the issue of health care financing has been politically sensitive. According to Siddiqi, in the very beginning, when WHO's tasks and role were to be defined, the United States vehemently opposed WHO involvement in what was referred to as 'socialized' medicine. The American delegate felt that health insurance should be left to the exclusive jurisdiction of the International Labour Organization. The Soviet Union, however, and several Scandinavian and other European countries with national health insurance programmes, argued that health and social security were interrelated, and thus the concern of WHO (Siddiqi, 1995).

The basic framework within which the PHC policies of WHO were developed can be said to be close to that of a publicly funded health system in the Scandinavian health services. It has been noted that though the statements on health care financing are cautious in the Alma Ata Declaration, they nonetheless clearly imply the desirability of an integrated, publicly controlled health care system (Gish, 1983). The WHO study in reorienting national health systems towards HFA drew attention to the balance between different levels of health care and the need for centralized responsibility for broad policy matters and localized responsibility for programme implementation (Kleczkowski et al., 1984). The HFA strategy emphasizes self-reliance and community responsibility for health, cost-effectiveness in health care technologies and services, decentralization and the reorientation of health care towards PHC (WHO 1981b, WHO 1987c). These elements give ground to those interpretations, which claim that the broad goals in health sector reform are in line with the HFA strategy. It has also been argued, however, that the use of the market may be regarded as an antithesis of the principles of PHC (Green, 1995).

The actual costs of PHC have been debated, especially in connection with selective primary health (Walsh and Warren, 1979) and also in the late 1980s when economic support to HFA policies became a crucial question (WHO, 1987c). One of the global indicators in the HFA strategy has been the allocation of at least 5 per cent of GNP to health, but in the 1990s the indicator has been changed to the mere percentage of GNP (WHO, 1981b; WHO, 1993b). As the potential to increase the health sector share from governmental resources and tax revenue was considered to be severely limited, attention was focused on other possible sources: charges to certain categories of users, or for particular services; health insurance or other local insurance; revolving funds; and voluntary contributions in cash or kind (WHO, 1987b).

While the Bamako Initiative was originally UNICEF's proposal and was launched without consulting WHO, WHO nevertheless later joined the

Bamako Initiative on community cost sharing in the provision of health services. In the late 1980s and 1990s the focus on changes linked to health reform has been more on the managerial issues and on the decentralization and reorganization of Ministries of Health (Mills *et al.*, 1990; WHO, 1990; WHO, 1991). The building of health infrastructure and the development of health systems has been emphasized in WHO's General Programmes, though the share of funding allocated to support for research and analysis on these issues has been very modest. A WHO study group report on recent changes in financing health services has also been published (WHO, 1993c), and a series of discussion papers on health sector reforms have been published in the Division of Analysis Research and Assessment. As an organization, WHO seems to take a managerial approach to health care reform, emphasizing the managerial issues and support for national capacities to adjust to health reform and to promote equity in health and access to health services.

There is a need for research, evaluation and information concerning the process of the health sector reforms implemented. There is also a need to strengthen WHO's capacities in the evaluation and assessment of policies applied in health sector reforms, especially with respect to equity and universal access, so that assistance may be provided to countries implementing the reforms. The locus of WHO work on health care reforms and health systems development has been in the Division of Strengthening Health Services and a large of share of the work has also been implemented through the Division of Intensified Cooperation with Countries (ICO) (WHO, 1994e; ICO, 1995). In 1996 the reorganization and formation of the Health Systems Development programme can be seen as a start in improving WHO capacities, analysis and action in this area. Health systems development and health care reforms have been high on the agenda especially in two regional offices, PAHO/AMRO and EURO. The PAHO/AMRO approach has been oriented towards strengthening the role of Ministries of Health and in elevating health on the political agenda (PAHO/WHO, 1997). The European office has had a slightly different approach, focusing more on comparative analysis and assessment of health care reforms implemented in the region (WHO, 1996d). At the 1996 May Executive Board meeting an *ad hoc* group on health systems development was formed in order to provide analysis and guidance for further strengthening WHO action on the issue.

UNICEF

The UNICEF role in the process of health reform might be defined as that of a practical intermediary. Through initiatives such as Bamako, Child Survival Strategy and Structural Adjustment with a Human Face, UNICEF has introduced and/or enhanced the selective provision of services targeted on the poor, and user charges, social funds and drug-revolving funds as methods of financing health services. Kanji has noted that in the Bamako Initiative UNICEF has gone a step further and aligned itself with the World Bank. This alignment is not surprising, as World Bank and donor support is crucial to UNICEF. It is therefore no coincidence that in the Bamako document UNICEF identifies the role of health delivery systems as being responsive to demand. Need no longer appears to be the criterion (Kanji, 1989). The UNICEF programmes focusing the resources of the health system on the most cost-effective interventions have also been extended by the World Bank through two publications on *Disease Control Priorities in Developing Countries*, and the *World Development Report 1993* (Walsh and Simonet 1995).

The emphasis on cost-effectiveness, as well as the need to reach the targets set in the Child Survival Strategy, have clearly deserved more attention than the organization and functioning of health systems. On the other hand UNICEF has been keen on innovating and catalyzing new approaches in health services financing, with an emphasis on community financing, self-reliance and participation in cash or kind in the development and maintenance of basic health services. The UNICEF interest in catalyzing and pilot projects has sometimes been seen as excessive in relation to the country's general health policy development (Cassels and Janovsky, 1992). As UNICEF tends to act more like a voluntary organization, it shares the concerns of nongovernmental actors in the health field. It is to be expected, therefore, that UNICEF would not oppose the privatization or contracting of services but rather promote these processes if there were promised gains; furthermore, it would have an interest in drug-related efforts for cost recovery, such as drug revolving funds.

Concerns and constraints

Concerns over the strategies promoted in health reforms have focused on the practical feasibility of the policies, and the equity and effectiveness of actions within the context of well-functioning health systems or spending on health in general, and also on the moral and political implications of these changes. While some of the constraints may be found in most of the countries, others have more relevance in developing countries. Many of the practices promoted in health reform have produced mixed results, not only in terms of equity but also in terms of efficacy and effectiveness. The broadest discussion has been focused on the effects of user charges, but recently other spheres of health care reform have become more prominent. As the role of the international organizations in health care or sector reform is most substantial in developing countries, the discussion on concerns and constraints emphasizes their experiences.

User charges

User charges in government health facilities have been promoted as a way to mobilize revenues, promote efficiency, foster equity, increase decentralization and sustainability, and foster private sector development (Shaw and Griffin, 1995). Concerns over the role of user charges have been focused on the same spheres, but with different expectations. The user charges and different types of additional private practice can be seen as a survival strategy for public sector employees when their salaries no longer cover their living expenses (Chabot and Brenner, 1988; Hien *et al.*, 1995). This aspect should be separated, however, from active promotion of user charges and private practice as an aim for health policies and a means of financing the provision of services.

Revenues derived from user charges differ widely from country to country. In practice, user charges have had a rather limited role in terms of cost recovery of health sector financing. A World Bank publication on user charges and insurance in sub-Saharan Africa notes that 'initial impressions are that revenues from user fees represent a small – at times an insignificant – share of recurrent government expenditures on health in Africa'. The same report, however, observes that community financing schemes have shown larger cost recoveries, and emphasizes the importance of the revenue left at the local or district level (Shaw and Griffin, 1995). Akin has concluded that the public sector could charge as much as the private sector for its services and still increase usage, if comparable quality were maintained (Akin *et al.*, 1995). If similar cost-recovery levels and strategies are to be applied in both public and private sectors, however, the role and aims of the public sector as compared to the private sector should be matters of concern.

The regressive equity impact of user charges has been brought up in several studies in several countries. These studies indicate that the poorer people are more likely to be put off by price increases than are the richer (Creese, 1991; Yoder, 1989; Mbugua *et al.*, 1995). The promotion of equity through user charges in Africa is mainly based on the argument that because the rich make disproportionate use of the health services, especially the tertiary hospitals, imposing fees for health services for those who can afford to pay and setting higher fees for tertiary level services, will free up more money to fund public-health goods and services and primary level health care. When user charges are linked with quality improvements, the poor will benefit more (Shaw and Griffin, 1995). The quality improvements may nevertheless have limits, as has been shown in Zaïre, where the improvements in the supply of drugs and technical quality of services did not compensate for the additional financial barriers created by the increased cost of services (Haddad and Fournier, 1995).

The role of user fees in enhancing equity is related essentially to the ability to exempt the poor and subsidize preventive health services. Exemption has not worked well in practice, and the effectiveness of the policy may be questioned (Russel and Gilson, 1995). Although the charging of user fees to improve the quality of local health facilities has been a widely approved principle, it creates a problematic incentive for health workers to neglect the exemptions in order to gain more resources for health facilities. This may well be a matter of concern in the case of such initiatives as the World Bank's promotion of incentive prizes for health facilities which achieve the largest degree of cost sharing (Shaw and Griffin, 1995). The costs of implementing a proper system of means testing have also been mentioned, and even with the necessary administrative capacity in place, in most countries the cost of implementing a strict means-testing programme might be greater than the revenue that could be collected from fees, especially where charges are low (Kutzin, 1995) In the United Kingdom, user charges were not collected in hospitals in the 1980s as it was not considered profitable enough when the exemption mechanisms were applied (Klein, 1984). In the 1990s prescription charges in the United Kingdom have been collected from only one fifth of the prescriptions, as others are exempted (Dean, 1994).

While the subsidization of public health-related services and of specific categories of people according to disease or other characteristics (children, maternity care, family planning) is part of user-charge policies in many countries, subsidies related to the treatment of sexually transmitted diseases (STDs) have been shown to be lacking in practice in many countries (Russel and Gilson, 1995). If the charge for treatment of STDs deters people from seeking care or causes a delay in their seeking it, as noted in Kenya, the potential health impacts are detrimental (Moses *et al.,* 1992). Regressive effects of user charges in child health have been demonstrated recently from the Philippines (Ching, 1995).The role of user charges in limiting the unnecessary use of health services has been shown to be very limited, if not nonexistent, especially in areas where opportunity costs to reach the health services are high (for example, when people have to pay for travel to the health services or walk long distances to reach them) (Abel-Smith, 1992; Gilson and Mills, 1995). The cultural and social constraints on claiming eligibility to exemption and the social effects of increased means testing and eligibility claims have so far received little attention.

Community and regional level self-reliance in financing is problematic. In community financing strategies, equity both within and between urban and rural areas may easily be compromised. The increased self-reliance in financing often connected with decentralization is of concern, especially if similar cost recoveries are expected in areas with different population and socioeconomic structures. The maintenance of health services is costlier in remote rural areas, and those living there may also be the least able to pay (Smith and Bryant, 1988). Emphasis on community financing strategies for rural areas can also develop a social and political dynamic of its own: an example is charging rural poor who are not likely to respond by exerting political pressure, while free services are maintained for urban pressure groups (Gilson and Mills, 1995).

The availability of drugs has been shown to have a substantial impact on the utilization of public health services (Unger *et al.* 1990, Litvack and Bodart, 1993, Waddington and Enyimayew, 1989). In many countries the availability of drugs has been a problem, and the role of drugs in the perceived quality of care is problematic. When the profits from sales of drugs have direct relevance to the prescriber, there is an incentive to over-prescribe. This has been observed, for example, in studies on Vietnam and China (Chalker, 1995; Kutzin, 1995). The persistence of polypharmacy in Nigeria (where charges are based on the drugs prescribed) also gives grounds for concern that cost recovery systems based on drug sales may create incentives for overprescription and the inappropriate use of drugs (McPake *et al.,* 1992). In Tanzania, pressures from patients to prescribe, lack of supervision and continuing education of health workers, prestige drug prescription and incorrect drug prescribing, as well as local beliefs about drug use, have been documented as factors influencing the irrational use of drugs (Mnyika and Killewo, 1991). In this respect the user satisfaction linked to drug availability and the perceived quality of health services may not always be compatible with sound medical practice.

Revolving drug funds have been one response to the challenge of financing drug supply (Cross *et al.,* 1986). In such revolving drug funds, supplies are replenished using monies collected from sales after an initial capital investment. They are one type of drug sales programme or cost-recovery scheme and an attempt to mobilize financial resources based on a demonstrated willingness of people to pay for health services. It has been further noted that unlike a public sector entity that receives a budget allocation from the government, and where management's principal financial concern is simply staying within that budget, a revolving drug fund must sell a product and, through sales, generate sufficient revenues to meet its cost recovery objectives. In many respects, management's concerns should reflect those found in private sector businesses – if the revolving drug fund is to survive and thrive (Cross *et al.*, 1986). These basic requirements on the management and orientation of revolving drug funds may have further long-term implications, however, especially when such funds are also used to finance the health care provision in the community. In addition to the problems related to the maintenance and sustainability of revolving drug funds as such (Courtois and Dumoulin, 1995; Cross *et al.,* 1986; Korte *et al.,* 1992; Kanji, 1989), the central importance of drugs may be problematic in the long term (Kanji, 1989). In schemes where health services financing is to be derived from profits from selling drugs – even essential drugs – the more drugs sold, the better the financing situation. This provides an incentive for pharmaceutically based curative care and thus undermines prevention and those conditions and strategies not based on the use of drugs.

User charges have been promoted as a means of directing patients to the correct level of treatment, but less attention has been paid to the relevance of medical indications as reasons for the direction of the patients and for the division of work between the facilities. While some people may be able to pay the fee, it still may not be wise to treat simple diseases in facilities oriented to the treatment of more complicated cases. Thus, economic incentives will not lead automatically to results justified on medical grounds. Similarly, the opportunity to reach 'untapped' resources and increase cost recovery in health services has been one of the key arguments in the promotion and practice of user charges, but less analysis has been focused on other potential uses of these resources. Such analysis is of essential importance in situations where exemptions do not work or where more emphasis is put on the private providers of health care.

People may be willing to pay more than they can afford and then be bound to sell assets or even land to cover the costs of health care. In Asian countries, where landlessness is a pressing problem (for example, in Bangladesh and Thailand), the cost of treatment for a family member constitutes one of the primary reasons for peasants selling their piece of land (Korte *et al,*. 1992). It has been concluded from observational data in Thailand that up to 60 per cent of involuntary land sales are due to the need to pay high medical bills (Baum and Strenski, 1989). In China 85 per cent of rural health care is paid for on a self-pay basis. Studies have found that 30 per cent of the people living below the poverty line became poor because of financial losses incurred during serious illness (Hsiao, 1995). While people may be accustomed to paying traditional healers for their services, traditionally the form and conditions of payment are determined by flexible methods to suit the family's ability to pay (Korte *et al.,* 1992). Rather little is known about how the costs of increased cost recovery in the health sector will be shared at the household level. According to Hammer, there are reasons to believe that the implementation of user charges is unlikely to be gender neutral. Usually women will bear a disproportionate amount of the costs which this policy imposes on households (Hammer, 1994).

Health systems and financing

User charges are imposed at a time when a person falls ill, whereas the benefit of risk-sharing schemes is that they may be paid for when there are more resources. This is of importance in rural areas, where income is dependent on season. There have been and still are many mechanisms by which communities have shared costs, and some traditional cost-sharing mechanisms have also been highlighted as a basis for health insurance development in rural areas (Arhin, 1995). In Niger the revenue generation *per capita* under a tax-fee method was two times higher than under the fee-for-service method, suggesting that the prospects of sustainability were better under the social financing strategy (Diop *et al.*, 1995). Many of the more collective cost-sharing strategies can still result, however, in the exclusion of those unable to pay their share or unwilling to share the costs involved in joining the scheme. In the cost-sharing insurance in Burundi, close to 30 per cent of households gave financial inability as one of the main reasons for not joining to the scheme, and in practice many joined the scheme only when in need of treatment (Arhin, 1994). If community cost-sharing mechanisms are to be ways towards broader and more sustainable strategies, strategies to avoid reproducing the problems in larger insurance schemes (for example costs of joining, exclusion of some persons, cost escalation tendencies) and exacerbating inequities at the community and inter-community level should be matters of consideration.

Health insurance is seen both as a problem and as a solution in health care reforms. The United States scheme, with its unregulated multiple private insurance funds and fee-for-service reimbursement, has been shown to fail both in containing the costs and in guaranteeing universal access (World Bank, 1993a). In OECD countries, the health systems based on general revenue appear to be simpler and more equitable ways to spread the risks, and they appear to have lower administrative costs when compared with health systems based on social insurance or private insurance (Schieber, 1995). The problems of cost escalation in insurance schemes have led to increased emphasis on provider payment and contract methods and incentives. This is also the area in which the role of the medical doctors is strongest – powerful enough to have shaped the provider-payment methods in several countries in favour of fee-for-service practice (Abel-Smith, 1992). The cure for cost-escalation problems in health care reform is often found in increased competition, which is claimed to have the potential to improve the performance of any payment method (Barnum *et al.*, 1995). This has also been the case in the countries in transition which have moved towards social insurance and the Bismarckian model of health care organization, with influence from the Central European models. In relation to the subsequent problems in health care organization and cost containment, the World Bank prescription for further reform suggests payment systems that create incentives for efficient service delivery, based as far as possible on health outcomes rather than diagnostic activities or treatment; monitoring quality and access for tight control of spending; and financing mechanisms that stimulate competition among providers, both public and private (World Bank, 1996a). While competition is often seen as the solution to problems faced in the health services, much less attention seems to be drawn to the preconditions of competition (in rural or sparsely populated areas, for example) or to ensuring that the medicine used does not cause hazardous side-effects in terms of increasing administrative costs and complexity, diminishing equity in access to health care, unnecessary over-supplying of services or the acceptance of sophisticated technology as the measure of quality.

In many developing countries, the population which is able and eligible to participate in insurance schemes is small. When formal employment is limited to a small fraction of the population, the employment-based models are problematic, and cost sharing can leave those who are most in need outside the insurance programmes. Universal health insurance can be compared to a specific tax. According to the egalitarian aims in health care, insurance cost sharing should be based on the ability to pay, without changes in benefits. This may be hard to achieve. The experiences from health insurance in practice have been problematic and it has been acknowledged that health insurance has acquired a bad name among many health administrators. In a number of countries it has grossly distorted health priorities by favouring urban at the expense of rural populations, encouraged curative medicine to the detriment of prevention, and created absurd waste and duplication of advanced technology (Abel-Smith, 1986).

In spite of the potential pitfalls, health insurance has been promoted in middle-income countries and lately also in low-income African countries (World Bank, 1993a; Shaw and Griffin, 1995). Shaw and Griffin have high-lighted two major considerations as far as equity is concerned : first, insurance for those who can pay will enable the government to privatize the costly tertiary level hospitals and thus concentrate on efforts to expand essential services for the poor. Second, insurance has direct equity-enhancing impact on partici-pants by providing benefits on the basis of need rather than income (Shaw and Griffin, 1995). While most would agree that health care should be directed according to need rather than income, the evidence supporting the suggested policies is equivocal in practice.

In countries with considerable insurance coverage and regulatory capacity, such as Korea and Thailand, the insurance schemes have led to competition regarding perceived quality. This has led to increasing use of sophisticated medical technologies and to questions as to whether the health care system will succumb eventually to the interests of providers and health industries (Yang, 1993; Bennet et al., 1994; Nittarayamphong and Tangcharoensathien, 1994). There are therefore real dangers that, rather than promoting equity, the schemes will foster the interests of health industries, medical doctors and those privileged enough to belong to the schemes. Within the context of sub-Saharan Africa, it has been asked whether privatization in health is basically a mis-allocation of public sector energy, as there is only one viable full-scale proprietary private hospital in the whole of sub-Saharan Africa north of South Africa: this hospital is expensive and exists predominantly to serve expatriate clients (Green, 1993). Attempts to create neo-private enclaves in public hospitals lead on balance to treasuries subsidizing élite services, not rich clients subsidizing core services for poor people (Green, 1993).

Privatization can be defined as a process in which non-government actors become increasingly involved in the financing and/or provision of health care services, but it is also often applied less accurately to policies that are designed to establish a 'public market' or an internal market, which encourages competition or market-like behaviour within the public sector without changes in public or private responsibility for health services financing and provision. In privatization problems with equity are likely to be greatest when the relative importance of the private for-profit sector increases in the absence of a government regulatory and monitoring role (Muschell, 1995). Government interventions are also needed where private practice is actually causing harm in the form of inadequate sterilization procedures, unskilled staff giving sophisticated treatments, refusal to treat emergency patients and extreme cases of dangerous or unnecessary treatments (Bennet *et al.*, 1994) Even when legislation on regulation exists, the problems involved in implementation may result in a situation where the unregulated expansion of the private sector causes more harm than good (Yesudian, 1994).

The basic problem in the public/private mix approaches and those emphasizing competition and the private sector is not only that of who eventually will subsidize whom (public sector vs private sector), but also that of accountability, regulation and whether the market mechanisms will end up being virtues or vices in the health sector, given the known possibility of market failure. According to Bennet, the rapid spread of private practitioners, and other profit and non-profit actors, in situations where a government lacks the willingness and/or capacity to regulate, may lead health sector reforms in developing countries to produce health care systems closely resembling that of the United States. Pluralism in health care funding and provision has been claimed to account for much of the inability to control health care costs in the United States. Diversity among the providers and a less comprehensive role for government in many developing countries tend to shift their policies towards a more pluralistic system. As today's policies shape the structure of health care systems for years to come, the pluralistic funding advocated by the World Bank has been viewed as warranting more critical consideration (Bennet, 1992).

Privatization may be implemented through changes in ownership, but also through contracting. Most commonly, contracting means that publicly funded services are purchased from private organizations. According to Smith and Lipsky, for public officials, particularly those with a conservative bent, a significant appeal of contracting with nonprofit organizations is the ability to achieve public goals without increasing the size of the public workforce. Government intrusion into society can be minimized, because private agencies will do the job. This form of privatization appears to combine the pragmatic objectives of keeping costs down and maintaining flexibility in policy options with the ideological objective of minimizing government's role in society, while directing charities and other community agencies towards playing their traditional roles. In the United States, however, contracting has resulted instead in an unprecedented growth of government involvement in the affairs of private organizations (Smith and Lipsky, 1992).

In many countries, some parts of the health services or nonclinical services are contracted by the government from either the profit or the nonprofit sector. Contracting has been seen as a means of introducing market mechanisms selectively in order to gain benefits from competition while limiting or avoiding the market failures of a purely private system (McPake and Ngalande-Banda, 1994). In order to gain from the contracts, governments need to have the skills necessary to establish contracts, evaluate bids and monitor contractor performances (Kutzin, 1995; Bennet *et al.*, 1996). Contracting also involves more administrative costs, which may outweigh the resources saved and thus not improve performance in the economic sense. The situations and fields in which contracting is actually needed are often those where competition is hard to achieve – for example, where there are plans to increase health service coverage in remote districts of developing countries, or to acquire specific skills or techniques in developed countries. Contracted services are often provided at lower cost (to the provider) than comparable government services; the price which government pays, however, may be higher than providing the service in house (Bennet *et al.*, 1996). Smith and Lipsky have noted that the efficacy of competition in contracting is weakened severely if there are few bidders, entry to the market is restricted, buyers have a stake in relationships with previous sellers, and sellers actively participate in structuring market demand. Experience in the United States in the 1980s also shows that the savings gained from contracting do not arise from market-driven logics, but from different conditions that structure wages in the public and private sectors (Smith and Lipsky, 1992). The problems associated with the bargaining positions of contracted institutions and with the general policy context of contracting have also been emphasized in developing countries (McPake and Hongoro, 1995).

In some countries, contracting to the nonprofit sector has been promoted because of the value-bound nature of nonprofit organizations. While such contracting may be a choice of convenience in many situations, the issue of value-based commitment is more problematic. When the contracting is done on the grounds of costs, the competition may make it hard for nonprofit organizations to survive in the long term. In the USA the nonprofit hospitals have over the years come more to resemble the for-profit hospitals (Relman, 1991). In many developing countries, the voluntary sector has become a more promising area for professionals to work in, and the rapidly increasing funding of the nongovernmental sector will have implications for the further development of this sector. In addition, the transfer of responsibility to the private sector (for-profit or nonprofit) will do nothing to improve the performance and accountability of the public sector, but does have potential to exacerbate the existing inequities (see Chapter 7).

The more elaborated models of contracting seen in the managed market reforms have been promoted as means to hinder both market and government failures, though they may be seen also as an extension of market mechanisms to the health sector. In the context of provision of hospital care it has been concluded that the negative effects on equity may be amongst the most important costs of managed market reforms, although these effects are frequently overlooked by those arguing in favour of such reforms (Broomberg,1994a; Broomberg, 1994b). The evidence relating to efficiency gains is ambiguous, as the managed market reforms have been implemented only recently and the experience gained in several developed countries does not provide evidence that competition enhances efficiency in health care markets (Maynard, 1993; Maynard, 1994, Finkel, 1993; OECD, 1994; Saltman and von Otter, 1995; Enthoven, 1993b). The market-driven reforms have been accompanied by reinforced and expanded regulatory measures. The most visible of these have been introduced in the pharmaceutical sector, and involve the introduction of reference pricing and/or positive lists (Saltman and von Otter, 1995). Reductions in costs of pharmaceuticals sometimes seem to have been the most observable reductions in costs when health care reforms have been implemented (Iliffe and Freudenstein, 1994; Karcher, 1994). If the reduced cost of drugs, due to increasing regulation of prescribing practices, is the major cost-saving change in the health sector reforms, the origin and nature of these savings should be presented more clearly. Furthermore, if the growth in the use of more expensive technology lies at the root of the escalation of health care costs, then none of the attempts to restrain costs, other than restricting the availability of expensive technologies, get to the root of the problems (OECD, 1994).

Decentralization

Decentralization can be defined as the transfer of authority, or dispersal of power, in public planning, management and decision making from the national to subnational levels, or more generally from higher to lower levels of government. Four main types of decentralization commonly found in practice may be distinguished: deconcentration, devolution, delegation and privatization. These reflect different degrees of decentralization of government authority and different approaches to decentralization (Mills *et al.*, 1990) (Box 9.4).

According to Kutzin, issues of concern in decentralization have been

Health Care Reforms

Box 9.4 Deconcentration, devolution, delegation and privatization

(Mills et al., 1990)

Deconcentration is applied to the handing over of some administrative authority to locally based offices of central government Ministries. It has been the form of decentralization most frequently used in developing countries since the early 1970s. Deconcentration implies establishing one or more additional management levels – for example, the district and/or region and delegating to this level certain administrative functions.

Devolution is the creation or strengthening of subnational levels of government (local government or local authorities) that are substantially independent of the national level with respect to a defined set of functions. They are rarely completely autonomous, but are largely independent of the national government in their areas of responsibility rather than subordinate administrative units as in the case of deconcentration. The experience of developed countries indicates that it is feasible to devolve health services to local government structures, but that this requires heavy state involvement in financing as well as considerable cooperation between local authorities to provide more specialized services.

Delegation involves the transfer of managerial responsibility for defined functions to organizations (often termed parastatal organizations) that are outside the central government structure and only indirectly controlled by central government. Governments may see delegation as a way of avoiding the inefficiency of direct government management, of increasing cost control, and of setting up an organization that is responsive and flexible. In the health field delegation has been used to manage teaching hospitals and to organize the provision of medical care financed by social insurance in some Latin American countries.

Privatization involves the transfer of government functions to voluntary organizations or to private -or non-profit making enterprises with a variable degree of government regulation. Privatization has been a practical solution in some countries and has lately become an ideological issue in others. As a slogan it conveys the ideal of free market, which is considered the ultimate in decentralization by proponents of a market system of health care.

interregional equity, the balancing of national health priorities such as family planning policies, and the potential to create a great deal of confusion about lines of authority and lines of accountability. The four common operational problems that face decentralized systems are: (1) local authorities lack the managerial capacity to run a decentralized system; (2) such a system results in an increase rather than a decrease in administrative expenditure; (3) it adds to the number of bureaucratic layers and creates more bottlenecks in decision making; and (4) the central ministry is unable to reorient itself to play a supervisory/monitoring role in a decentralized system as opposed to the earlier focus on direct service delivery. Decentralization does not, by itself, solve any problems. In a decentralized system the local managerial authorities are in a better position to respond quickly to local needs than in a system in which all important decisions must be taken at the central level – but local management must also have the capacity to respond appropriately (Kutzin, 1995).

While decentralization has been considered an important tool for implementing PHC policies, more recently it has also been promoted as a means of improving the efficiency, management and responsiveness of government health services (Kutzin, 1995; World Bank, 1993a). The World Bank also tends to emphasize the role of locally collected funds as a means to true decentralization, in which districts and communities should have more control over money and health-system inputs (Shaw and Griffin, 1995). In principle the interregional inequities may be balanced through a central redistributive system. When decentralization is linked with increasing self-reliance in funding, however, problems of interregional inequity may become evident. In Papua New Guinea the existing inequities between provinces were perpetuated and even heightened following decentralization (Thomason *et al.,* 1991, cited in Kutzin, 1995, Thomason *et al.,* 1994).

Collins has called for a critical and political analysis of decentralization in order to avoid its becoming something of a wolf in sheep's clothing. Decentralization may be interpreted as deepening and sustaining inequities and power structures when decentralization is consistent with a reduced role of the state system in social affairs, when it is pursued as a means of dispersing and defusing social and political conflict, when it reinforces the access of local dominant groups in decision making and resources allocation, and when decentralization expands central government control over the periphery (Collins, 1989). According to Collins and Green decentralization is clouded in ambiguities as a concept. It is a political issue that lends itself to different interpretations by social and political groups with contrasting interests. It involves a restructuring of the state system with significant implications for systems of political domination, the access of groups to the centres of decision making, and the character of public policies. Collins and Green therefore criticize the tendency of decentralization to be associated with state limitations and the potential of decentralization to strengthen political domination and inequality at the local level (Collins and Green, 1994). Similar notions are presented by Packard *et al.,* who claim that the process of PHC implementation and decentralization was also designed to serve as a means to maintain the interests of the élite groups, and that it was implemented in Latin America in order to achieve other political and economical goals (Packard *et al.*, 1989).

Challenges and future prospects

Politics of health care reform

According to Walt and Gilson, attention to the content of health sector reform neglects the actors involved in the policy reform as well as the processes contingent on developing and implementing change and the context within which the policy is developed. While prescriptions abound as to what health policy reforms in countries should introduce, little attention has been paid to how countries should carry out reforms, and even to the question of who is likely to favour or resist such policies (Walt and Gilson, 1994). In addition, while attention has been drawn to the poor as a general category, there is little information on the implications of health sector reforms by gender (Standing, 1997).

There are obvious reasons to ask about the origins of the differences between resources spent on health, the actual state of health of the populations and the perceived qualities of health services in different countries. It is also clear that social policies and health care are connected to the aims, values and emphasis on redistribution inherent in the general development policies of particular governments and, increasingly, of the wider international community as well. There are obviously limits to government spending on the health sector, but there are also large differences in reported allocations to the health sector even within government budgets. While there are substantial differences in health expenditures between many of the OECD countries with similar health outcomes, in some developing countries both the absolute and relative shares of health expenditure are very small (World Bank, 1993a). Health expenditures and access to health care need also to be linked to differences in health within the population and to the share of population with access to health care. While increasing attention has been drawn to health care costs, it could be time to take a closer look at to the broader set of economic and public policies that have been implemented, and at their returns to the health and social well being of whole populations and groups within these populations.

In a comparison of European countries with the United States, Wagstaff and Doorslaer concluded that tax-financed systems tend to be mildly progressive, social insurance systems regressive, and private systems even more regressive. In most countries out-of-pocket payments are an especially regressive means of raising health care revenues (Wagstaff and Doorslaer, 1992). Experience to date suggests that the introduction of competition-based reforms has proved expensive. To the extent that these and additional expenditures reflect new transaction costs associated with market-based reforms (contract negotiation and litigation, advertising, higher personnel salaries), as well as costs of national monitoring and evaluation activities, these higher costs have been recurring. The evidence to date also suggests that finance-side competition, at least as currently conceptualized, generates more problems than it resolves (Saltman and von Otter, 1995). It has also been argued that most of the conditions required for successful implementation of these reforms are absent in all but a few richer developing countries (Broomberg 1994a, 1994b). According to Maynard and Bloor, the recent reform 'epidemic' has been driven by rhetoric, incomplete theorizing and little evidence (Maynard and Bloor, 1995). The World Bank, the aid agencies and others have taken up positions on the value of market approaches in improving the efficiency of the public health sector in developing countries. Such policy prescriptions are being advanced, however, despite an almost total lack of knowledge on whether these solutions are likely to be any better than the systems they are intended to replace (Mills, 1995).

Professionals and power in health care reform

In some countries, such as Sweden, one of the motives leading to reform has been to gain more power over the professional autonomy of medical doctors (Dahlgren, 1994). In Britain the role of planned market mechanisms has been to shift a degree of authority away from physicians towards managers, reducing the value placed on physicians' independent clinical role (Harrison, 1995). Markets or the threat of markets have been seen as a means to change professional hierarchies and power relations, market mechanisms also introduce other emphases and incentives to the professionals. Perceiving physicians as entrepreneurs primarily interested in their earning possibilities will also enhance these elements in the profession. It has been claimed that the exchange of ideas and innovations that can help preserve the quality of care has become more difficult in the competitive atmosphere, and cooperating, not competing, has been emphasized as the means to improve health care (Berwick and Smith, 1995). In the United States the invasion of commerce into medical care has been seen as an epic clash of cultures between commercial and professional traditions, where the invasion of commercialism poses severe hazards for the care of the sick and the welfare of communities: the health of the public and the public health (McArthur and Moore, 1997). Professional activity governed by duty executed in a knowledge-based manner, may also be more cost-effective than the creation of bureaucratic regulation in public and private markets. In the United States estimated management costs have indicated that 15–17 per cent of expenditure has been used to monitor behaviour (Maynard and Bloor, 1995).

In developed countries a widely emphasized aspect of the health care reforms has been maintaining or increasing the patient's choice of the medical practitioner, but this is a practical possibility mostly in areas where a larger number of medical practitioners are available. In remote areas choice soon becomes very limited, and in medicine choice has different implications and meanings than in a grocery store. Perhaps more gains could be achieved through improving patients' rights, continuity of care, and a consideration of the more humane aspects of medical care. Markets are not a prerequisite for choice in health care and strategies to improve choice may be linked with trade-offs and choices in other aspects of health care which may further limit the choice of those with more limited financial resources.

The role of professional and managerial power should also be of concern because of lessons learnt from the corporatization of power in the USA. The health care industry forms a major economic power base in terms of employment and economic activities in the United States, with increasing merging of the ownership of the providers and purchasers of health care (Salmon, 1995). It has been noted that the markets introduce their own changes, enhancing the merging of the different actors in the field (Saltman and von Otter, 1995). Specific attention has already been drawn to the fast pace of growth amongst the for-profit providers in the United States, as well as their corporatization in larger chains (Robinson, 1996; Bond and Weissman, 1997; Imersheim and Estes, 1996; Fuchs, 1997).

Equity and health as social right

The general egalitarian principle in health care has been defined as receiving treatment according to need and paying according to the ability to pay (Wagstaff and Doorslaer, 1993). The current emphasis on health care reform has the potential to lead increasingly to the provision of health services and treatment according to willingness to pay, a trend which undermines the principle as far as both paying according to the ability to pay and provision of care according to need are concerned. In a health system the use of sophisticated health technologies should be based on need and the medical relevance of the problem, while the proposals for health care reform tend to emphasize the relevance of cost efficiency and willingness to pay as the primary criteria.

Conflicts between different policy objectives (efficiency or effectiveness vs equity) and between different reform instruments (negotiated contracts vs patient choice) have confused implementation. One key conflict between efficiency and equity has emerged in the debate about the contents of a 'basic package' for health services. Attempts to define such a package are a response to the continued expansion of clinical capacities, on one hand, and the constrained public sector on the other. The notion of a basic package is essentially a routinized form of health care rationing, reconfigured as an administrative device (Saltman and von Otter, 1995). The danger that particular political decisions may be dealt with as technical and administrative issues should always be a concern in the debate on health sector reforms. According to Klein, there have been recent attempts in Sweden, New Zealand and the Netherlands to define priorities in health. These attempts have resulted in the rejection of an economic approach – that is, ranking services according to the ratio between costs and benefits (Klein, 1995). While there are problems in practice, questions may be posed also in relation to other implications of the exercise (see Chapter 8). The concern with allocative efficiency, as usually envisaged by the economists, is not necessarily shared by the general public; and allowing cost-effectiveness to assign priorities in health care may impose an excessively simple value system upon decision-making about resource allocation (Nord *et al.*, 1995). From another point of view, if the basic package includes proven, cost-effective therapies, why should consumers buy private insurance for unproven, cost-ineffective interventions (Maynard and Bloor, 1995)?

In some countries, universal access to even a limited range of services may be beyond reach at the moment, but the long-term effects of creating a two-tier system in health care should be of concern wherever the reforms are implemented. Concerns about the development of two-tier health care are related to the increasing emphasis on contracting, the involvement of private providers, and competition in the financing of health care. Changing and reforming health systems is a slow and complicated process involving different actors and interest groups. It is clear that without a commitment to social rights and to the fate of the most vulnerable groups of the society, other aims will predominate. The current emphasis on the provision of at least some services to all may be seen as an achievement in many countries. The process by which this is to be achieved, however, seems to involve choices which may become a hindrance to equitable health policies in the long run.

10

Drug Policies

The pharmaceutical question

The Third World experiences a wide range of problems in relation to pharmaceutical drugs: vital drugs are often inaccessible while worthless or harmful drugs are abundant; bad and misleading information on drugs; improper use; the high share of drugs in health costs; and the lack of measures to regulate drug markets. In recent years heated debates have concerned the financing of drugs and use of drugs in the financing of health care.

The search for rational and equitable pharmaceutical policies has been part of the Third World initiative for the establishment of a New International Economic Order (Patel, 1983a). Essential drugs became one of the eight basic elements of PHC with the adoption of the HFA strategy. The strategy made the need to regulate the use of drugs even more urgent, because its adoption would entail a large increase in the supply. The Alma Ata Conference recommended that member states should

> formulate national drug policies and regulations with respect to import, local production, sale and distribution of drugs and biologicals so as to ensure that essential drugs are available at the various levels of PHC at the lowest feasible cost; that specific measures are taken to prevent the over-utilization of medicines; that proven traditional remedies are incorporated; and that effective administrative and supply systems be established (cited in Jaysena, 1985).

In the 1960s and 1970s the governments of several Third World countries tried to rationalize their purchase of drugs. Building up national industries, nationalizing the existing pharmaceutical industry and introducing generic prescribing were some of the measures thus tried. There has been considerable opposition by the multinational industries to all rationalization measures, however, and changes in the economic situation along with the implementation of structural adjustment policies have defeated many of the attempts (Mamdani, 1992; Bidway, 1995; Chowdhury, 1995a).

The drug situation

Drug consumption in 1994 was estimated at about US$259 billion, with the top 20 manufacturers supplying about 48 of this total. North America, Japan and Europe dominate in consuming the drugs, with an 83 per cent of share of sales (Euromonitor 1995). African people account for less than 2 per cent of the worldwide spending (Chetley, 1993), and the Third World countries together account for 21 per cent of the world's pharmaceuticals (OTA, 1993). WHO has estimated that in 1985 between 1,300 and 2,500 million people had little or no access to essential drugs (WHO, 1988c).

Drug production is centred in North America (30 per cent of the world's production), Europe (28 per cent) and Japan (20 per cent) (Euromonitor, 1995). In 1989 eight of the top 15 pharmaceutical companies were US-based multinationals (OTA, 1993). The big drug exporting countries in 1982 were the USA, Germany, the UK and France (Taylor, 1986). The developing countries' share of global production of pharmaceutical products in 1990 was 18 per cent (Ballance *et al.*, 1992; cited in Correa, 1996), and a large part of this production was carried out by the same multinational companies which, in general, control two thirds or more of the markets in developing countries (Correa, 1996). It has been estimated that of the money spent on drug research, 4 per cent at most is used to research drugs needed for disease conditions especially encountered in the Third World (WHO, 1988c).

It has been estimated that 20–30 per cent of the drug production involves international trade, while the remaining amount consists of drugs that are produced and consumed within individual countries (Use of WHO Certification Scheme, 1994). In 1987, 45 per cent of the exports of the pharmaceutical industry of the European Community were to Third World countries. In addition a considerable volume of raw materials was exported to the Third World for local production (van der Heide, 1991).

Alternative medicines, including herbal medicines, commonly used in Third World countries, have become increasingly popular in industrialized countries. The botanical industry is growing rapidly, and in several European countries alternative drugs are an integral part of conventional medicine (Marwick, 1995). Multinational pharmaceutical companies are increasingly surveying plant life in Third World regions (Correa, 1996), and firms marketing these products are being bought as investments by leading pharmaceutical manufacturers (Marwick, 1995). The role of regulatory authorities concerning the use of herbal medicines is under discussion in several countries (Marwick, 1995; Cottrell, 1996).

Despite minor spending on drugs in absolute terms, drug budgets have been a substantial part of the small health budgets in most Third World countries: volumes as high as 50–80 per cent of public health expenditure have been cited (Peretz, 1983). In the public sector, drugs generally account for between 10 per cent and 30 per cent of total recurrent costs (World Bank, 1993a). The share of the private sector in the provision of drugs is 80 per cent or above in monetary terms in many Third World countries (AIDAN and VHAI, 1986). During the 1980s countries looked increasingly to international agencies to pay their bills, and in a number of African countries these agencies were paying for a major part of the drugs consumed (Kanji, 1989).

Quality

Many of the drugs used in Third World countries are either useless or even harmful. According to Hartog's investigation, only 16 per cent of the drugs exported by major European companies to Third World countries were essential drugs (Hartog, 1993). Approximately one out of every four drugs exported from West Germany to the Third World was never sold in West Germany or had not been marketed there for at least 15 years (van der Heide, 1991).

For the poorest Third World countries one major problem is the entry of substandard drugs, partly due to the absence of adequate control laboratory facilities (Jaysena, 1985). According to the All India Drug Action Network and Voluntary Health Action of India, 20 per cent of the drugs in India have been found to be substandard, and over half the sampled drugs of substandard quality were manufactured by multinational companies (AIDAN and VHAI, 1986). In Bangladesh substandard drugs have been found to be produced mainly by small units and some medium-sized enterprises, accounting in total for only a minimal share of the total market (Chowdhury, 1995a).

Drug promotion

Inadequate drug promotion practices are of worldwide concern. While drug promotion is better controlled in industrialized countries than has been possible in Third World countries, it is also true that in industrialized countries new drug promotion strategies have been adopted that have so far escaped direct prohibition. There has been concern, for example, about the use of the Internet in the promotion and selling of drugs (Gilbert and Chetley, 1996). Recently WHO has called on its member states to close the loophole on the control of drugs that has been opened by the Internet (Siegel-Itkovich, 1997).

Drug promotion in the Third World countries has included the presence of an abundance of retailers (in some countries equal to the number of physicians), gifts to the physician including very expensive commodities (such as a car) in addition to free samples, and misleading information on drugs, in the form of both labelling and advertising (Melrose, 1982). Drugs exported from the United States are required to have the same drug labelling as in their home market, but a survey of drugs imported by Third World countries through US-based companies exposed serious labelling faults (OTA, 1993). In a follow-up study improvements in drug promotion practices in Third World countries were found. Most cases of irrational promotion involved domestic firms: of these 40 per cent were multinationals and 60 per cent were local firms. A clear case of double standards was still found between marketing practices in the United States and those in Third World countries (Silverman *et al.*, 1986).

Regulation in the Third World countries

In recent years Third World countries have adopted legislation on drug licensing (Bruneton *et al.*, 1996) but their power to regulate drugs or information about the drugs available is very limited. Few Third World governments have succeeded in imposing successful controls on private drug sales (Melrose, 1983), and in some countries up to 75 per cent of the drugs moving in the market may be outside the control of the Health Ministries (Sterky, 1985).

WHO has estimated that only 5 per cent of Third World countries possess an effective drug regulatory administration (WHO, 1988c). The small regulatory authorities are vitally dependent on authoritative, reliable and independent information generated in the exporting country (Guiding Principles, 1989). It has been claimed that the rule of thumb in many Third World countries is that any drug approved in an industrialized country is suitable for use in their own country (Jaysena, 1985).

The possibility of Third World countries ensuring the appropriate use of drugs may be even more remote. As mentioned above, drug promotion practices are often unethical. Moreover, in many countries a great number of drugs are sold over the counter without prescription and by untrained personnel. Relying on the information and advice they receive, poor people often spend their money on unnecessary or useless drugs, instead of on commodities that they really need, such as food or curative drugs (Melrose, 1982). In the future, the power of governments to regulate the selection of drugs, as well as their use, promotion and price, is more likely to become weaker than stronger, as a result of the economic policies imposed by the World Bank and the IMF, the Final Act of a new international trade treaty under the Uruguay Round of GATT, and the emergence of a new global regime under the WTO, further discussed below. Furthermore, with the trend towards harmonization of drug licensing for universal sale, there is a danger that requirements set by individual countries may be ignored as countries are pressured to give licences to whatever drugs have been licensed elsewhere (Weerasuriya, 1996).

Regulation in the exporting countries

The USA has prohibited the export of drugs not approved in the USA. Since 1986 this policy has been relaxed somewhat, and export to a limited number of countries with good regulation systems is permitted (OTA, 1993). Since 1986 attempts have been made to prevent members of the European Union from exporting pharmaceuticals which have been banned, withdrawn, or restricted within the EU market, or which have not been registered for that market. The industry has opposed such initiatives strenuously. A very limited proposal on the drawing up of a list of products banned or withdrawn within the EU was adopted in 1989 (van der Heide, 1991) and EU countries had to translate this policy into national law by 1991. Many countries have adopted additional regulations or retained regulations that supplement the weak EU law, but serious loopholes remain in the legislation of all countries. For example, most European countries allow the export of products that have never been licenced, or have been delicensed in the exporting country, while France and Switzerland still allow licensing 'for export only' (Bruneton *et al.*, 1996).

Policies

WHO

Until the early 1970s WHO's concern with drugs was limited mainly to an attempt to harmonize drug standards in international commerce; imposing quality controls over the chemical and physical properties of drugs (Stenzl, 1981; cited in Mamdani, 1992). The thalidomide disaster in 1961 forced WHO to focus on drug safety and efficacy (Mamdani, 1992). WHO's constitution requires the organization to 'develop, establish and promote international standards with respect to food, biological, pharmaceutical and similar products' (WHO, 1994a). In 1969, WHO endorsed requirements for 'Good Practices in the Manufacture and Quality Control of Drugs'. These guidelines were the starting point for the 'Certification Scheme on the Quality of Pharmaceutical Products Moving in International Commerce' adopted in 1975. The WHO Certification Scheme provides Third World countries with a mechanism for obtaining information on the quality of pharmaceuticals imported into a country, such as whether they are approved for use in the country of export and, if approved, what labelling is used there (OTA, 1993). The majority of WHO member states subscribe to the WHO Certification

Scheme (Drug regulation, 1993), but in practice the scheme is not used effectively (Use of WHO Certification Scheme, 1994). Other long-term harmonization activities include, for example, the WHO Model List of Essential Drugs, the WHO Model Prescribing Information and the WHO Guidelines for Good Clinical Practice for Trials on Pharmaceutical Products (WHO, 1996e).

A United Nations Council for Trade and Development (UNCTAD) study published in 1975 (Lal, 1975) outlined the basic elements of the pharmaceutical policies needed for Third World countries. It called for a list of priority pharmaceutical needs in Third World countries, national buying agencies, exclusion or alternatively shortening of patents for pharmaceuticals, adoption of generic names for pharmaceuticals, vitalizing the development of national pharmaceutical industries and creation of regional cooperation in production. The concept of essential drugs was introduced by WHO in 1975, and national drug policies were identified as a top priority for developing countries. Essential drugs were defined by WHO as 'those considered to be of utmost importance and hence basic, indispensable, and necessary for the health needs of the population. They should be available at all times and in proper forms to all segments of the society' (Mamdani, 1992).

WHO's Drug Policies and Management unit (DPM) was created in 1977, and the first head of the unit was Dr. H. Nakajima (the Director General of WHO since 1988). DPM's overall idea was to improve drug supplies in Third World countries by encouraging them to produce locally. In 1981 DPM was abolished and the Action Programme on Essential Drugs (DAP) was created (Walt and Harnmeijer, 1992).

At the beginning of the 1980s (now under the leadership of the Dane Dr Ernst Lauridsen and after changes in the organizational structure), the DAP became a more practical programme attracting fair amounts of extra-budgetary funds (Walt and Harnmeijer 1992). The execution of the DAP programme relied mainly on drug kit systems. Although it made the 'essential drugs' concept known and affected drug policies, the kit system, instead of being an intermediate stage leading towards an integrated system, became an end in itself (Kanji and Hardon, 1992). The vertical nature of the DAP is evident from the way it reacted to requests from Third World countries: it failed to give its full support in the early stages of policy formulation in Bangladesh, and did not allow Mozambique to purchase drugs outside UNICEF's Supplies Division (Kanji, 1992). The DAP evaluation also found that seven of the thirteen countries evaluated used ready-packed kits, mainly imported from Europe and often from UNICEF's Supplies Division in Copenhagen, and that external funding was sometimes conditional on the purchase of kits. The major funders of the DAP between 1984 and 1989 were Denmark and the Netherlands (LSHTM/KIT, 1989).

A WHO conference of experts on the rational use of drugs was held in Nairobi in 1985. It was agreed that governments were responsible for regulating marketing, but industry extracted major compromises: essential drugs policies were targeted on Third World countries and on their public sectors only; the conference did not accept an international code on drugs, nor did it endorse the 'medical need' criterion for the approval of drugs (Hardon, 1992).

In 1986, the WHA endorsed a revised drug strategy based on the outcome of the Nairobi conference. The rational drug policies identified by WHO in 1988 had the following major components: (1) essential drugs lists, composed of a limited number of generic drugs; (2) legislation, registration and quality assurance; (3) procurement and distribution; (4) local production; (5) education and training; (6) information to the public; and (7) research (WHO, 1988d).

The formulation of the new pharmaceuticals policy put to the test WHO's reputation as a sober and technologically competent organization that had stayed out of politics (Walt and Harnmeijer, 1992). The United States baulked several times at the essential drugs policy, the code for breast milk substitutes, and the restrictions on promoting unsuitable weaning products (Chetley, 1990). During the WHA in 1986, the US took the strong position that the WHO should not be involved in efforts to regulate or control the commercial practices of private industry, even when the products related to health: infant food products, pharmaceuticals, tobacco and alcohol were all mentioned (cited in Chetley, 1990). In 1986 and 1987 the US withheld its contribution to the budget of WHO, allegedly because of its disapproval of the policies on breast food substitutes and essential drugs. Later the US announced its new contribution to WHO in 1988 during the same session at which Dr Nakajima was elected as Director General (Hardon and Kanji, 1992). Soon after that the importance of DAP was diminished by removing it and the Pharmaceuticals Unit out of the Director General's office and putting them into a new division. Donor dissatisfaction has resulted in the withdrawal of funds from the programme (Walt and Harnmeijer, 1992).

While WHO earlier emphasized issues like promoting local production, procurement and distribution as tools for lowering prices on drugs, these emphases have not been prominent in the 1990s. According to Vaughan *et al.*, rather than having a strong advocacy role combined with policy formulation and development, the DAP is currently putting more emphasis on implementation in individual countries, and the main challenge is the application of drug policies in a context of health sector reform (Vaughan *et al.*, 1995). The highest DAP priority is direct country support and the development of practical tools and training materials (WHO, 1996f). WHO's guidelines on drug promotion were published in 1996. In 1996 the WHA endorsed a revised drug strategy

Box 10.1   Rational drug policies and their survival

In countries where rational drug policies were introduced successfully, substantial improvements and savings were achieved. According to the World Bank some countries achieved savings of 40 to 60 per cent in pharmaceutical expenditure by improving selection and by competitive purchasing (World Bank, 1993a) – but pressures from Western governments, the drugs industry and the Bretton Woods institutions, along with the economic recession and political changes within the countries, have made it difficult for the new policies and their achievements to survive.

In Bangladesh a national drugs policy was launched in 1982. It included essential drugs lists, the use of generic names for the most basic drugs, measures for quality control, reorganization of the pharmacies, the relaxing of regulations concerning patents, and other measures to favour local production (Chowdhury, 1995a and 1995b). As a result of the policies the proportion of local production rose to 60 per cent, and the proportion of essential drugs of all local production rose from 30 to 80 per cent. The cost of essential drugs was reduced and the government's procurement procedures improved. Serious problems persisted, however, in access to drugs, prescribing patterns and quality control. The problems were not eased by the immense pressures from the pharmaceutical industry and the various Western countries with major drugs exporting industries. The pressure from governments was not insignificant, since 80 per cent of the Bangladesh development budget consisted of foreign aid (Reich, 1994).

WHO, having stumbled in failing to give permission for the translation and distribution of the essential drugs list, and to support the drug policy publicly in the early stages (Chowdhury, 1995a; Kanji, 1992), was now strongly supportive (Reich, 1994). According to Chowdhury several explanations for the cautious behaviour of WHO may be surmised. One may be the reluctance of the US government, a major funder of WHO, to endorse the policies. Other possible explanations include the medical and technological orientation of the organization, and the intention to take apolitical and neutral stands (Chowdhury, 1995a).

In 1992 the head of the Industry and Energy Unit of the World Bank's office in Bangladesh wrote a letter to the joint secretary of the government's economic relations division, in which he made specific recommendations pertaining to pharmaceuticals: to allow the introduction of new products by using free sales certificates, to lift all controls on prices, to remove the control on advertising from the drugs licensing authority, to remove existing restrictions on foreign firms in the area of what drugs they can produce, and to abolish controls on the import of pharmaceutical raw materials. Concern over the national drugs policy

Box 10.1 cont.

led WHO and UNICEF to defend it, and to contacts with the World Bank. As a result the World Bank wrote another letter to the government official, starting with the assurance that the World Bank was in favour of the essential drugs policy. The letter went on to argue that the present controls could be replaced by more liberal policies/procedures without sacrificing the objective of increasing availability of good quality and affordable essential drugs. Even with these changes, the World Bank's position still promoted foreign commercial interests over the health interests of the people of Bangladesh. Curiously enough, at the time of these events another division of the World Bank's office in Bangladesh, the Population and Health Unit, was finalizing agreement with the government and with major donor agencies on a programme that included a significant component on rational drugs use (Chowdhury, 1995a and 1995b).

In Mozambique, although many difficulties existed after the first years of the new drugs policy, there were many achievements: in 1979 the drugs tender system gave rise to 41 per cent savings, and it was able to exclude harmful, ineffective and useless drugs (Martins, 1983). In Bolivia a promising start to the new drugs policy was hampered first by the opposition of the pharmaceutical industry and the pharmacy system, and then by a change of government. As in many countries, the main controversy around pharmaceuticals was over whether they should be looked upon from the health perspective or from the industrial and commercial point of view (Prudencio and Tognoni, 1987).

which pays attention to the new challenges occurring with the private drug sector playing an increasingly important role (WHO, 1996f) (Box 10.1).

UNICEF

UNICEF has always played an important role in supplying basic drugs and vaccines to organizations such as WHO, as well as to country programmes, but it did not become more deeply involved in the essential drugs concept until 1981, when the Joint Committee on Health Policy (JCHP) initiated a joint programme on essential drugs (Walt and Harnmeijer, 1992) – although UNICEF and many NGOs had started their first projects with fees for drugs at the end of the 1970s in Kenya (Bennett, 1989).

With the launching of the Bamako Initiative, UNICEF became an important actor in drug policies. It should be noted that the Bamako Initiative aims at implementing the supply of essential drugs, which become the basis for primary health finances. Since the aim is self-reliance in financing of PHC, it is surprising that the pilot projects have relied largely on drug kit systems from UNICEF's Supplies Division, making the transition towards self-reliance after the first phase more difficult.

According to its health strategy, UNICEF will place more emphasis on assisting countries in creating innovative financing mechanisms and accessing economies of scale in the global market place through UNICEF procurement services (UNICEF 1995c). In 1996 the former drugs specialist of the World Bank was appointed chief of UNICEF's Health Section. The implications of this appointment for UNICEF's drug policies are not yet clear.

The World Bank

The World Bank has included pharmaceutical policies in its agenda since 1980 (World Bank, 1980), but its more substantial involvement in pharmaceutical policies came much later. The World Bank has been involved with drugs and pharmaceutical industries on the three levels of its actions: promoting 1) free trade and deregulation at the international level, 2) private investments and the use of essential drugs at the national level, 3) drug revolving funds at the project level.

The World Bank finances pharmaceuticals by US$300 million a year. According to the former pharmaceutical expert of the Bank, Denis Broun, drug procurement using World Bank funds should be limited to essential drugs only, and the drugs should be procured under generic names (Broun, 1995). While endorsing the use of essential drugs, other policies supported by the World Bank have often supported the liberalization of the pharmaceutical trade and the encouragement of private pharmacies, resulting in a situation where the actual drug supply available can be quite different from the supposed emphasis on essential drugs. The extension of the essential drug policies to the private sector seems to come mainly through encouragement of the pharmaceutical industries to market generic products to the private sector (Health Horizons, 1995).

In Mali, for example, the World Bank policies at the beginning of the 1990s (linked with structural adjustment) required liberalization of the pharmaceutical supply and distribution sector. Brunet-Jailly has claimed, therefore, that the aim of realizing essential drugs policies has become impossible to achieve, because of the other measures imposed by the World Bank (Brunet-Jailly, 1993).

In Laos, the spread of the private sector pharmacies as result of economic liberalization quickly led to the private sector supplying 80 per cent of the drugs. This created concern that the cheap generic drugs rationally dispensed may not be attractive to pharmacists, whose livelihoods depend on a large turnover. It was also found that 60 per cent of drugs were obtained directly from pharmacies without prescriptions. In addition to a large proportion of substandard drugs, irrational combinations were found, such as those involving corticosteroids and vitamins. There was also inappropriate use, involving polypharmacy and including overuse of antibiotics and injections. A study of the development of a pharmaceutical market in Laos has concluded that for the national drugs policy to have a substantial effect, it would have to include all outlets, both formal (state or health care institutions) and informal (private sector, especially pharmacies and drug shops where practices are often irrational) (Paphassarang *et al.*, 1995). Restricting the supply of drugs to essential drugs as a means of controlling public sector costs may provide cost-efficient savings in the public sector, but does not necessarily correct the problem of inappropriate use. There is thus a risk that the World Bank prescription on pharmaceutical policies may lead towards two-track policies, where the increased markets in the private sector may be of much larger significance than the public sector's efforts to rationalize drug use and savings from essential drugs in the public sector. If national drugs policies are to be effective in the broader sense, a more comprehensive approach is needed.

The World Bank approach to the essential drugs and pharmaceutical policies in Africa gives a picture of World Bank drug policies. The Bank has pointed out that the value of drugs received by the consumer is only 12 per cent of the public sector budget allocation for drugs, indicating a substantial inefficiency and waste in the public sector and the need for national drug policies. The solutions provided by the Bank may be problematic in the long run, however, and in any case would require considerable regulatory ability on the part of the governments. The Bank suggests that the national drug authority should aim at working through consensus building, while policies based on 'prohibition and repression' are seen as less effective. It is suggested that the operational responsibilities for wholesale drug purchase and distribution should be assigned increasingly to the nongovernmental sector. To facilitate this process, governments should foster the development of private commercial and noncommercial drugs sectors, reinvigorate public sector distribution efficiency, and promote cost-effective means of supplying essential drugs on a sustainable and affordable basis to the poorest groups in society. The Bank further notes that the international drugs manufacturers typically realize full economies of scale with higher quality standards at non-African production facilities than would be possible in most African countries in the foreseeable future. Therefore, because of the extremely competitive world market in generic drugs, the production of drugs should not be started in countries lacking a pharmaceutical manufacturing tradition (World Bank, 1993b).

GATT/WTO

The GATT/WTO Uruguay Round Treaty came into force in the beginning of 1995. The WTO, like the World Bank and the IMF, will become a powerful force for dictating moves towards deregulation and liberalization in the trade politics of developing countries (Watkins, 1994). While the role of GATT has traditionally been restricted to international trade in goods, the new agreement extends to intellectual property, such as patents, copyrights and trademarks including trade-related aspects of intellectual property rights (TRIPs) (Chaudhuri, 1993).

According to the new regulations, there is an obligation to grant patent protection in all fields of technology, and equal treatment regardless of the product's origin (Correa, 1996). The term of a patent would be 20 years from the date of filing the application, and since a process patent is also available, it might be possible to extend it for another 20 years (Balasubramanian 1996). Since, according to the TRIPs Agreement, there is no longer any obligation to exploit the innovation in the country where the patent is held, the Agreement is consistent with the trend towards internationalization of production and marketing by multinational companies (Correa, 1996). The Third World countries were allowed a transitional period.

Generally-speaking, industrialized countries have applied patent laws on pharmaceuticals that reflect the development stage of the domestic industry. The US pharmaceutical industry trade association had an important role in formulating government policy support for strict international protection of intellectual property, a central goal of US international economic policy (Weissman, 1996). In line with this policy and its various expressions – a US Trade Act and the inclusion of intellectual property rights in the North American Free Trade Agreement (NAFTA), and finally in the GATT/WTO Agreement – many countries, particularly those in the Third World, have been pressured to amend their patent legislation (Correa, 1996; Weissman, 1996; South Centre, 1995) even against the interests of their domestic drug policies and pharmaceutical industries.

Although it has been claimed that the introduction of TRIPs would stimulate transfer of technology, encourage foreign direct investment, strengthen research and development and innovation, and ensure early introduction of new products in developing countries, there is little evidence in support of these assumptions (Balasubramanian, 1996; Correa, 1996). Bidway has summarized the direct effects of the Treaty on the pharmaceutical sector rather differently: strengthening of patents (through a product patent system instead of a process patent, as well as by extending their duration) and thus strengthening monopolies; treating importation as equivalent to working the patent (instead of requiring the patent holder literally to work the patent in the country of issue); near abolition of compulsory licensing, which used to require the patent holder to grant non-exclusive licences to competitors; and the reversal of the burden of proof in charges on theft of a new invention (Bidway, 1995). The negative implications for Third World countries, especially those with their own pharmaceutical industries, are feared to be: (1) higher consumer prices of drugs; (2) larger foreign exchange outflow due to higher imports and lower exports; (3) smaller employment generation due to lower domestic production (Chaudhuri, 1993).

Although naturally occurring substances are not patentable, only mildly altered chemical substances are (Correa, 1996). Serious concerns have been expressed about the possibility of patents on biological materials, many of them traditionally used by ordinary people in the South (Khor, 1995; Raghavan, 1995). Shiva has noted that the transnational corporations that accuse the Third World of piracy, and have created TRIPs to stop this piracy, are themselves engaged in large-scale piracy of biological wealth and intellectual heritage from the Third World, including medicinal plants (Shiva, 1995).

Thus the new GATT/WTO Agreement leads to an erosion of the sovereign decision-making power of national governments in respect of intellectual property rights, control over drug prices, tariffs and duties, subsidies for the health care system, and the scope of public intervention in the pharmaceutical market. Similarly, the likely effect of NAFTA and new economic ground rules within the European Union will be to homogenize policies while eroding autonomy (*Development Dialogue,* 1995). In the EU drugs are dealt with mainly as part of industrial policies and, according to Hancher, at the EU level the pharmaceutical industry is viewed as one of Europe's best-performing high-technology sectors. It is the primary goal of European pharmaceutical industry policy to remove existing territorial barriers created by national legislation to ensure that European innovative firms enjoy a sufficiently large market (Hancher, 1996). In the EU sales licensing is harmonized (*Lancet,* 1995c), and the entry of drugs approved in any EU country to other countries is facilitated (Taylor, 1993).

The pharmaceutical industry

As has been shown above, the pharmaceutical industries are important actors not only in the making of pharmaceutical policies, but also in health and trade policies. During recent years, TNCs have increased in size while their number has decreased as a result of continuous mergers of companies in a context of intensive competition for markets and products (Hamrell and Nordberg, 1995; *Lancet,* 1995d). In 1996, 10 leading corporations accounted for 34 per cent of the worldwide pharmaceutical sales in one of the industry's most profitable years (*Financial Times,* 1997).

Research on drugs is dominated by research done or financed by pharmaceutical companies. Research organizations and public institutions are increasingly dependent on industry funding (Rosenberg, 1996), and companies may prevent the publishing of research that is nor favourable to their products (Coney, 1992; Pearce, 1992; McCarthy, 1996). Furthermore, concern has been raised over secrecy in regulation, which means that neither the basis of sales licensing nor the quality of regulation can be scrutinized by the public or by the scientific community (Statement, 1996; Ollila and Hemminki, 1996).

The Geneva-based International Federation of Pharmaceuticals Manufacturers Association (IFPMA) comprises largely multinational research-based companies controlling about 80 per cent of the world market. WHO established official relations with the IFPMA in 1971 and the IFPMA lobbied WHO throughout the 1970s, and protested vigorously against the essential drugs concept, regarding it as completely unacceptable (Walt and Harnmeijer, 1992). In response to the pressure for more controlled pharmaceutical policies, IFPMA produced its own code in 1981, which concentrated strictly on marketing (IFPMA, 1981). In the course of time it has become evident that improvements in marketing practices have been more likely to result from regulations and from opportunities to control than from internal control by the industry. Consumer and professional organizations have played an important role in watching over the industry.

Several programmes in WHO have collaborated with IFPMA, including the Special Programme for Research and Training in Tropical Diseases, the Special Programme for Research, Development and Research Training in Human Reproduction, the Division of Mental Health, and probably others as well (Antezana, 1990). For the drug companies collaboration with WHO may be beneficial for their image. By 1983, 52 companies had agreed to provide some 140 drugs and vaccines included in WHO's model list of essential drugs at favourable prices. In addition some 11 companies had offered to second experts to WHO in such specialist areas as logistics, distribution and procurement (Peretz, 1983). Lately WHO has sought closer collaboration with the industry in the field of vaccines (Beardsley, 1995).

While the World Bank may have a basic orientation towards looking at pharmaceutical policies from the industry's point of view, more recently it has sought even closer collaboration with the IFPMA. A World Bank/IFPMA fellowship meant for assisting 'the Bank and its borrowers in the development and evaluation of health sector projects containing pharmaceutical components and undertaking appropriate policy and analytical work', has been announced. According to this announcement IFPMA will choose the fellow from a field of candidates proposed by member companies, and the successful applicant's company will pay most of the two-year fellowship's costs. In addition to opposition from some World Bank employees, there have been protests by advocacy organizations for the rational drug policies, such as Health Action International (HAI) and the Medical Lobby for Appropriate Marketing (MaLAM) against this plan (HAI-Lights, 1996).

In 1989 the industry associations and regulatory authorities from the European Union, Japan and the United States initiated the International Conference on Harmonization of Technical Requirements for registration of Pharmaceuticals for Human Use (ICH), coordinated by a secretariat provided by the IFPMA. At a later stage observer status was granted to the WHO, along with the European Free Trade Area (EFTA) and Canada. The ICH agenda is set largely by the multinational industry. The aim is a global dossier and speedy access of drugs to the world market. The work of the ICH focuses on developing technical consensus, which should result in guidelines for drug approval. Although the ICH thus far has focused mainly on new molecular entities and their premarketing requirements within the industrialized countries with reasonable resources for regulatory control, it is believed that the implications of this initiative are much broader than has been recognized. Already in the US the requirements for generics have been increased in the name of harmonization (Hodgkin, 1996).

Concerns and constraints

The pharmaceutical industry is an increasingly powerful actor in drug policies, while the power of nation states to regulate their drug markets is decreasing. Many WHO programmes are seeking closer collaboration with the pharmaceutical industry. As regards pharmaceutical policies, WHO seems to have taken a more technical approach, although there have been efforts to respond to the need for tools of regulation in the new market-oriented environment. The World Bank, according to its own statements, is going to be more active in the area of the pharmaceutical policies. UNICEF continues to emphasize revolving funds for drugs and low price procurement through UNICEF. UNICEF, WHO/DAP, the World Bank and the EU have started regular meetings to discuss coordination at both global and country levels: technical and political pharmaceutical issues are discussed (Essential Drugs, 1996).

The future of rational drug policies is of serious concern. According to Prudencio and Tognoni the critical aspect of the drug problem is not procurement or selection, but purely a conceptual and political question. Apart from opposition by the industry and pharmacists, the basic controversy arises around the nature of drugs. Are they a 'fast' sector of the economy, generating riches, envy and profit, or a self-sustaining service which should be available to the whole population (Prudencio and Tognoni, 1987)? In Bolivia, for example, the centrally controlled agency for medicines (which had a rational drugs policy based on WHO's principles) was closed down in accord with the priorities of trade liberalization and the encouragement of the private sector (Prudencio and Tognoni, 1987).

In the health policy debate, the perception of drugs has shifted over the past twenty years: from seeing essential drugs as part of basic needs and as something that should be made accessible and available to all people at a feasible price, towards seeing drugs as a means of paying for health care, and even as far as seeing drugs solely as commodities. Whereas in the first half of the 1980s, solutions aimed at reducing the costs of drugs were based on policies such as the rational choice of drugs, public distribution systems, the use of bulk importers, the use of generic names and the domestic production of drugs (Patel, 1983b), in the 1990s the solutions are sought increasingly in private drug suppliers, competition and 'the untapped financial resource: patients' payment for drugs' (Cross *et al.*, 1986). Looking from the trade perspective, Cross *et al.* have mentioned that one of the most important factors in the failure of revolving funds is the resistance to thinking of the fund in business terms (Cross *et al.*, 1986). The regionalization and globalization processes also emphasize the trade aspects, and play their part in making drugs the stuff of industrial rather than health policies. According to Wolffers (1995), pharmaceuticals and access to them can have connotations that relate to political and economic change in the country in question. This can become evident especially in the former socialist countries. Restrictions on access to pharmaceuticals, on the grounds of their toxity for example, may be interpreted as 'old-fashioned' state control.

Whereas in the 1970s the debate was over the *need* for drugs, it now centres on the *demand* for drugs. In the most extreme distortion of this perspective, the importance of health professionals in selecting drugs for the funds is seen as one factor modifying the individual preferences of those buying the drugs (Cross *et al.*, 1986). A survey of the industry's perspectives for the future in the 1980s revealed that 'the most important requirements for drugs will continue to be for antibiotics, cough and cold preparations, vitamins, analgesics, hormones and tonics' (Information Research Ltd, 1980, cited in Melrose, 1983).

The advances achieved by good national drug policies in many countries – whether by way of promoting essential drugs or encouraging a strong domestic pharmaceutical industry – are today threatened by GATT/WTO, regional trade and economic compacts, and the global trend towards 'harmonization'. 'Harmonization' has some positive features in areas of drug regulation and resource sharing, but it can have extremely negative effects on national health programmes, social welfare schemes and national drug policies. The new global trend may have the effect of removing the constraints placed upon pharmaceutical transnational corporations by countries in response to their price excesses and unethical practices. There are no guarantees of sanctions in place to prevent a removal of these constraints, and many Third World countries look especially vulnerable (*Development Dialogue*, 1995).

11

Population Policies and Reproductive Health

The rise of the population issue

According to Davis, population policies are concerned in principle with all attributes of population, including age structure, geographical distribution, racial composition, genetic quality and total size. But Davis notes further that, by tacit understanding, population policies are concerned only with the growth and size of population, and the policies labelled 'population control' do not deal with mortality and migration but only with the birth input (Davis, 1967). Population policies concerning Third World countries still concentrate on trying to affect fertility levels. In this book, too, population policies are dealt with mainly as policies aimed at affecting fertility levels.

Although the origins of population control reach back to the intellectual currents and social movements of the nineteenth and early twentieth centuries, population control as a major international development strategy only dates back to the period immediately following the Second World War (Hartmann, 1995), and the interest and international activities concerning population growth in Third World countries increased most markedly during the 1950s and 1960s.

The Population Council was established by the Rockefeller Foundation in 1952, and the International Planned Parenthood Federation (IPPF) was founded in the same year (Wolfson, 1983). In the decade from 1962 to 1972 a series of resolutions on population were adopted in the governing bodies of UN agencies (Finkle and Crane, 1975). The World Bank, UNFPA, WHO and UNICEF took their first steps in the area of family planning in the 1960s. The resolutions were usually initiated and supported by Western and Asian countries, including Sweden, the United States and India (Finkle and Crane, 1975). Sweden was an early and strong advocate of population assistance: when the Swedish International Development Authority (SIDA) concluded an agreement with the government of Sri Lanka to provide assistance in family

planning in 1958, population became a priority concern of Swedish development cooperation (Wolfson, 1983). USAID established an office of population in 1964 (La Cheen, 1986), and became an important funder of population activities by the early 1970s (Hartmann, 1995). During the 1960s governments of many of the recipient countries became increasingly tolerant of efforts
to create or strengthen international population assistance (Finkle and Crane,
1975). From 1966 onwards India has implemented population control programmes, and even in the early 1950s there was an implicit population policy
in the country (Bose, 1988). We can examine the evolution of international
interest in population policies by looking at the United Nations conferences on
population.

United Nations conferences
and the evolution of population policies

The first world population conference, concentrating on information about
demography, was organized in 1954 by the International Union for Scientific
Study on Population (IUSSP) and the United Nations. At the 1965 World
Population Conference in Belgrade population was discussed as a policy issue for
the first time (Ashford, 1995). These meetings were not gatherings of official
government representatives but technical and scientific assemblies (Johnson,
1995).

The first major attempt to address the issue of population growth in an
international forum was the UN Conference on Population held in Bucharest
in 1974. The North was interested in the implementation of effective
population control policies in the South, but this was resisted violently by the
Southern countries, who shifted the debate to larger development issues
(Amalric and Banuri, 1994; Karkal, 1995; Miró, 1977; Finkle and Crane,
1975). Population targets and growth rates were a controversial issue: in the
final World Population Plan of Action, targets were mentioned only in an
oblique way, related to other assumptions about mortality and population
growth rates (Johnson, 1987). 'Development is the best contraceptive', was the
slogan of the Third World countries, and attention was drawn to the widening
gap in the distribution of wealth between the South and the North, and to the
need to accelerate socio-economic development in general and to bring about
a more equitable international economic order (Karkal, 1995; Finkle and
Crane, 1975). In the Plan of Action 'the basic human right of all couples and
individuals to decide freely and responsibly the number and spacing of their
children' is recognized (World Population Plan of Action, 1975).

The Plan of Action also stated, however, that 'the responsibility of couples
and individuals in the exercise of this right takes into account the needs of their

living and future children and their responsibilities towards the community'
(World Population Plan of Action, 1975). The discrepancy between individual
need and will, on one hand, and the needs of society and the responsibilities of
individuals towards the society on the other hand, has constituted one of the
key issues of population policy and family planning programmes throughout
the history of the programmes. The question has been to what extent
reproductive rights are recognized as the overriding principle, and to what
extent the nation's right is taking precedent over that of the individual to define
the needs of future generations and responsibilities towards the community. In
the past a greater emphasis on the nation's right has sometimes resulted in the
acceptance of coercive population policies, both anti- and pronatal.

By the time of the population conference in Mexico City in 1984, there was
more consensus among Third World countries, as well as donors and NGOs,
about the need to limit population growth. The economic situation of the
Third World countries had worsened, their dependence on Western aid had
increased, and their political bargaining power had lessened (Lee and Walt,
1995; Finkle and Crane, 1985). In Cairo in 1994 they were even more
subdued (McIntosh and Finkle, 1995). According to Lee and Walt, the degree
of influence of family planning activities has depended on both the political
ideology of policy élites in the Third World countries and on their economic
relations with Western countries. When economic problems have been
perceived as urgent by policy élites, family planning has tended to be higher on
national policy agendas (Lee and Walt, 1995).

Influenced by its internal politics and the coming presidential elections, the
United States introduced its changed position on population policies in
Mexico City: dropping the previous emphasis on the need for vigorous
government programmes to reduce the rate of population growth, it stated that
those countries with population pressures should reduce government
interference in their economies in order to promote economic growth and
thereby reduce fertility. The statement clearly indicated that the economic
reforms advocated were those consistent with a market economy. Thus while
in Bucharest it was the Third World countries that expressed the need for
economic reforms, in Mexico City it was the United States (Finkle and Crane,
1985; Johnson, 1987) – although the content of the suggested reforms was
quite different.

The third UN population conference, the International Conference on
Population and Development (ICPD), took place in Cairo in 1994. According
to the United Nations Population Fund (UNFPA, 1995d), the ICPD was the
start of a new era in population and development. UNFPA further states that
the Programme of Action explicitly places human beings, rather than human
numbers, at the centre of population and development activities, and encourages the international community to address global problems by meeting

individual needs, while maintaining the responsibilities and sovereignty of governments. The Programme emphasizes the need for gender equity and equality, and ennunciates the right to universal, comprehensive reproductive health care, including family planning (UNFPA, 1995d).

The Cairo conference was preceded by unforeseeable discussion and participation on the part of NGOs, including women's movements. The women's movement mounted a spirited ethical critique of the demographic approach to population growth and the instrumental and narrow approach to family planning. In its place women advocated a broad range of voluntary family planning services integrated into a programme of reproductive and sexual health care. In addition, women activists from the Third World criticized the development models that had been applied by the colonial powers and postcolonial development organizations, especially the World Bank and the IMF. At the pre-conference meeting, the women's demands were accommodated by including two new chapters and some language revisions (McIntosh and Crane, 1995). On the threshold of the ICPD, Vandana Shiva from India wrote: 'The most important challenge in Cairo is whether it will be able to transcend the 'demographic fundamentalism' of the US and the 'religious fundamentalism' of the Vatican and put Third World women at the centre of the population discourse'. (Shiva, 1994b).

Before having a closer look at the achievements of the Cairo conference, and major issues of interest and concern, we consider the policies of major international actors in the field of population/reproductive health. The policies of UNFPA have been dealt with in Chapter 6.

Policies

WHO

In 1952 WHO decided not to undertake population programmes. The Catholic nations had strong objections to having WHO undertake any research or technical assistance in the areas of population control and family planning. In the 1960s, however, there were increasing demands, especially from the USA, to address population questions. The decision of 1952 not to undertake population control programmes was cautiously reversed in 1966 when WHO agreed to give technical advice on the development of family planning activities, but only on request, and only as an integral part of health services, without impairing the normal functions of preventive and curative services. Until 1970 WHO made only minor resource allocations to family planning. With the World Bank entering the field in close cooperation with UNFPA, however, WHO responded by upgrading its activity in the field (Finkle and Crane, 1976).

In 1966 the Division of Family Health was created, and in 1969 family planning became an integral part of the maternal and child health programme. WHO's Special Programme of Research, Development and Research Training in Human Reproduction (HRP) was founded in 1972 (Vaughan *et al.,* 1995) (see also Box 11.1). The Safe Motherhood Initiative was launched in 1987. It has, however, been noted that thus far WHO has played a minor role in that initiative (Stenson and Sterky, 1993). The Global Programme on AIDS (GPA), under WHO's administration, was transferred to the Joint United Nations Programme on AIDS (UNAIDS) from January 1996 (Box 11.2). Recently the units most relevant to family and reproductive health – those concerning the health of children, adolescents, and women, nutrition, technical support and research on reproductive health technologies – have been gathered under a common division, the Division of Family and Reproductive Health, in an attempt to improve the coordination and cooperation of these linked areas of work.

Box 11.1 Special Programme of Research, Development and Research Training in Human Reproduction (HRP)

HRP was founded in 1972, initially as part of the WHO's Family Health Division (Vaughan *et al.,* 1995). According to Finkle and McIntosh (1994), funding provided for WHO's Expanded Programme in Human Reproduction was a way of getting WHO more involved in family planning. In 1988 HRP became a programme sponsored by UNDP, UNFPA, WHO, the World Bank and other bodies, UNFPA being the major funder. In 1991 the largest funders were the United Kingdom, UNFPA, Sweden, Norway, the World Bank and Denmark (Khanna *et al.,* 1992).

To begin with the WHA was the principal governing body. With the exception of the need for research on infertility, however, the concerns expressed by the WHA were not followed by deliberate programme efforts. In the early years the most critical post as far as external influence was concerned was that of chairman of the Advisory Group, for many years held by Swedish scientists. In 1988 the Policy Coordinating Committee was established, but it seems to have had little influence on actual priority setting (Vaughan *et al.,* 1995).

The HRP agenda is said to be unresponsive to other internal actors within WHO, and to be influenced largely by programme staff, with support from colleagues in the international scientific community represented in the Scientific Advisory Group (STAG). It has been further observed that little attention has been given to collaborative priority setting between the different HRP units. For

Box 11.1 cont.

example the major programme on research collaboration with China was established without any formal decision in the programme advisory bodies (Vaughan *et al.,* 1995). Stenson and Sterky (1994) have observed that although no direct link between the origin and destination of the grants is to be seen, many of the major donors to HRP also receive large grants. They question the cost-effectiveness of transferring large sums of money through WHO and back to the country of origin.

The HRP programme areas are research and development, resource building for research, statistics and data processing, and programme management, along with administrative activities. Half of the budget goes to research and development, which in turn consists of technology development and assessment, research on technology introduction and transfer, epidemiological research on reproductive health, and social science research on reproductive health. The social science research has accounted for only about 6 per cent of the budget. Vaughan *et al.* (1995) have noted that the balance between research on technologies for fertility regulation and broader reproductive health concerns, as well as between bio-medical and social science research, is a matter of ongoing debate in the programme.

The main task of HRP has been the development of new contraceptives. For example, HRP has made efforts in the development of anti-fertility vaccines, heavily criticized by a number of women's groups (Stemerding, 1994). The role of HRP may sometimes be controversial: on one hand, it is one of the developers of new contraceptives, and on the other hand, an evaluator of new technologies. It is possible that HRP's involvement in innovation may hamper its role as an impartial evaluator.

Over the past 20 years, WHO has collaborated with 130 countries on MCH/family planning projects, funded mainly by UNFPA to the tune of over US$300 million (Kessler, 1994). The emphasis on reproductive health at the Cairo conference is in line with WHO's priorities. WHO has its mandate in the area of health, and therefore its emphasis is on integrating family planning with primary health care. The WHO involvement in reproductive health includes at least three main functions. It is a normative and technical body involved in efforts to develop tools for the amelioration of reproductive health and to implement these through health services. It is a coordinator of contraceptive development. Being a health organization, it also addresses larger issues on women's and girls' health that influence reproductive health.

Box 11.2 HIV

WHO was the first UN organization to take up AIDS as a critical issue in 1986. WHO's Special Programme on AIDS, which soon became the Global Programme on AIDS (GPA), expanded quickly, stimulating programmes in over 100 countries in the first 18 months of its existence. In 1988 WHO and UNDP entered an Alliance to Combat HIV/AIDS. The GPA emphasized a medical and epidemiological approach, and considerable attention was paid to AIDS in male populations in the industrialized countries, whereas the UNDP highlighted more the socioeconomic consequences of the epidemic (Bailey, 1994).

The choice of HIV as a priority of the donor agencies, development banks, and technical agencies of the UN system, which together finance a substantial proportion – up to a half of the total budget – of the public expenditure on health in many African countries, has resulted in a large number of policies, projects, programmes and institutions dealing with the issue (Lancet, 1995e). Furthermore, in India, for example, the AIDS control budget comprises about one fifth of the public health budget (Prakash, 1994). Because the total support to the health sector in Third World countries has remained constant, the support must have been withdrawn from other parts of health care (Lancet, 1995e). Lack of coordination between the HIV programmes of different donors has left many countries with parallel vertical interventions, often isolated from national development strategies (Bailey, 1994).

Notably 95 per cent of the annual global AIDS budget has been spent within high-income countries (Lancet, 1994b). AIDS research in Africa centred on efforts to understand why the African experience was different from the Western one (Packard and Epstein, 1991; Mann and Chin, 1988). While much attention was paid to research, other areas, for example health education, were less well covered. Other forms of sexually transmitted diseases have been neglected (Laga, 1995). Measures being taken to control the spread of HIV infection in Africa have been mainly concerned with increasing the safety of blood transfusion and the promotion of condom use through health education (Sanders and Sambo, 1991). Packard and Epstein (1991) further claim that the research was handicapped by limited Western knowledge about the disease and the African culture. According to Sanders and Sambo (1991), failure to identify and address the social and economic factors underlying the spread of HIV infection in Africa has led to an overwhelming concentration on sexual behaviour. There is also a lack of studies on how the African epidemic will affect the supply of, demand for, and quality of health care (Lancet, 1995e). Very little attention has been paid on the linkages between the HIV epidemic and globalization, including the linkage of globalization with the increased movement of people (migration, migrant labour, displacement, tourism,

---

Box 11.2 cont.

occupying military forces), weakening systems of social support, greater social inequity and human insecurity, and reductions in the public services, including those of health care (Lee and Zwi, 1996).

In 1994 a decision was taken to transfer the GPA to a joint UN programme on AIDS, sponsored by WHO, UNDP, UNICEF, UNFPA, UNESCO and the World Bank (Bailey, 1994), while retaining some HIV-related issues under WHO. UNAIDS became effective at the beginning of 1996. It aims to emphasize the broad social, economic and development issues related to the HIV epidemic.

UNICEF

UNICEF's main activities in the field of reproductive health, and especially in family planning, include: (1) policy discussions during country programming, (2) information, education and communication activities, and (3) activities connected with maternal and child health.

UNICEF's family planning policy dates back to the mid-1960s. The emphasis was on 'responsible parenthood' and the inextricable link between safe motherhood and spacing through strengthening maternal and child health services (Jolly, 1993). In 1967 it was agreed in the UNICEF/WHO Joint Committee on Health Policy that UNICEF assistance would be given for the development of maternal and child health services, but that this assistance would exclude the provision of contraceptives (Lee, 1994).

Along with its efforts in the area of women's empowerment and the improvement of health care services, UNICEF emphasizes advocacy, information, education, communication (IEC) and community-based programmes in its family planning efforts. As far as IEC activities on responsible sexual behaviour are concerned, UNICEF has broadened its coverage from mothers to include men and adolescents. When appropriate, UNICEF may assist in providing family planning services, usually as an integral part of MCH services. UNICEF does not provide contraceptive supplies from its own resources. UNICEF does not provide support for abortion services, nor will it in the future support abortion as a method of family planning (Jolly, 1993; UNICEF, 1993b, 1995d). More recently UNICEF has paid increasing attention to the reproductive health of adolescence and women.

UNICEF's late and cautious involvement in family planning has been associated with opposition from Catholic and Soviet-bloc countries (Lee,

1994). Even today, family planning continues to be an issue which raises controversy among donors and other interested parties. For example, the Vatican recently withdrew its core support from UNICEF in protest against UN participation in birth control projects, although it continued to support individual UNICEF programmes with the same symbolic amount of money as before (Vatican withdraws, 1993). In the 1990s UNICEF has also been attacked for keeping children alive in communities with a rapid population growth, and for not doing enough to address the issue (King, 1991; King and Elliot, 1993). Thus UNICEF has landed in a difficult position, with pressures from both sides of the family divide.

In recent years UNICEF has spent more than US$70 million a year on work related to family planning. Of this amount, 4 per cent has been spent on reproduction, the family and family planning, 72 per cent on morbidity and mortality, and 19 per cent on counselling and guidance, training, and dissemination or communication (personal communication with UNICEF's Health Promotion Unit, 1995). Although the earlier level of collaboration has been described as virtually nonexistent (Mendehlson *et al.*, 1993), according to Jolly (1991a) (Deputy Executive Director of UNICEF in 1991), UNICEF is collaborating increasingly with UNFPA (Jolly, 1991a). UNICEF has also been an active partner in processes relating to the Cairo conference (UNICEF, 1995d). In a report entitled *The State of the World's Children 1992*, UNICEF stated that 'family planning could bring more benefits to more people at lower cost than any other single "technology" now available to the human race' (Grant, 1992). Increasing attention to population growth can also be surmised from UNICEF's analyses concerning the PPE (poverty-population-environment) spiral, where the three elements are seen to form a vicious circle drawing in the attendant evils of disease, hopelessness, loss of self-respect, breakdown of families, alcohol and drug abuse, increasing violence and the abandonment of women and children (Grant, 1994).

The World Bank

'The World Bank is concerned above all with economic development, and the rapid population growth is one of the greatest barriers to the economic growth and social well-being of our member-states.' On the basis of this rationale, World Bank President MacNamara announced the new involvement of the Bank in this field in 1968. Concern over the ultimate size of the world's population and the ability of the earth to support it were other World Bank concerns (Nassim and Sai, 1990).

In 1969 the Population Projects Department was established. From 1975 onwards, health components were introduced into the population projects, and in 1979 the Population, Health and Nutrition Department was established. When the era of structural adjustment policies began, Population and Human Resource Divisions were created in Country Departments (Nassim and Sai, 1990). The Bank's involvement in the population field has grown rapidly. In monetary terms, the Bank's contribution was as large as that of UNFPA and about half that of USAID in 1986 (Nassim and Sai, 1990). Preliminary estimates show that in the fiscal year ending 30 June 1995 the World Bank approved more than US$450 million in lending commitments to finance population and reproductive health activities (World Bank, 1995c).

The influence of the World Bank in the population field may be even greater than one would expect on the basis of its share of lending. The World Bank includes population issues in policy discussions with countries needing loans (Conable, 1988; Nassim and Sai, 1990; Sai and Chester, 1990; World Bank, 1986, 1994d) and can make effective population programmes conditions for such loans (Sai and Chester, 1990). Furthermore, the Bank has an influence on the direction of socio-economic development in its debtor countries, including social development affecting the level of fertility. A population perspective has also been incorporated into work in other sectors, such as agriculture, labour and poverty (World Bank, 1994d).

The Bank seeks ways to alter the demand for children. Methods include improving the health of children, improving female education, increasing job opportunities for women, and promoting women's property rights (World Bank, 1994d). Incentive schemes, where families with few children are given extra benefits, have been seen by the bank as a means of transferring to parents more of what society gains if they limit the size of their family (World Bank, 1986). Further shifting to parents of the cost of raising children (for example, the introduction of fees for post-primary education and for curative health services) is seen as one of the ways to persuade people to have fewer children. The Bank also seeks to expand family planning services by means of private channels, social marketing and, when the commercial sector fails, the public sector. According to the World Bank (1994d), the nonspecific content of mass media messages, particularly those that expose audiences to new values and the concept of choice, can play an important role. When the private sector is expected to play a more prominent role, government involvement may still be required to provide financial support or to remove legal and regulatory obstacles, including medical regulations that in the Bank's view unnecessarily increase the amount of time and money that individuals have to expend (World Bank, 1986; World Bank, 1994d). While the Bank seeks to increase free trade through measures which include the removal of barriers to contraceptive marketing, it is worth noting that even the World Bank supports the WHO baby milk formula code, as it recognizes that 'unnecessary changes in breastfeeding practices jeopardize the health of infants and undermine any rise in contraceptive prevalence' (Tinker and Koblinsky, 1993).

USAID, other government donors, and nongovernmental organizations

USAID established an office of population in 1964, and began funding direct family planning activities in 1967 (La Cheen, 1986). Ever since the initiation of population assistance, the United States has been the major source of funds. The US government has pushed harder than any other Western government for Third World countries to adopt population policies. It has further been the pillar of multilateral efforts through the UN system, including the World Bank, and a number of private organizations such as the International Planned Parenthood Federation (IPPF) (Finkle and Crane, 1985). Between 1989 and 1991 the USA provided yearly an average of US$293 million, or 44 per cent of the total population aid; direct bilateral aid accounted for 55 per cent of the aid and 45 per cent was given through NGOs (World Bank, 1994d). The allocation for 1994 was US$ 500 million. Guaranteeing universal access to reproductive health services is an issue of US national security (McCarthy, 1994). Direct operational support for family planning services, together with service-related activities such as training, information dissemination and contraceptive supplies, have accounted for over three quarters of overall USAID assistance for population. USAID has emphasized the role of the private sector and social marketing. USAID's approach has been criticized for inadequate attention to cultural and behavioural factors influencing demand, and heavy-handedness in pushing contraception and insufficient emphasis on the quality of care (Conly *et al.,* 1991).

Between 1989 and 1991 the most important government donors after the United States were Japan, Germany, Norway, Sweden, the United Kingdom and the Netherlands (World Bank, 1994d). Excluding the US funding, 60 per cent of donor contributions were channelled through the UN in 1990 (Conly and Speidel, 1993).

The average total annual government aid between 1989 and 1991 was US$670 million, and about equal proportions of the total aid were given as bilateral aid, multilateral aid and aid through nongovernmental agencies. The major proportion of the multilateral population assistance from governments is channelled through UNFPA (World Bank, 1994d): in 1994 this amounted to US$265 million (UNFPA, 1994). The other multilateral agencies include WHO and UNICEF (World Bank, 1994d). In addition to its assistance to governments, the average World Bank lending for population assistance between 1989 and 1991 was US$215 million (World Bank, 1994d). Preliminary estimates show that in the fiscal year ending 30 June 1995 the World Bank approved more than US$450 million in lending commitments to finance population and reproductive health activities (World Bank, 1995c).

According to Conly and Speidel (1993), the Nordic countries (especially Sweden), the Netherlands, France and Switzerland have in general favoured a broad approach that integrates family planning with other activities, such as health and women's development programmes. The United States is more focused on family planning, and has also taken the lead in providing contraceptive supplies and introducing social marketing. The United Kingdom, Canada and Australia have also been said to be moving towards a strategy that emphasizes family planning. This difference in views has led the Nordic donors, along with the Netherlands, to urge the World Bank and UNFPA to integrate family planning efforts into a broader framework of maternal and child health services, and to suggest that the IPPF should soften its traditional focus on contraceptive services – while the United States, along with some other donors, has criticized these institutions for lacking focus and contributing too little to family planning (Conly and Speidel, 1993). The European Union is also becoming an important actor in international development assistance. Between 1991 and 1993 the EU committed an average of US$21 million annually in population assistance; in 1994 this figure rose steeply to US$38 million (Conly and Rosen, 1996).

The other main channel for international population assistance consists of private organizations, which receive funds both from governments and from private foundations in the industrialized countries. The largest private foundations giving funding for population assistance over the three-year period 1989–91 were the Rockefeller foundation, the MacArthur foundation, the Population Council, the Hewlett Foundation, the Ford Foundation and the Mellon Foundation, all based in the United States (World Bank, 1994d).

The major international NGOs receiving funds for population assistance are the IPPF, the Population Council, the Association of Voluntary Surgical Sterilization, the Program for Appropriate Technology in Health (PATH) and Pathfinder International (World Bank, 1994d). As regards service provision and related assistance, local NGOs in developing countries have been quite limited in their activities. In some countries, Family Planning Associations affiliated to the IPPF have been major providers of family planning and related services. A number of women's organizations have been active in training local health and family planning workers (Cassen and Bates, 1994). In other countries, such as India and Bangladesh, women's health advocates have played an important role in bringing attention to coercive practices included in population control policies.

Concerns and constraints

Population and sustainable development

The ICPD was the first in the series of population conferences that explicitly linked population and development. The way this linkage was made, however, has raised concern among researchers and activists in the fields of women and development issues. Although in academic circles the debate on the relationships between population and development is far from over, the ICPD document is based on the belief that population growth is a problem at all levels of aggregation: local, national, and international (Amalric and Banuri, 1994), and it regards early stabilization of the world population as a key goal in achieving sustainable development (UNFPA, 1995d). In the words of Nafis Sadik, the Executive Director of UNFPA, population may be the key issue that will shape the future as regards economic growth, environmental security, and the health and well-being of countries, communities and families. She further states that there can be no long-term environmental security, development or peace, North or South, without slower population growth (Sadik, 1992).

The ICPD's Programme of Action has come under fire for neglecting the right to development, the access to resources and to an unpolluted environment; and the urgency of alleviating poverty, international debt and unequal trade relationships (Simons, 1995). Grimes has claimed that the draft document was completely neo-Malthusian in its outlook (Grimes, 1994); according to Karkal, poor women are again blamed for global consumption, for which they are not responsible (Karkal, 1995). Others have noted that while in Bucharest development was seen as the best contraceptive, in Cairo contraceptives were seen as the best development.

International population policies have often been based on the belief that rapid population growth will lead to major global problems. Earlier in the course of population programmes the perceived threats were expressed quite bluntly. The United States National Security Memorandum on international population policy, issued in 1974, feared adverse socio-economic conditions generated by population factors could contribute to increasing levels of child abandonment, juvenile delinquency, unemployment, petty thievery, organized brigandry, food riots, separatist movements, communal massacres, revolutionary actions and counter-revolutionary reprisals. The Memorandum pointed out that such conditions would also detract from the environment needed to attract foreign capital. It also feared that rapid population growth could endanger the world's mineral supplies, which increasingly come from the developing countries. This could happen if population growth frustrated the prospects of Third World country citizens for economic development and social progress, undermining the conditions for expanded output and sustained flows of mineral resources. The political consequences of current population factors in the least developed countries were seen as damaging to the internal stability and international relations of countries in whose advancement the United States was interested, thus creating political or even national security problems for the superpower (United States International

Population Policy, 1982). The national security interest guiding US population policies has been reemphasized recently (McCarthy, 1994), but otherwise such perceptions of the effects of population growth in the South no longer surface in official documents. Many of above perceptions are still cited in less official connections, however (see, for example, Johnson, 1995; King and Elliot, 1993), and may affect the manner in which we think about children and their parents in Third World countries and the types of intervention we hold to be justified.

According to McNicoll, after the effects of population growth as identified by the proponents of population control had been downplayed by the Reagan and Bush administrations, these pundits felt a need for political help and turned to the environmental movement. They gave greater attention to the environmental and poverty effects of population growth and its implications for the welfare of women and children; in a more speculative vein, political consequences were explored, reflecting topical concerns with ethnic conflict and state failure (McNicoll, 1995).

While few would deny that it would be beneficial for the ecosystem to have slower population growth, blaming population growth for the phenomena caused mainly by inequality and poverty not only simplifies the questions, but can also mislead the search for the solutions. Hartmann has stated that blaming poverty and environmental degradation on population growth obscures the real causes of the current global crisis: the control of resources – economic, political, and environmental – by ever more tightly linked international élites (Hartmann, 1993). Even when the unsustainable patterns of consumption in the industrialized world are recognized alongside population growth in the Third World in discussions about the ecological future of the globe, the actions required tend to concentrate on reducing population growth.

The unmet need

In the early era of family planning programmes it was believed that making family planning services available would rapidly bring population growth down. Another assumption was that high fertility was supported by cultural values and attitudes and that this would be overcome with information concerning modern contraceptives and offering family planning services (Ahlberg, 1989). The role of family planning programmes in slowing the pace of population growth was supported by Knowledge-Attitudes-Practices (KAP) studies, which became abundant early in the era of population concern. Since then the extent to which people in Third World countries feel an unmet need for family planning services has been a topic of heated debate. Warwick has claimed that the early KAP studies were closer to advocacy for population projects and their funding than to research. The Population Council – while simultaneously funding and doing research on contraceptive development and acceptability, and also implementing programmes – took a leading role in encouraging these studies, often conducted as an initial step in the process of planning a population programme for the country in question (Harkavy, 1969; Warwick, 1994). While the data from more recent contraceptive prevalence studies, such as the World Fertility and Demographic and Health Surveys is better in quality, the validity and reliability of such data remain open to question (see for example Bongaarts, 1991; Ahlberg, 1989).

Lee *et al.* state that in their study of eight countries they found a surprising lack of evidence that popular demand had an important influence on the initiation of family planning policies and programmes. Nor did they find any evidence of a perceived 'surplus' of children. The study concluded that the policy élites had played a key role in initiating and sustaining family planning policies. The investigators also found that in some countries family planning remained high on the agenda because of the demands of donors (Lee *et al.*, 1994).

The proportion of married women, not pregnant, fecund, at risk of pregnancy, and not wanting to conceive in the near future, but not using a modern contraceptive is quite small: around a few per cent or less (Pritchett, 1994; Westoff, 1988; Bongaarts, 1991). The conclusions made from these analyses have varied: in 1988 Westoff concluded that the basic supply problem has been met, and Pritchett (1994) that family planning efforts are generally not a dominant, or typically even a major, factor in determining fertility differences. Bongaarts has suggested that the proportion of fertility produced by this small fraction is significant, and further that the demand in time is augmented by those not in need of contraception at the time of the survey. Bongaarts estimated that the level at which the prevalence rates of contraceptives would plateau in the future, if fertility preferences were completely met, would mean an additional 17 per cent of contraceptive users amongst married women in the 15 developing countries studied. While by 1992 Westoff had come to agree in principle with Bongaarts that the fertility produced by this small fraction with unmet need could be significant, he also pointed out that about half of those in the unmet need group reported that they did not intend to use a contraceptive method. According to the Bongaarts estimate, there would be about 87 million married women (or their husbands) with an unmet need for contraception. Estimating the proportion of unmarried individuals with an unmet need for contraception, Bongaarts reaches a total of about 100 million couples or unmarried individuals. Although this investigation did not look at the reasons for the unmet need, they are said to be likely to include a variety of factors such as limited access to and poor quality of family planning services, dissatisfaction with and/or lack of knowledge of available methods, weak motivation to implement reproductive preferences, and opposition from the husband (Bongaarts, 1991).

Ahlberg (1989) has pointed out that, even when women are motivated to limit family size and postpone the next birth, there are many factors prohibiting contraceptive use, such as economic costs, limited and irregular supplies, programme management, perceived health risks, religious beliefs and social structures. According to this author, family planning programmes have largely failed to conceptualize reproduction in its complex social and cultural dimensions and patterns (Ahlberg, 1989). According to Warwick, until recently there was little research on the impact of economic development on client interest in the practice of family planning, the politics of implementing family planning programmes, the strategies and tactics of international donor agencies, and the link between culture and client interest in family planning. In the 1990s, population research covers a broader range of topics, but donor funding is still slanted towards studies with benefits for population limitation (Warwick, 1994).

Human rights, incentives and coercion

Several ways of affecting the demand for children and of using incentives and disincentives – or even coercion – were suggested in order to reduce population growth successfully, despite inadequate knowledge of the complex social and cultural dimensions and pattern of reproduction, and by inadequate programme implementation and technologies, (see for example Davis, 1967; Berelson, 1969; Green, 1977).

Serious violations of human rights have been reported as a consequence of coercive policies (Hartmann, 1987; Warwick, 1982). For example, there is some evidence to suggest that in Bangladesh sterilization was still being made a condition for the granting of food aid in some areas in the 1980s, and even that military forces were used to fetch women for sterilization (Hartmann, 1987). China's one-child policy has also included forced abortions during late gestation and forced sterilizations (Aird, 1990). Recently China introduced a law to reduce the number of 'inferior' births by means of compulsory premarital and prenatal testing, including attempts to detect those with mental illnesses and infections such as Hepatitis B. It was also stated that births of 'inferior' quality are a serious problem among 'the old revolutionary base, ethnic minorities, the frontier and economically poor areas' (Dickson 1994; Nature, 1994; Lancet, 1995f). Western authorities have been reluctant to take positions against the violations inherent in such policies, pleading cultural relativism in defining human rights (Nature, 1994).

Many programmes were target-oriented, with a minimal choice of methods, and numerous experiments were undertaken with incentives and disincentives (Finkle and McIntosh, 1994; McIntosh and Finkle, 1994). The pressure to achieve targets in India has distorted the family planning pro-gramme: generally, the client's needs have been neglected by family planning workers (Townsend and Khan, 1993), and incentives given to the client have even led to the sterilizing of the same people twice, and to sterilizing both spouses (Banerji, 1985).

The Cairo document does not approve of the use of incentives, dis-incentives or other forms of coercion. Amalric and Banuri have claimed, however, that there is an apparent contradiction between the two main principles of the draft document – to stabilize world population and to respect people's rights. They question what guarantees there are that people's rights will not eventually be sacrificed to the goal of population control (Almaric and Banuri, 1994). Starting from the view that rapid population growth leads to increased poverty and deprivation in Third World countries, Hernandez concluded in his article on the ethics of fertility reduction policies in Third World countries that these policies appear justified. According to this author, Third World countries may prefer socioeconomic development and positive incentive policies, but may feel compelled to employ negative incentives and sociopolitical pressures and coercion in their desire to achieve major fertility reductions (Hernandez, 1985). The pressures from the medical profession to take a more demographic view of family planning services have been increasingly strong during the 1990s (see, for example, King, 1990; *Lancet*, 1993b; Smith, 1993; Smith and Leaning, 1993). King and Elliot have argued in the journal *Lancet* that ecological constraints take no account of our ethics or of 'human rights'. Their conclusion is that the option of a two-child world is already gone, that it has to be a one-child world, and they are waiting for academia and the UN agencies to recognize this (King and Elliot, 1994). They have also raised the possibility of introducing Chinese-style incentives and penalties in severely trapped communities (King and Elliot, 1995).

The Programme of Action of the ICPD recognizes 'the basic right of all couples and individuals to decide freely and responsibly the number, spacing and timing of their children and to have the information, education and means to do so, and the right to attain the highest standard of sexual and reproductive health'. The reliance of the Cairo document on individuals rather than society to reduce population growth has also drawn criticism from members of the population establishment (Johnson, 1995; McIntosh and Finkle, 1995). These critics maintain that it is inadequate to rely on a policy focused on the individual in those areas of the world where there is little demand for contra-ception, where economic development is stagnant or declining, and where religion and culture tend towards pronatalism (McIntosh and Finkle, 1995). The relative emphasis given in the future to reproductive rights, on one hand, and to the reproductive responsibilities of Southern people towards their society and towards the globe, on the other hand, remains to be seen.

The incentive and disincentive schemes have been supported by many organizations providing population assistance, including the World Bank, UNFPA and USAID (World Bank, 1986; World Bank, 1990; Hartmann, 1987, see also Chapter 6). More recently, incentive and disincentive schemes have been increasingly shifting towards indirect measures, including an emphasis on changes in factors influencing the cost of and demand for children (World Bank, 1994d).

Potential demand

Suggestions for affecting the desirability of children in the Third World were made early in the course of international population policies (see, for example, Davis, 1967; Zeidenstein, 1977). The World Bank (1994) recently emphasized efforts to reduce the desire for a large number of children and there are indications that population policies are increasingly part of broader social policies. There is also some wishful thinking about directing the bulk of development aid towards measures conducive to lower family size (see, for example, Jain, 1995). While such thinking is relevant in so far as it is about promoting better socioeconomic conditions and decreasing inequality between geographical areas, genders, and racial, ethnic and socioeconomic groups, there is also a danger of starting to see socioeconomic development in poor countries predominantly as subordinate to population policies.

Several approaches to creating demand for family planning have been used in the course of population policies and programmes. First, the aim has been to commit national governments to undertaking effective population measures. In this connection, policy discussions, along with the conditionality of aid or a World Bank loan on effective population policy, has been a powerful tool (Nassim and Sai, 1990; Sai and Chester, 1990).

A second approach is to make the service delivery system and the public aware of the problem so that they will act accordingly. In addition to different incentive and disincentive schemes, attempts have been made to get people to need smaller families. Along with socio-economic and other measures, such as a higher level of women's education and more work opportunities outside their homes, there has been a stress on modernization and Westernization. Often, however, modernization and the importation of Western values and practices have eroded practices traditionally controlling sexuality, and hence fertility – resulting sometimes in higher fertility than before (Ahlberg, 1991; Mamdani *et al.,* 1993). In some cases the greater workload of women, the need for further children and the breakdown of extended-family structures have resulted in increased fertility (Mamdani *et al.,* 1993). Ahlberg (1989) has maintained that high fertility is a result of the breakdown of cultural systems which previously regulated and controlled fertility rather than a phenomenon deriving from existing cultural values and attitudes. Amalric and Banuri (1994) have pointed out that the breakdown of collective management of resources following the integration of local communities within a larger political and economic realm accounts in a large measure for environmental degradation and the persistence of high fertility rates in the rural areas of Southern countries.

Social marketing of contraceptives

The term 'social marketing' refers to the use of mass media to market medical products and ideas (for criticism of the approach, see also Chapter 4). Social marketing is an approach favoured by the World Bank, USAID and UNICEF. The practical effects of emphasizing social marketing and free advertising of contraceptives can be many. Especially in countries where practically only sterilization or other semi-permanent methods (IUDs) have been available, social marketing of condoms and oral contraceptives may increase the accessibility of contraceptives.

Social marketing of any easily administrable prescription drug is like selling it over the counter, as mechanisms for monitoring are often inadequate. Furthermore, USAID has expressed concern about the medical barriers introduced by listing clinical procedures and exclusion criteria for hormonal contraception, and by combining reproductive health issues with those of contraception (Shelton and Calla, 1991). Similarly, according to the World Bank there are in general too many restrictions limiting the scope of contraceptive delivery (World Bank, 1994d), and a World Bank discussion paper calls for removing limitations on private sector advertising of contraceptives (Tinker and Koblinsly, 1993). At the same time, the quality of the information on contraceptives can be below an acceptable level. For example, in a study on a Brazilian slum area it was found that a substantial proportion of pill users had contraindications against hormonal contraception (Giffin, 1994). It has been argued that the demand for contraception will be so high that increased user fees or prices on contraceptives will have a minimal effect on prevalence of use – although the effects of contraceptive price changes on prevalence can be sizable. In Indonesia a significant reduction in the prevalence of contraceptive use in poor households was found when prices were raised (Jensen et al.,, 1994). In Bangladesh an increase in the price of condoms was followed by a dramatic decrease in sales, but the effect of an increased price on oral contraceptive sales was less dramatic (Ciszewski and Harvey, 1994).

The status of women and their empowerment

For decades the women's movement has striven for the empowerment of women as a goal in itself. The early initiatives for reproductive rights consisted primarily of campaigns for birth control. In much of Latin America, for instance, the inability to obtain safe and effective contraception and the denial of abortion rights drew women into political action. In many Asian countries, on the other hand, women have been politicized by their experiences of coercive policies that gave them no right to refuse contraception or sterilization. Campaigns for reproductive rights have since become increasingly located within a broader framework that also includes the right to sexual autonomy, to safe motherhood, and to a healthy environment for child rearing (Doyal, 1996). Recent publications have stressed social needs that erode reproductive and sexual choice for the majority of the world's women, who are poor (Correa and Petchesky, 1994). Some writers point out that while the ICPD document pays attention to women's empowerment, the larger socio-economic and cultural issues are not addressed. According to Basu, 'the poor, illiterate, unskilled men may exploit their women at home, but they can be described as advantaged in very relative terms'. The empowerment, reproductive health and autonomy of poor men need also to be addressed (Basu, 1996).

Apparently in response to the effective lobbying of the women's movement (McIntosh and Finkle, 1995), the concept of reproductive rights is recognized in the Plan of Action of the Cairo Conference, as we have seen. Feminist demands, such as women's empowerment or women's control over their bodies, were accepted by all parties at the conference – the fundamentalists of all religions, the right-to-life organizations and the population control agencies (Yuval-Davis, 1995). According to Petchesky (1995), because it embeds the language and conceptual framework of reproductive rights and gender equality – and to some extent sexual rights – in population and development discourse, the ICPD document is a major historical achievement. Others have felt more uneasy, however, because they have felt that the meaning of those feminist demands had changed critically (Yuval-Davis, 1995; Simons, 1995). Petchesky answers that the meaning of that language will depend on the future commitment of the women's movement (Petchesky, 1995).

Organizations working in the population policy field generally recognize that enhancing the status of women and their decision-making power has an important role in reducing fertility (see, for example, World Bank, 1994d). But critics have claimed that gender equality has become the social tool by which the UN seeks to ensure that its goal of population control is achieved (*Lancet*, 1995g); they also point out that in the latest UNFPA report on the state of the world's population, based largely on the results of the Cairo conference, health is defined in a one-dimensional manner: as existing only within the reproductive context. 'When seen through the lens of fertility control, the notion of "health" is distorted beyond all recognition.' (*Lancet*, 1995g).

While empowerment from above for an *a priori* goal contradicts the very concept of empowerment, there is a role that can be played from above: that of enhancing women's rights through legislation, regulations and access to credit. Bottom-up activities aimed at empowerment cannot be driven from above, however: when the goals are set from above, empowerment is limited to fulfilling these goals. An Indian Women's Development Project is reported to have turned away from the initial objective of empowering women and become a vehicle for inundating the villages with information and programmes that served market interests in encouraging the use of 'hazardous contraceptives' (State's Role, 1994).

The importance of the involvement of men in fertility regulation activities has been recognized. The integration of family planning into maternal and child health services, along with the fact that most methods of fertility control are for the use of women, has resulted in men's exclusion from family planning efforts, and sometimes made men unnecessarily suspicious of family planning. At the same time, in situations where there are considerable efforts to reduce fertility, where the methods offered are those for the woman's use, and where women have less power to make decisions than men, the emphasis on involving men in responsibility for family planning may in practice result in using men to persuade women to use a method, in spite of the woman's dissatisfaction (see, for example, Amatya et al., 1994).

Women's health and reproductive health

According to an analysis conducted by WHO and the World Bank, 30 per cent of women's and 12 per cent of men's overall burden of disease and disability is related to reproductive ill-health (WHO, 1995e). While such figures are bound to be rough estimates, it is nevertheless clear that a large proportion of the health problems of women, men and children are problems other than those relating to reproductive health.

While socioeconomic differences in health should not be forgotten, women and girls in many countries have special needs for health care in sectors of health other than that of reproductive health, largely because of the consequences of their inferior status. These special needs have received little attention (WHO, 1992; Vlassoff, 1994; Okojie, 1994; Key, 1987). There are indications that girls with older sisters (Muhuri and Preston, 1991), unmarried women and infecund women are especially vulnerable.

In China, India and South Korea, the traditionally weak position of women has led to inverse female/male ratios (Xu et al., 1994; Ren, 1995; Freed and Freed, 1989; Han, 1994). While inverse female/male ratios have not been found the majority of other developing countries, according to Hill and Upchurch (1995) a pervasive pattern of female disadvantage emerges, when adjusted for the 'standard historical level of female advantage' (the historically observed lower female mortality levels, assumed to be at least partly of genetic origin). The mechanisms of the inverse ratio are many: the nutritional status of women is less favourable than that of men; women reach health care less often than men, regardless of the need; they are disadvantaged as far as education and property ownership are concerned; female infants and foetuses are subject to straight killing and abandonment, and girls to worse nutrition and care (WHO, 1992; Xu *et al.,* 1994; Freed and Freed, 1989; Craft, 1995). Strong pressures to reduce fertility have exacerbated the situation. In China the adoption of the 'one-child' policy appears to have had adverse effects on female survival (Ren, 1995). Modern technologies enabling the identification of female foetuses and their subsequent abortion – ultrasound, amniocentesis and chorionic villus sampling – are commonly available in India, where the government has estimated that several thousand female foetuses are aborted annually (Nandan, 1993; Chhabra and Nuna, 1993). There are also indications of the same trend in China (Yi *et al.,* 1993), and in South Korea (Han, 1994). It is curious that research focused on practical methods of sex determination was one of the many actions that were recommended for solving the population problem in the 1960s (Berelson, 1967).

The concept of reproductive health was developed during the process that led to Cairo. According to the Cairo document, reproductive health implies that people are able to have a satisfying sex life and that they have the capability to reproduce and the freedom to decide if, when and how often to do so. Implicit in this last condition is the right of men and women to be informed about and have access to safe, effective, affordable and acceptable methods of family planning of their choice, as well as other methods of their choice for the regulation of fertility which are not against the law, and the right of access to appropriate health-care services that will enable women to go safely through pregnancy and childbirth and provide couples with the best chance of having a healthy infant.

According to WHO, reproductive health must address, as its basic elements, sexual behaviour, family planning, maternal care and safe motherhood, abortion, reproductive tract infections including sexually transmitted diseases and HIV/AIDS, and certain reproductive tract malignancies such as cervical cancer (Safe Motherhood, 1994). Reproductive health must be a component of all primary health care services, and must incorporate all aspects of reproductive health throughout the individual life span (WHO, 1994f). One of the special aspects of reproductive health that in recent years has gained increasing attention, has been the genital mutilation of females, and large campaigns have been launched to abolish such practices.

According to recent estimates by WHO and UNICEF, about 585,000 women died from pregnancy-related causes in 1990. Maternal mortality ratios are particularly high in sub-Saharan Africa. In the area of the WHO's regional office for Africa the ratio was estimated to be 940 maternal deaths/100,000 live births (WHO and UNICEF, 1996). The health of the mother used to be neglected in the maternal and child health services, but in recent years, in addition to the overwhelming emphasis on birth control, attention in the area of reproductive health has been paid to reducing maternal mortality. Maternal morbidity (Graham and Campbell, 1992), sexually transmitted diseases (Laga, 1995) and especially infertility have received less attention.

Box 11.3 Research on New Contraceptives

Hartmann has argued that research on contraceptives has focused over-whelmingly on the female reproductive system, and on systemic and surgical methods, and more on efficacy issues than on safety concerns (Hartmann, 1987). Until recently little emphasis has been given on male, barrier and user-controlled methods.

Because of the liability issues raised mainly by the IUD known as the Dalkon Shield in the USA at the beginning of 1970s, the drug industry, especially in the USA, lost interest in contraceptive development. The development was largely transferred to nonprofit institutions. According to Mastroianni et al., nonprofit organizations supplement the role of government agencies while avoiding many of the political and other constraints government faces. The US public sector remains the major source of funding for contraceptive development. Important nonprofit organizations involved in contraceptive research include the Popula-tion Council, Program for Appropriate Technology in Health (PATH), Family Health International (FHI), universities and university-based programmes such as Contraceptive Research and Development Program (CONRAD), and international organizations such as WHO and the World Bank (Mastroianni et al., 1990)

Many of the contraceptives recently developed or under development, including Norplant and antifertility vaccines, have attracted heavy criticism from women's health advocates (Richter, 1993, Mintzes et al., 1993). There have been claims that research in the area of contraceptive development has had a demographic orientation. It should also be borne in mind, however, that because of the long time span of contraceptive development, today's contraceptives reflect largely the ideologies of twenty or thirty years ago.

As a result of the work done by women's health advocates and growing awareness of the HIV pandemic, research on methods capable of preventing sexually transmitted diseases has been given more attention of late. According to Hagenfeldt (1994), research priorities for the 2000s could involve methods that can be controlled by women, can be used by adolescents, can be used by breast-feeding women, will protect against sexually transmitted diseases, and are easily reversible.

Today 57 per cent of married women of child-bearing age are using contraception (Grant, 1994). Although there has been a significant increase in the prevalence of contraceptive use, there is still a need to improve accessibility of family planning services in many areas, including those of the former Eastern Europe (Pierotti and Blayo, 1994). In recent years, increasing attention has been paid to the reproductive health care needs of adolescents. Beyond the achievement of expanding coverage, however, lies the challenge of improving the quality of services (Kessler, 1994). While a perfect contraceptive still remains to be found, Hartmann (1987) has pointed out that enhancing the suitability of contraceptives may often be linked more with the quality of family planning services and the power relationships between the client and the provider than with the features of the method itself (see also Box 11.3. for Research on New Contraceptives).

The pandemic of the HIV infection has attracted much attention, but as far as prevention and treatment are concerned, there has been little success (see also Box 11.2). Recently there has been evidence that proper treatment of conventional sexually transmitted diseases (STDs) will prevent HIV infections (Grosskurth et al., 1995), and STD case management has increasingly been included in the HIV prevention strategies (Laga, 1995). The demographic impact of AIDS is most immediate and serious in sub-Saharan Africa and in parts of the Caribbean, where falling life expectancy and increasing infant and child mortality have been observed. Given the high proportion of the population already infected and the high mortality resulting from the disease, a demographic impact over the next two decades is inevitable in these areas (Armstrong and Bos, 1992).

Abortion has been a subject of heated debates (see also Box 11.4 on Abortion). In the Mexico Conference the USA took a firm stand against abortion, and stated that it would not extend population assistance to or through any international or nongovernmental organization that supported abortion or coercive family planning programmes. Following the Mexico Conference the USA withdrew its funding from the IPPF, and in the following year also from UNFPA (Finkle and Crane, 1985; see also Chapter 6). Following heated debates on abortion, the Cairo document states that it should not be promoted as a method of family planning and urges that the health impacts of unsafe abortion should be dealt with as a major public health problem. The need for abortion should be reduced by expanded and improved family planning, but the right to abortion is left to be determined at the national or local level according to the national legislative process. Hempel (1996) has noted that while consensus was reached in the ICPD on difficult topics such as access to safe abortion, services and education for adolescents, and sexuality, it was achieved less through a change of perspective than through finding language that will allow different interpretations.

Box 11.4 Abortion

Estimates of abortions performed annually in the world are bound to be, at their best, informed guesses. Henshaw has estimated that there are 40–50 million abortions per year, of which 30–50 per cent are illegal (Henshaw, 1990). In 1993, 41 per cent of the world's population lived in countries with legislation allowing abortion on request, 22 per cent in countries where termination of pregnancy was possible on broad social and socio-medical grounds, and 37 per cent in countries with restrictive laws ranging from strict to very strict, including some countries where abortion was prohibited without exception (Unsafe abortion, 1993). Experience in Romania showed the dramatic rise in maternal mortality which can occur when abortion is made illegal (Stephenson, 1992). Even when abortion is legal, the question of accessibility often remains serious (Henshaw, 1990). In India, where abortion is allowed on broad social and socio-medical bases, it has been estimated that illegal abortions are 10–11 times more common than legal ones. In 1990 almost 12 per cent of maternal mortality in India was due to abortion (Chhabra and Nuna, 1993). The abortion pill will not necessarily provide a safe alternative to unsafe abortions, not even if safe surgical abortion procedures are developed as a back-up. If an abortion induced by means of the abortion pill is incomplete and complications occur, which according to Le Grand could occur in 4–5 per cent of cases, surgical interventions will be necessary. Furthermore, there is a danger that the abortion pill could leak into unregulated markets in Third World countries, in which case its safe use is questionable (Le Grand, 1992).

The integration of reproductive health services

The debate on how to organize family planning services – within the health care infrastructure, or outside it – has been going on since the mid-1960s (Allman *et al.,* 1987). After the population and development conference in Cairo, the debate has extended to the organization of reproductive health services. While a consensus has emerged that reproductive health services, including the former MCH/FP and STD/HIV services, should be integrated in the PHC system, the content, priorities and practical means of doing it are still to be discussed and developed (Mayhew, 1996). It has been noted that the financial commitments mentioned in the ICPD document to providing services other than family planning do not even come close to matching the resources for family planning (Centre for Reproductive Law and Policy, 1994).

WHO has favoured linking family planning with MCH as a means of organizing family planning services (Kessler, 1994), and the population organizations traditionally have been in favour of separate structures (Finkle and Crane, 1976). In the early phase of the efforts to limit fertility, it was recognized that the health care system was limited in extent and inaccessible to millions of couples. A separate vertical approach was favoured in these circumstances. Furthermore, from the point of view of the proponents of population limitation, leaving the implementation of population programmes in the hands of health professionals would lead to downgrading of the demographic objectives, to weak management, and to insufficient attention to motivating people to limit their fertility (Finkle and Crane, 1976). A debate has been going on as to whether the integration with health service components will improve the effectiveness of family planning services (Allmann *et al.*, 1987, DeGraff *et al.*, 1986). The population organizations have feared that the integration of existing separate programmes (Allman *et al.*, 1987), or the inclusion of new elements in the existing family planning programmes (Finger, 1994), might hold back the family planning effort. Evidence on the issue has been insufficient, although some efforts have been made to study the effects of the implementation of components of health care on contraceptive prevalence rates (see for example Phillips *et al.*, 1984; DeGraff *et al.*, 1986).

Since population programmes were integrated in the existing public health care systems, the growing emphasis on family planning and the overwhelming support of the development agencies in this field have, according to WHO, prompted the MCH divisions in Third World countries to undertake family planning as an additional aspect. In practice the emphasis on family planning in some countries outgrew MCH, so that in some countries the MCH work suffered (Ko Ko, 1990). In India, for example, the budget for family planning programmes was greater than that for the health services during the seventh five-year plan (1985–90) (World Bank, 1992c). While the integration of family planning services with health care can be seen as generally desirable, in India the integration efforts have led to a neglect of primary health care (Banerji, 1985; Banerji, 1992). Banerji believes, however, that the most important reason for the worsening of maternal and child health care has been the use of coercion in the sterilization programme, which has led to loss of faith in the health care workers. Hartmann has claimed that in countries where governments are not committed to taking care of the basic needs of their people, there is a tendency for integration to lead to an emphasis on population control at the expense of health care (Hartmann, 1987). One can ask, however, to what extent individual governments have been independent in their decision making, and how much the decisions concerning population programmes have been linked with negotiations with their major donors of development assistance.

The organizations outside the state sector provide a major component of total health care in many developing countries (Green, 1987). The role of

NGOs in population policies has been important in some countries, as they have been used as channels for family planning efforts when action through the government has been impossible, reluctant or ineffective. The voluntary and for-profit agencies in developing countries have been favoured especially by USAID as implementers of family planning programmes, as part of the Reagan administration's identification of the private sector as the proper locus of social and economic growth. In the family planning field, this focus has fostered the multiplication of voluntary and for-profit agencies in developing countries (McIntosh and Finkle, 1994). In addition to private family planning services, privatization has been encouraged through cost-recovery and cost-sharing systems, and through the provision of contraceptives by means of social marketing schemes. It is noteworthy, however, that the promotion of non-governmental sources in the provision of integrated reproductive health services may bring new problems, or at least exacerbate some existing ones. The private sources are more interested in the curative elements of these services, while the 'public good' aspects, such as immunizations, may not be of interest to them. It is clear that private provision is not monolithic. In many countries, it includes a sizeable non-profit sector that is more likely to provide 'public good' services (Berman and Rose, 1996). However, in areas in which a substantial proportion of health services are provided by NGOs linked to religions that oppose contraceptive use and abortion, provision of comprehensive reproductive health services may be constrained. The for-profit sector, on the other hand, is more interested in taking over services likely to bring good profits. A well-known example of the danger of reliance on private, for-profit organizations in the provision of reproductive health is the favouring of caesarean sections over normal delivery. New medical possibilities resulting from scientific innovation are more likely to include a profit prospect than long-term and low-profile services. In the absence of adequate ethical guidelines and regulation, the increasing availability of techniques such as foetal sex determination tests, used to identify female foetuses for their subsequent abortion, may also exacerbate ethical dilemmas and create future problems such as unbalanced demographic structure.

Petchesky has noted that while on the level of rhetoric the ICPD document does acknowledge the dire impact of 'public sector retrenchment' and structural adjustment programmes on the social sector in many countries, the document also aims at promoting 'increased involvement of the private sector' in producing and marketing contraceptives and providing reproductive health services, as well as the 'selective use of user fees' and 'social marketing' techniques. Petchesky thus concludes that with regard to global economic and political structures, implementation mechanisms, development models, and the enabling conditions necessary to realize reproductive and sexual rights, the Cairo Programme is no achievement at all (Petchesky, 1995).

12

Conclusions

International organizations in the making

Traditionally international organizations have been understood in the light of power play between nation states and their interests, as the institutional means by which powerful military and economic states have tried to achieve their ends (Lee, 1995). In this book we have had a different perspective, focusing on international actors and their basis and value framework for action as such, thus seeing them as more than extensions or battlegrounds for national self-interests.

Different policy emphases separate the various international organizations; but they are not homogeneous entities within themselves. Different divisions within one organization may have their differences; sometimes even their contradictions. In the case of the World Bank, for example, divergent perspectives on the Bangladeshian drug policy between the Bank's Industry and Energy Unit and its Population and Health Unit were evident (see Box 10.1). In addition, international experts form a transient species moving from one organization to another; it is possible that what might be seen as an organizational position may to a large extent reflect personal views and expertise. Nevertheless, organizations have history; they exist within a global political and economic context, where they are influenced by diverse power relations; and they have mandates, policies, aims and practices that connect but also distinguish them.

Mandates and roles in international health policies

The mandates and activities of United Nations organizations have attracted increasing attention during recent years, with attempts to identify the relative strengths and advantages of each organization and to enhance the effective and appropriate functioning of the whole UN system. At present there is some

206

duplication of activities, and at times contradictory policies and interventions. While several attempts to reform the UN system have been initiated, for example by the Nordic countries, the United States and the United Nations Association, they have concentrated on the technical efficiency of the United Nations system (Lee, 1995). Fundamental conflicts in values, beliefs and interests have not been addressed.

In the United Nations system the agencies differ from each other not only in terms of their areas of action, but also in their focus. While agencies such as WHO and the ILO have a global mandate, the United Nations funds have their focus on developing countries. Even though UNICEF has extended its sphere of action to a more global level on issues such as the rights of children, the UNICEF mandate is to give assistance, particularly to the Third World countries, in the development of permanent child health and welfare services. WHO has the global mandate on health policies. According to its constitution, WHO should 'act as directing and coordinating authority on international health'.

WHO's mandate is normative, whereas the mandates of UNICEF and UNDP, for example, emphasize development cooperation. While the contact level for WHO is Ministries of Health, in the donor countries UNICEF and UNDP usually deal with national Development Agencies. The World Bank deals primarily with Ministries of Finance and national Development Agencies in the donor countries. The problem inherent in these relations is the lack of common policies in health between the donor country Development Agencies, which allocate funds to multilateral cooperation, and the Ministries of Health, which decide upon international health policies. Thus it has been possible, within the donor countries, to divert resources from policies and programmes in line with global policies on health towards agency activities not necessarily compatible with building a sustainable and well-functioning health system. While there has been criticism amongst the donor countries over the activities of the international organizations, there has been rather less analysis of the distorting impact of donor countries on the practices and policies of these organizations. The problems of donor 'distortion' may be seen as reflecting different national interests, but often also derive from the different national alliances favoured by Ministries of Health and Foreign Affairs, with their respective views on the actors and contents of global health policies.

From the latter half of the 1970s until the latter half of the 1980s WHO executed its health mandate in the larger political context, especially as regards advocacy and promotion. In the late 1980s WHO began to move towards a narrower approach, with more emphasis on the technical and biomedical aspects of health, and less emphasis on health policies or health in the larger policy context. In spite of the past lessons from disease eradication efforts and the proven necessity of a sufficient institutional basis for carrying out sustainable activities in vertical programmes, pressures continue to engage in more focused disease-oriented activities. In the late 1980s and 1990s the role of WHO in international health policy formulation has been decreasing while the role of the international financial institutions and health industries has expanded. At the International Conference on Harmonization (described in more detail in Chapter 10), for example, WHO had to resign itself to observer status, regardless of its constitutional mandate.

WHO's tendency to interpret itself only as an international organization of Ministries of Health, rather than as *the* global health organization, has limited its scope unnecessarily. When major international agreements such as GATT/ WTO are negotiated, WHO should be in the forefront making proper analyses in advance of the anticipated health effects of such treaties, instead of restricting its role to assisting the Health Ministries in their efforts to cope with the effects afterwards. The WHO mandate on health is broad and demands a broad analytical capacity and knowledge basis. This has been lacking in the broader fields of action beyond clinical or experimental medicine, and it is clear that, without further strengthening of its capacity in these fields, WHO will be unable to fulfil its mandate effectively.

To a large extent health is determined by policies and action in areas outside the health sector. At the global level health is defined within the framework of complex global economic policies, and international organizations such as the WTO, the IMF, the World Bank and the OECD have a major role in defining this framework. The liberalization of trade and expected subsequent increase in global competition has been reflected in policies aimed at 'right-sizing' the public sector and in public sector reforms. The World Bank has entered the fields of health and social welfare more extensively, and in the 1980s and 1990s it has often done so within the framework of social and health sector reforms. The World Bank agenda has been focused on financing and has been linked with public sector reforms which emphasize market mechanisms and competition, privatization and regressive health system financing mechanisms such as user charges. As WHO wavers, failing to assert the leadership role in international health policy formulation and coordination envisaged by its constitution, other influential parties contemplate the possibility of handing this mandate to the World Bank (Berkley, 1996). The World Bank has no mandate in health policy formulation, however, and the focus of its activities deny it any truly global perspective on health policies. Any claims for the World Bank's comparative advantages on issues concerning health should be seen in the light of the actual mandate, decision-making strategy, power relations, focus of action, and constitutional limitations as an international forum in health policies.

The most crucial question with respect to the World Bank's financing of health is not the quantity of lending for health, but its role in agenda setting through lending practices, debt servicing, policy prescriptions and joint financing of health projects. While there have been calls for an increase in World Bank lending on social issues and health, its lending policies on health should be based on policy prescriptions in line with the agreed global policies formulated in the World Health Assembly. In addition, there is a need to assess the social and health impacts of the World Bank Group (IBRD, IDA, IFC, MIGA) activities as a whole with respect to determinants of health and in terms of implications for health system development. This is important in order to ensure that the other policies and practices of the organization do not act against the maintenance and/or development of the social capital and institutional basis necessary for public health and the provision of health care services that are universally accessible and affordable.

In the 1970s UNICEF was advocating a multisectoral approach in health, but since the 1980s policies have emphasized selective approaches to primary health care. Furthermore, it has emphasized cost containment in the services, in the form of developing revolving fund systems for primary health care. The health policy practised by UNICEF has moved closer to that of the World Bank. UNICEF, as a United Nations development fund, places more emphasis on project implementation. In comparison with WHO, UNICEF has been much more efficient in building alliances for childrens' rights and in providing a broader ground for advocacy support on specific issues such as landmines and child labour, especially within the developed countries. As a fund, dependent on voluntary contributions, however, it is also more vulnerable to donor shopping, and has to be clear and attractive in presenting its goals, targets and achievements.

The UNDP has a broad mandate, and the number of staff dealing specifically with health is limited. It therefore needs to cooperate with other organizations – but UNDP's interagency role has changed from that of its original mandate. According to the Nordic UN Project, the role of the UNDP as the central funding and coordinating agency has been substantially reduced and marginalized in the field of development cooperation. The mandate of UNFPA relates to population and family planning activities in the developing countries. In 1994 the International Conference on Population and Development linked population and development more intrinsically, moving from demographically orientated population policies towards policies placing human beings in the centre of development; and from family planning service provision approaches towards reproductive health services. In the post-Cairo era, there may be some confusion concerning, on one hand, the respective mandates of UNFPA and UNDP on development and, on the other hand, the roles of UNFPA and WHO in reproductive health. Differences remain in the interpretations developed by these organizations. UNFPA and WHO put different emphases on the various aspects of reproductive health. Similarly, while

UNDP sees development in a broader and more complex framework, UNFPA sees a slower population growth as an important prerequisite for development.

In recent years there have been calls for UNDP coordination of multilateral development policies, including those of the Bretton Woods organizations. At the same time more resources have been directed through IDA than through the UNDP, rather undermining the UNDP's possible role as grand coordinator. The major question of importance in terms of mandates and practice is the role of the Bretton Woods institutions. The World Bank has clearly extended its sphere of action in normative functions and donor coordination on areas and activities – a role more suited to the mandates of other international organizations more able to provide global forums for dealing with the issues. The relative shifting of mandates from United Nations agencies towards the Bretton Woods institutions has been the aim of some developed countries (Beigbeder, 1997). On the other hand, the World Bank's move towards the social sector and the reaffirmation of its poverty focus may also be seen as the result of pressures from NGOs and some donor countries, such as the Nordic countries, the Netherlands and Canada, with support from the United Kingdom and France (Culpeper, 1997).

The concept of 'civil society' has had a secure place in the rhetoric of the 1980s and 1990s. In practice, civil society has been interpreted too often as NGOs, without further attention to the nature of these organizations. The category of NGOs is diverse, however, telling more about what they are not than about what they are. They range from transnational industries and large charity organizations to grassroots organizations and public interest groups. At the international level the largest NGOs are of the same magnitude as some aid agencies and United Nations organizations. Clearly they need to be assessed in terms of their policy aims, accountability and relation to civil society in order to ensure that mechanisms intended to empower civil society are not diverted for the promotion of commercial, professional, private or career interests. Lobbying tends to enhance those with more resources, and intervention is needed to include the voices of those with less resources, with special reference to social movements and networks in developing countries.

Accountability and forums of decision making in international health

The emphases of accountability and transparency towards the communities and countries for which the policies, programmes or projects are provided, and towards the mandates and democratic decision-making structures of the organization, may be diverted by donor-driven policies in development aid. Accountability and transparency may instead become a requirement of the donors, stressing the monetary and managerial aspects rather than those that have more to do with value bases, choice of policies, and processes of decision making. Emphasis on the managerial and monetary aspects of accountability and transparency tends to lead to a further move in the direction of vertical approaches and the setting of easily quantifiable outcome measures and targets, where achievements can be seen in the short term, rather than aiming at improved comprehensive health policies with multiple effects that may not be measured easily nor achieved within the timespan of a project cycle. In a world with increasing inequalities and increasingly hard economic conditions for the poorest, it is important to consider whose perspectives these organizations adopt, and to ensure that the voices of the poor, forming the great majority of the world's population, are not lost in a process dominated by the voices of those making major monetary contributions.

The United Nations specialized agencies are accountable mainly to their member states. Decision making in the United Nations system generally follows a 'one state, one vote' principle. In the case of WHO, the organization is accountable primarily to its member states, as represented by the Health Ministries in the WHA. The UN funds – UNICEF, UNFPA, UNDP – are in principle accountable primarily to the member states of the UN system, as represented in rotation on their executive boards. Because the whole budget of a fund is comprised of voluntary contributions, however, their accountability to the funders cannot be neglected in practice. This is the case also with respect to the extrabudgetary funds in WHO. The accountability of the World Bank is primarily to the major financiers on the Board of Governors. The relevance of the views prevailing in the capital markets may not be disregarded, as the World Bank functions as a borrowing agency. The governments are usually to be considered as accountable for the outcome of World Bank projects and loans. This is also the case with respect to regional development banks.

It is important to draw attention to the nature of loans and grants in development financing, as well as to the broader impacts of programme aid, donor coordination, and the amount of recipient country resources tied in by the conditions imposed. In the poorest countries even a single large infra-structure project may crowd out other government efforts. In support aimed at providing changes – health care reforms, for example – the catalytic role of the external support may be seen as efficient from the point of view of that organization. The recipient countries, on the other hand, may have embarked on policies or initiated changes according to prescriptions which they may not be able to carry out, or which may be inappropriate or distorting in the long term. The nature of international bidding for contracts and consultancies easily creates a distorted policy environment where in-depth understanding of the feasibility and further impact of the policies, programmes or projects is compromised by perceived 'efficiency'. In addition, the use of local resources and the improvement of local capacities for addressing local questions may be compromised. When the international consultants have long since departed, the recipient country is left – in addition to the sometimes ill-defined policy prescriptions and their consequences – with the payment of the loan taken to buy this advice and the implementation of the changes suggested.

Traditionally, governments have been assigned the responsibility of seeing that people are provided with possibilities to attain health. In the process of the 'right-sizing' of public sectors, there is a danger that governments in practice are given a way out of this responsibility. While the WHO Health for All strategy clearly assigns this responsibility to governments, the World Bank agenda is much less clear, with its emphasis on a government role in public health but private funding for 'personal health services'. In the provision of health services the 'opting out' of the rich is seen as a means of securing the publicly funded health services for the poor, often with little attention to the long-term consequences of this strategy. The NGOs are no doubt an important group of actors with various accountabilities, but more often than not they have little to do with civil society, and too often represent charities or professional and commercial organizations involved in health with a lesser emphasis on empowerment and rights. The increasing role of nongovern-mental actors in the health sector should also be seen in the light of the retrenchment of the state and the use of NGOs as efficient global charity and poverty services.

There is also a clear global trend towards the corporatization of health-care, mainly in the form of private insurance companies and managed-care chains, supplemented by 'voluntary health care' with an increasing role for informal care and NGOs in the provision of health services for the poor. While the World Bank has recognized the necessity of a government role, one of its basic functions is to promote private foreign investment and it has paved the way for the public/private mix in health care within countries. The development of the WTO agreements in trade in services also has relevance to the future of public sector contracting of services. The recent moves of the pharmaceutical industry towards owning health care services further complicates the issues of account-ability protection of the interests of patients.

Clearly, some international organizations may enhance the role of health care markets yet neglect regulatory and legislative needs, impacts on health systems development and, ultimately, impacts on household spending and long-term health security. Meanwhile, the retrenching state has created space for the legitimacy of many nongovernmental actors: NGOs, private voluntary organizations and religious institutions. If there are more markets for private actors in health care, there are also markets for organizations and institutions involved in charity. In terms of the Health for All strategy and access to health care as a social right, these trends are disturbing.

Experiences and challenges in international cooperation in health

The problems of 'donor shopping' between multilateral agencies may be seen in the moulding of the activities of these agencies. Specialized United Nations agencies give higher priority to activities which have been able to attract external funding, while other areas, including the original normative and information functions, have suffered a relative decline. Moreover, the expansion of technical cooperation has been subsidized partly by regular budget resources (Nordic, 1991). WHO has been no exception in this respect. The stringency of funds in its regulatory budget has directed the organization towards greater emphasis on its operational role through the increasing relative importance of extrabudgetary funds. While WHO may not be seen as a development agency, in practice its current role and the nature of its funding render it vulnerable to changes in development policies and funding priorities. The technical and normative roles of WHO have sometimes been divided too rigidly, and there is a clear need to understand the normative activities in broader terms. The WHO role in technical cooperation is part of its commitment to equity and should be seen as providing the building blocks for sustainable health systems development in countries with the greatest need.

Current attempts to improve coordination of United Nations agencies at country level are welcome – but better coordination of multilateral and bilateral actors should not mean sidetracking of their national counterparts in recipient countries, and should not lead to the overriding of national policies. The role of the UNDP has been emphasized at international meetings, such as the Social Summit. The World Bank has been active in donor coordination efforts and its coordination arrangements can be seen as a means to ensure that donors adhere to the particular policy framework advocated by the Bank. While both the WHO and the UNDP have formal mandates to coordinate, this role has been increasingly challenged (mainly covertly) by the World Bank and UNICEF at country level (Buse and Walt, 1996). There is thus a need to improve national capacities for guiding and setting the agenda of national policies, and to ensure that the external actors involved will support – and not confuse or distort – these policies. In this the United Nations specialized agencies and the UNDP could have a more supportive role.

The sprawling bureaucracy of the United Nations system has been widely criticized, but in terms of funding and number of personnel, the criticism may not be justified (Childers and Urquhart, 1994). At present the United Nations system outside the Bretton Woods agencies suffers from a vicious circle: lack of resources makes the work more difficult and less effective, and this lack of effectiveness in turn becomes a reason for withholding resources or shifting them to other systems (Jolly and Singer, 1995). While obviously there are problems and a need for change, it is also evident that some of the criticism of the agencies acts in a counteractive way and is leading to a marginalization of the United Nations. There is also a major difference when the United Nations agencies are compared with other international actors such as multinational corporations. For example, the marketing and sales personnel of a medium-large multinational pharmaceutical company such as Pfizer exceeds the total personnel of WHO (*Financial Times*, 1997). Salary levels in the United Nations agencies are lower than in the World Bank, and new grades of lower-cost employees have been introduced, such as national professional officers. If the UN specialized agencies are to have more capacity in research, analysis, assessment and evaluation on a longer-term basis, they need the human resources to implement these tasks. A part of this work may be contracted, but it is clear that there is a need for a proper in-house knowledge base and understanding in order to avoid fragmentation and administrative hollowness. The professional basis of the different international organizations may also need further assessment. Of more importance than professional expertise as such – 'professionalism without purpose' – could be its linkage with the experience and understanding of broad public health issues and commitment to the aims and value basis of the organizations.

It is important to delink the organizational reforms from streamlining. Studies have urged the renewal of staffing management and rewarding practices in UN organizations, including better use of termination for unsatisfactory performance (Beigbeder, 1997). Some staffing practices within the specialized agencies and Bretton Woods institutions have led to top-heavy administration and distortion in the formal mechanisms of governance. It is clear that a perfect organization, whether public or private, cannot be found: issues and problems need to be dealt with on a continuous basis. It should also be born in mind, however, that a process of continuous reform, reorganization and streamlining may divert too many human resources from achieving the actual aims of the organization.

Global policies on health, equity and social justice

International health policies may be seen in the light of cooperation between the international actors. It may be prudent to ask, however, whether this is a time for actual global health policies and for a global forum on health. The process of globalization, here understood mainly as liberalization of trade, emergence of information technologies, increased travelling and global environmental change, will have direct and indirect implications for social well-being and health. Globalization or globalism, however, may also apply to specific policy choices and prescriptions for health sector reforms implemented in different parts of the world.

It is clear that the process of globalization does provide complex new dilemmas with respect to health. Global environmental issues and climate change have placed new issues on the policy agenda with specific implications for health. Travel and technology are also managed on a global scale and the protection and promotion of health necessitates a global agenda and surveillance systems. International trade agreements may have very important implications for health, which may not be given sufficient attention in the present context of decision making. The implementation of healthy public policies at the national level may be hampered by trade consideration; health, safety or quality considerations may become covert means for trade policies. For example, the Uruguay Round Intellectual Property Rights (TRIPs) regime has wide implications for drug policies and for possible public sector regulation, as well as for the domestic and multinational pharmaceutical industries. Furthermore, global policies lend significance to policy actors working at a global level. In practice this means improved possibilities for transnational corporations and their interests, which are not necessarily in line with health considerations, as has been shown in terms of policies on tobacco or breast-milk substitutes. It is clear that the global policy level is of increasing importance for normative health activities, advocacy, and analysis of the health implications of globalization.

Globalization is a process where all people are global; but some people are more global than others. The normative rule-setting issues at a global level gain importance as the globalization process tends to limit the role of national governments, leaving less room to manoeuvre in designing pro-employment policies, pensions, unemployment insurance and compensation for unpaid work, such as caring for the sick and the elderly (UNDP, 1996). Thus it is necessary to consider human development impacts of the globalization process and global liberalization of trade. There is also a need to assess to what extent the globalization agenda is driven by beliefs and ideologies (see, for example, Krugman, 1996). International competition tends to be seen as one of the factors necessitating the 'right-sizing' of the public sector, with clear consequences for health systems development.

Addressing of human, social and environmental impacts of the process means strengthening the role and relevance of international forums such as the United Nations specialized agencies, and supporting their research capacities and normative functions on human development issues. Instead, current policy making seems to be giving ground to the growing role of institutions more involved in promoting productivity and economic growth, such as the WTO, the World Bank and the OECD. This means a change not only in the policy forum, but also in some of the basic values and aims of policy making. There is a clear difference, for example, when pharmaceutical policies are viewed from the perspective of trade interests rather than from the perspective of health.

Equity and social justice are not merely nice words far away from the real world of self-interest; they are building blocks for health and sustainable health systems. It has been shown, not only on the global level but also within the developed countries, that inequality is bad for health (Wilkinson, 1996). In the 1990s the large differences between people and population groups within countries can not be ignored. Experience in the United States has shown that, even with high health care costs, inequities in health and access to health care may remain substantial. It is clear that with respect to equity and social justice the two major initiatives on health, WHO's Health for All strategy and the health reforms of the World Bank, differ in their emphasis. While HFA is based on equity, health reforms are seen as consequences of efficiency gains in the World Bank's perspective. A pressing question is whether many of the World Bank policies promoted in the name of health reforms are in fact compatible with the aims of the Health for All strategy.

International organizations and actors in the health policy field have their histories, mandates, policies and aims. Their work and scope of action are based on their constitutional mandates, and different organizations have different emphases in their values, knowledge bases, decision-making structures and strategies. In the light of recent shifts in policy making, with many actors on the scene and global challenges ahead, it may be the time to consider how and in which forum we want to deal with international policies.

The context of international policies

Over the last decade there have been many positive developments in international health. The average lifespan has increased, the global infant mortality rate has decreased, and the target of 80 per cent vaccination coverage has been reached. However, there are widening gaps between the rich and the poor, between one population group and another, between age groups, and between the sexes (WHO, 1995a).

While the current international policies are characterized predominantly by globalization, the promotion of free trade and an emphasis on economic growth, during the last decades the gap has widened between the rich and the poor, both between developed and developing countries as well as within many countries (UNDP, 1992). There has been a disproportionate flow of resources from the developing to the developed world – poor countries paying money to rich countries – because of debt servicing and repayment and as a consequence of prices for raw materials that favour the latter at the expense of the former. Structural adjustment policies aimed at improving economic performance have often made the situation worse (WHO, 1995a). While environmental questions, social action, women and democratization have been among the issues highlighted in international development policies, the priorities in the policies may not have been conducive to fostering these aims in the long run. The incompatibilities between the expressed and practised priorities in global policies seldom receive adequate attention. As even national governments have become vulnerable to international policies and are often at the mercy of the terms of trade, people-centred development is in danger of becoming increasingly difficult in the integrated global economy. While the terms for the multinational actors have become easier, it is the citizens worldwide who will have to adjust.

The division into blocs of industrialized and Third World countries is changing, and the differences between population groups within countries are tending to become pronounced in the industrialized countries as well. Economic growth is not automatically associated with increasing employment, and social inequalities are increasing in many countries. With the increasing emphasis on competition, economic growth and productivity, those without consuming power are in danger of becoming 'surplus' people in the eyes of those within the spheres of economic productivity. The situation of the unemployed or those struggling in the various spheres of the informal sector easily becomes worse, and this may lead to the partition of populations into people of value and those who are less valuable.

At the global level regional structures such as NAFTA and the European Union have gained ground in international policies, while the increasing emphasis on globalization as the creation of a single common marketplace has become the new framework for integration. This new framework not only poses a threat to the integrity of nations but also seeks to displace the United Nations and proposes a major and historic revision of the whole model of a political organization of human affairs (Kothari, 1995). Integration has had its repercussions on the functioning and role of the international institutions. The role of Bretton Woods institutions (World Bank, IMF, GATT/WTO) has been increasing, and meanwhile the restructuring process of the United Nations in the 1990s has de-emphasized its role in economic analysis and policies, and put greater emphasis on operational activities (Adams, 1994). The Social Summit in 1995 tried to increase the coordination and cooperation between the international actors, including the World Bank and the IMF.

The global environmental issues, including climate change, ozone layer depletion and loss of biodiversity, have gained ground in international policies. The effects of pollution and environmental degradation on health have been emphasized. The global environmental concerns have also placed more emphasis on population growth, often perceived as a major source of existing environmental problems at both local and global levels. In this context it is often the poorest whose increased fertility is of most concern. The increasing emphasis on population growth as a cause and explanation of diverse problems, ranging from ethnic conflicts to poverty and climate change, not only undermines the importance of the other factors and processes involved, but also creates an environment fostering coercive practices in the name of our global future. Respect for human dignity and human rights is a prerequisite for socially and ecologically sustainable development in the future.

In the 1990s information spreads fast, and more people now receive more information about many of the problems around the world. The role of the media in awakening global concern and creating ground for action is substantial. Widespread publicity is given to such things as catastrophes, hunger, threats caused by new viruses and the spread of epidemics. While human suffering receives much attention in the media, the structures, politics and history of such events may not be covered, and this often results in undue emphasis on the short-term alleviation of suffering and on simplistic technical solutions. The re-emerging infectious diseases have received substantial attention. Though many of these diseases have been known for centuries, their re-emergence has often been connected with overcrowding and population growth, and little emphasis has been placed on social and economical structures, or on the neglect of public health policies.

Health policies

Health and its improvement are often taken as self-evident aims for policy making. The values and framework by which and in which health policies operate are often not expressed or even perceived. A major step forward has been acknowledging the role of health as a means to achieve general development, but the trade-off involved may be undermining health as a social right and aim in itself. Economic arguments tend to dominate the current discussion on health. This may be helpful in diminishing the waste of resources. At the same time, however, inherent values and political choices get hidden behind the argumentation, which is often believed to be value-free and sometimes perceived as the only possible way forward. It is also believed to be the only choice without a hidden agenda.

Currently health is often defined as a commodity, a definition which emphasizes the consumer aspects. While this may highlight issues concerning quality, communication and relations between the client and the providers of health services, those without consuming power will be left aside more easily or face increasing means testing in order to receive treatment. In this context, access to health care as a social right may be undermined.

The political implications of increasing nongovernment resources in order to provide additional resources for health care are important. Decisions concerning the share of responsibility governments take in providing resources to the health and social sectors are essentially political and value based. Furthermore, decisions on how the costs of health care will be divided are political. The difference in the redistributive effect is substantial according to whether the costs of health services are to be covered through taxation, through the user charges paid by the sick, or through private insurance, universal social insurance or other types of collective cost sharing. In the debate over health care costs, the emphasis has been on prioritizing diseases and shifting the costs to private sources, while less attention has been focused on the assessment of the relevance and justification of health care technologies and of the public health interventions implemented. While it is clear that prioritizing in the area of health care is being undertaken and will be undertaken in future in most countries, the values inherent in the process, and the moral and political implications of the different choices, should be brought up and discussed openly.

The new technologies in health not only need assessment in terms of cost, relevance and justification, but are also open to a wholly new set of ethical and political concerns. As what is technically possible no longer determines the action, other issues need to be assessed. The implications of the new genetic technologies for health care and policies may be considered as having little relevance in the global context. Nevertheless, it is clear that the development process and choices of new technologies will influence subsequent choices in clinical care and in public health policies, as well as how the problems of health and illness are perceived.

When health is seen as a commodity, it is more easily perceived as something which can be bought and sold. This has implications not only for preferences in treatment practices but also for how the human body comes to be perceived. The trade in human beings is not new in the light of the history of prostitution or slavery. However, cases of trade involving parts of the human body may represent a modern medical version of this phenomenon. Furthermore, the possibility of choosing the qualities of children to be born may also result in a trend towards reducing the births of children perceived to be of lesser value and productive capacity – for example, children who are disabled or of the wrong gender.

The more health care becomes a domain of market-led private interest, the more easily it will also become a domain of health-related industries such as insurance companies, pharmaceutical companies and firms involved in technologies for treatment and diagnosis. These industries tend to be for profit, which means that they are not likely to collaborate with governments, doctors, researchers or international organizations unless they expect advantages for themselves. These advantages may be mutual. It is likely, however, that attention will be diverted towards policies which will be profitable for these industries while not necessarily being the optimal choices for those receiving the services, or for those paying for the costs, or for health sector development as a whole. In practice this could mean, for example, an emphasis on private insurance within health systems, or the promotion of curative technical fixes rather than preventive measures resulting from public health intersectoral policies. The international atmosphere of deregulation and free trade, with the scope that this gives to multinational industries, will also have implications for health and health sector development.

Population policies have been criticized for lacking emphasis on socio-economic concerns and reproductive rights, and more recently social and reproductive rights have received more attention. Now that these topics have moved into mainstream rhetoric, their interpretation and contextualization can distort the original aims. Reproductive rights have been interpreted increasingly through a concept of reproductive health emphasizing the positive health effects of family planning, and building on responsibilities in reproductive health. Moreover these reproductive responsibilities have come to cover the individual's responsibility for her/his reproduction towards the society and the future generation, thus actually undermining rights and highlighting the responsibility not to reproduce. Similarly, efforts to increase self-reliance in health may lead to a responsibility to stay healthy rather than the right of access to health services. The universal right of access to health services may be undermined by the simultaneous emphasis on means testing.

The biomedical interpretation of health runs the risk of neglecting the issues of human dignity and the social context in which decisions are made. While the role of the health services in the 'production' of health is often limited, they should have a major role in alleviating the suffering of the ill. Consumer choice has been promoted as a means to combat the arrogance of medical professionals, yet respect for human dignity will be gained only by those able to pay. Moreover, competition involving consumer satisfaction may not be a sufficient basis for the sound development of health services and treatment practices. The more humane approach in medical services ultimately needs more emphasis on respect and human dignity.

Development cooperation and health

The Alma Ata conference strongly emphasized a comprehensive approach to health, but the rhetoric was stronger than its implementation in practice. Development cooperation is, in fact, becoming increasingly focused on separate problems to be solved by narrow universal and technical solutions within a limited time frame. Many well-known indicators of socioeconomic development have turned into goals in themselves and have at the same time been disconnected from their wider context. Although improvements in the indicators are often important as such, the larger context which the indicator used to represent may become forgotten. Even if they are achieved, such goals may be difficult to sustain, because the infrastructure needed for sustainability may be lacking. The successive vertical projects with their narrow target setting have also had implications for long-term efforts to build health systems. Experience in vaccination efforts has also shown that the attainment of targets does not guarantee their sustainability. The best public health policies with multiple benefits may often not be implemented in terms of clearly set measurable targets and a short time perspective.

Many explanations may be offered for the prevalence of short-term, target-oriented programmes in development cooperation. First, it may be linked to a fragmented understanding of the context of realities in the Third World countries, and to a technocratic view of the problems and their solutions. Second, it may be connected with the vulnerability of the donor funding mechanisms, largely based on voluntary donations. The simplified models of action are easily communicable during fund-raising activities. With the increasing demands for proven cost-effectiveness, the vertical approaches with clearly defined, narrow goals may provide a better means to reach the targets set. Universal targets for goal achievement can be effective in advocacy work in donor countries. However, universal targets may not be consistent with national priorities, and striving for their achievement may distort national priority setting and resource allocation. Third, these practices may be linked to the donors' commercial interest in promoting their products. When the donors are part of the solution, for example as suppliers of the products used in the projects, the opportunities to extend markets may seem attractive.

The values and expectations inherent in development cooperation often take a concrete form in the use of expertise. Expertise in one aspect of health is expected to be universal and transferable as such. Experts often identify and plan projects in different settings in a short time with a standard frame, and often offer standard technological solutions. Local abilities, knowledge and special characteristics remain unacknowledged, or are even perceived as hindrances. Solutions unfamiliar to the funder or implementer may be rejected, rather than those unfamiliar to the receiver.

The concept of reproductive health calls for a comprehensive approach, as opposed to the target orientation of previous population programmes. As the aims in social and health development have become increasingly subordinated to the pressures to limit population growth, the integrated approach is in danger of being determined by the ability of each individual intervention to further reduce fertility, rather than by the social or health needs themselves. Legitimization of social and health rights on the basis of their fertility-reducing capacity devalues the inherent worth of such rights.

HIV/AIDS has become the new challenge for medicine. While the devastating effects of the HIV pandemic are widely known, it is not clear whether diverting health budgets from primary health care towards HIV projects is necessarily serving best even those areas affected by the disease. Nor is it clear to what extent the efforts of the international HIV projects carried out under the aegis of development cooperation have served those affected in Third World countries. Prevention through health education, treatment of sexually transmitted diseases, or through changes in the content of population programmes seem to have gained only limited ground thus far, while more effort seems to have been put into finding a vaccination or cure through medication. The question remains, however, whether the majority of those falling ill in the poorer countries would ever be able to have access to the cure if it existed.

Universal access to health services and family planning have become a high priority in health policies. Reliance on private providers for those who can afford them, however, and the channelling of government services to the poorest, may in the long run be a dangerous solution. Those not dependent on government services may no longer feel responsible for funding them or bother about their quality, which may eventually lead to deterioration and decay of the government-funded health services. While such deterioration inevitably has been and is a problem in many countries already, a question of concern is whether the prescribed cure will consist of more of the same medicine. A transfer of responsibilities to the private sector exacerbates inequality, and as such will not do anything to improve the accountability and performance of the public sector. The increasing use of nonprofit and value-based organizations has often been seen as part of the solution. However, the reliance on the benevolence of NGOs may prove to be as problematic as the earlier reliance on the benevolent state has been. Building more on charity than on collective responsibility, it may also legitimate a narrower interpretation of the social responsibilities of the state in future.

Introducing competitive elements in publicly funded health care provision is an important part of the health reform policies. The evidence of increased savings resulting from these policies is so far very limited, even in the developed countries where these have been implemented. The management and information needed to implement policies often create additional administrative costs and constrain the management capacities of governments. There seems to be an increasing tendency to adjust the capacities of governments to fit these models, instead of trying to enable those governments committed to improving the health of their citizens to implement policies which would fit their capacities. The international actors in development policies are also very interested in acting as a catalytic force, or searching for new approaches and solutions. While this is important, the long-term aims in building a functioning health system may be compromised in the search for new solutions. The catalytic interpretation also tends to undermine the support which is needed much later, when the problems and realities of these approaches become evident.

It seems that in development cooperation there is always a search for a kind of magic bullet that will solve the problems for us, without the need to tackle the issues of inequality or redistribution. There are continually new initiatives, new technological solutions and new types of organizational and financial structures. Development efforts, however, require will, commitment and long-term struggle, while the fruits may materialize only years later. The evidence has shown that issues in social development and health are value-based and political. Looking beyond prioritization and the current debate on whether we can afford health services or Health for All, this could be the time to ask whether we can afford not to take seriously health as a social right, the interrelatedness of health and social justice, and the need for intersectoral action expressed in the Alma Ata Declaration.

Bibliography

Abel-Smith, B. (1986) 'Funding health for all – is insurance the answer?', *World Health Forum,* 7: 331.

Abel-Smith, B. (1992) 'Health insurance in developing countries: lessons from experience', *Health Policy and Planning,* 7: 215–26.

Abel-Smith, B. and Eawal, P. (1992) 'Can the poor afford "free" health services? A case study of Tanzania', *Health Policy and Planning,* 7: 329–41.

Abel-Smith, B., Figueras, J., Holland, W., McKee, M. and Mossialos, E. (1995) *Choices in Health Policy. An Agenda for the European Union.* Office for Official Publications of the European Communities and Darthmouth Publications Ltd: Aldershot.

Abrams, H., Anderson, H., Anderson, J., Ashford, N., Baker, D., Beaumont, P., Bergeisen, G. *et al.* (1996) 'Letter to World Health Organization, International Labor Office, United Nations Environment Program and International Program on Chemical Safety', *Archives of Environmental Health,* 51: 338–40.

Adams, N. (1994) 'The UN's neglected brief – "The advancement of all peoples"? ', in Childers, E. (ed.) *Challenges to the United Nations. Building a Safer World.* Catholic Institute for International Relations and St Martin's Press: New York.

Ahlberg, B. M. (1989) 'A critical review of family planning programmes with special reference to sub-Saharan Africa', *International Journal of Prenatal and Perinatal Studies,* 397–416.

Ahlberg, B. M. (1991) *Women, Sexuality and the Changing Social Order. The Impact of Government Policies on Reproductive Behaviour in Kenya.* International Studies in Global Change. Gordon and Breach: Philadelphia.

Ahlberg, H. and Lovbraek, A. (1985) *UNDP in Action.* Utrikesdepartementet Ds UD: 1, Stockholm.

AIDAN and VHAI. (1986) *A Rational Drug Policy. Problems, Perspective, Recommendation.* All India Drug Action Network and Voluntary Health Association of India: New Delhi.

Aird, J. S. (1990) *The Slaughter of Innocents: Coercive Birth Control in China.* American Enterprise Institute: Washington.

Akin, J. S., Guilkey, D. K. and Denton, E. H. (1995) 'Quality of services and demand for health care in Nigeria: a multinomial probit estimation', *Social Science and Medicine,* 40: 1527–37.

Allain, A. (1991) 'Breastfeeding is politics: A personal view of the International Baby Milk Campaign', *The Ecologist,* 21: 206–13.

Allman, J., Rohde, J. and Wray, J. (1987) 'Integration and disintegration: the case of family planning in Haiti', *Health Policy and Planning,* 2: 236–44.

Almroth, S. and Latham, M. C. (1995) 'Rational home management of diarrhoea', *Lancet,* 345: 709–11.

Alternative Copenhagen Declaration. (1995) *Finnish Official Report of the Social Summit, 6–12 March 1995 in Copenhagen.* Ministry of Foreign Affairs: Helsinki.

Amalric, F. and Banuri, T. (1994) 'Population: malady or symptom', *Third World Quarterly,* 15: 691–706.

Amatya, R., Akhter, H., McMahan, J., Williamson, N., Gates, D. and Ahmed, Y. (1994) 'The effects of husband counselling on Norplant[R] contraceptive acceptability in Bangladesh', *Contraception,* 50: 263–73.

Anand, S. and Chen, L. (1996) *Health Implications of Economic Policies: a Framework of Analysis.* New York: UNDP Office of Development Studies.

Anon. (1985) 'Wanted: a new breed of doctors (roundtable)', *World Health Forum,* 6: 291–309.

Anon. (1986) 'A discussion document on the concept and principles of health promotion', *Health Promotion,* 1: 73–6.

Anon. (1991) 'Supportive environments for health: the Sundsvall Statement', *Health Promotion International,* 6: 297–300.

Anon. (1992) 'Let them eat pollution', *The Economist,* 8 February 1992.

Anon. (1994a) 'African NGOs call for change in International Monetary Fund and World Bank policies', *Third World Resurgence,* 49: 28–31.

Anon. (1994b) 'Enough is enough, say US NGOs', *Third World Resurgence,* 49: 32–6.

Anon. (1997) 'Joint NGO statement on issues and proposals for the WTO ministerial conference', *Third World Resurgence,* 77/78: 29–37.

Antezana, F. (1990) 'A view from the World Health Organization. Cooperation between WHO and industry on projects in the Third World', in *Proceedings of the IFPMA International Seminar: Pharmaceutical Industry Projects in the Third World, Geneva, 13-14 December 1989.* Geneva: IFPMA.

Apffel-Marglin, F. (1990) 'Smallpox in two systems of knowledge', in Apffel-Marglin, F. and Marglin, S. (eds), *Dominating Knowledge. Development, Culture, and Resistance.* WIDER Studies in Development Economics. Oxford: Clarendon Press.

Arellano-Lopez, S. and Petras, J. F. (1994) 'Non-governmental organizations and poverty alleviation in Bolivia', *Development and Change,* 25: 555–68.

Arhin, D. (1994) 'The health card insurance scheme in Burundi: a social asset or a non-viable venture?', *Social Science and Medicine,* 39: 861–70.

Arhin, D. (1995) 'Health insurance in Africa', *Lancet,* 345: 44–5.

Armstrong, J. and Bos, E. (1992) 'The demographic, economic, and social impact of AIDS', in Mann, J., Tarantolam, D. J. and Netter, T. W. (eds), *A Global Report. AIDS in the World.* Cambridge, Massachusetts and London: Harvard University Press.

Ashford, L. (1995) 'New perspectives on population: lessons from Cairo', *Population Bulletin,* 50, 1: 1–44.

Ashton, J., Grey, P. and Barnard, K. (1986) 'Healthy cities – WHO's new public health initiative', *Health Promotion,* 1: 319–24.

Askwith, M. (1994) 'The roles of DHA and UNDP in linking relief and development', *IDS Bulletin,* 25: 101–4.

Awuonda, M. (1995) 'Swedes support UNAIDS', *Lancet,* 345.

Ayres, R. L. (1983) *Banking on the Poor. The World Bank and World Poverty.* Cambridge, Massachusetts: MIT Press.

Backet, E. M., Davies, A. M. and Petros-Barvazian, A. (1984) *The Risk Approach in Health Care. With Special Reference to Maternal and Child Health, Including Family Planning.* Public Health Papers. Geneva: WHO.

Bailey, M. (1994) 'UNDP – healthy development? The case of HIV', *Health Policy and Planning,* 9: 444–7.

Balasubramanian, K. (1996) 'Heads – TNCs win: tails – South loses or GATT/WTO/TRIPS Agreement'. Paper presented at HAI seminar on WTO/GATT, Pharmaceutical Policies and Essential Drugs, Bielefeld, Germany, 1996. Amsterdam: Health Action International.

Ballance, R., Pogany, J. and Forstner, H. (1992) *The World's Pharmaceutical Industry. An International Perspective on Innovation, Competition and Policy.* Vermont: E. Elgar.

Banerji, D. (1985) *Health and Family Planning Services in India. An Epidemiological, Socio-cultural and Political Analysis and Perspective.* New Delhi: Lok Paksh.

Banerji, D. (1990) 'Crash of the immunization program: consequences of a totalitarian approach', *International Journal of Health Services,* 20: 501–10.

Banerji, D.(1992) 'Family planning in the nineties. More of the same', *Economic and Political Weekly,* 27: 883–7.

Banerji, D. (1993) 'Simplistic approach to health policy analysis. World Bank team on Indian health sector', *Economic and Political Weekly,* 28: 1207–10.

Banuri, T., Hyden, G., Juma, C. and Rivera, M. (1994) *Sustainable Human Development: from Concept to Operation, a Guide for the Practitioner.* New York: UNDP.

Barer, M. L., Marmor, T. R. and Morrison, E. M. (1995) 'Health care reform in the United States: on the road to nowhere (again)?', *Social Science and Medicine,* 41: 453–60.

Barnes, J. N., Grosman, E. and Reid, W. V. (1994) *Bankrolling Successes: a Portfolio of Sustainable Development Projects.* Friends of the Earth, National Wildlife Federation, World Resources Institute.

Barnum, H., Kutzin, J. and Saxenian, H. (1995) 'Incentives and provider payment methods', *International Journal of Health Planning and Management,* 10: 23–45.

Basta, S. (1989) *Evaluation and Analysis of UNICEF's External Relations Policies and Functions.* New York: UNICEF.

Basu, A. M. (1996) 'ICPD: what about men's rights and women's responsibilities?', *Health Transition Review,* 6: 225–9.

Baum, B. H. and Strenski, T. (1989) 'Thailand: current public health perspectives. short communication', *International Journal of Health Planning and Management,* 4: 117–24.

Baum, F. E. (1993) 'Healthy cities and change: social movement or bureaucratic tool ?', *Health Promotion International,* 8: 31–41.

Baum, F. E. and Sanders, D. (1995) 'Can health promotion and primary health care achieve Health for All without a return to their more radical agenda?', *Health Promotion International,* 10: 149–60.

Baum, W. C. and Tolbert, S. M. (1985) *Investing in Development. Lessons of World Bank Experience.* Washington, DC: Oxford University Press and World Bank.

Baza, A., Hakizimana, A., Hanson, K., Kwizera. F. and van der Geest, S. (1993) 'Health insurance and the Bamako initiative in Burundi: value for money?', *International Journal of Health Planning and Management,* 8: 129–35.

Beardsley, T. (1995) 'Better than cure', *Scientific American,* January: 68–75.

Beattie, R. and McGillivray, W. (1995) 'A risky strategy: reflections on the World Bank report "Averting the old age crisis"', *International Social Security Review,* 46: 5–21.

Behague, D. (1993) 'Growth monitoring and the promotion of breastfeeding', *Social Science and Medicine,* 37: 1565–78.

Beigbeder, Y. (1997) *The Internal Management of United Nations Organizations. The Long Quest for Reform.* London and New York: MacMillan Press and St Martin's Press Ltd.

Bellamy, C. (1996a) 'Statement by Carol Bellamy to the WHO-UNICEF Joint Committee on Health Policy, Geneva, 15 May 1996', internet: gopher://gopher.unicef.org:70/00/.cefdata/ speech/96.027, April 1997.

Bellamy, C. (1996b) *The State of the World's Children 1996.* New York: UNICEF, Oxford University Press.

Bennet, F. J. (1989) 'The dilemma of essential drugs in primary health care', *Social Science and Medicine,* 28: 1085–90.

Bennet, S. (1992) 'Promoting the private sector: a review of developing country trends', *Health Policy and Planning,* 7: 97–110.

Bennet, S., Dakpallah, G., Garner, P., Gilson, L., Nittayaramphong, S., Zurita, B. and Zwi, A. (1994) 'Carrot and stick: state mechanisms to influence private provider behaviour', *Health Policy and Planning,* 8: 113.

Bennet, S. and Tangcharoensathien, V. (1994) 'A shrinking state ? Politics and private health care in Thailand', *Public Administration and Development,* 14: 1–17.

Bennet, S., Russel, S and Mills, A. (1996) *Institutional and Economic Perspectives on Government Capacity to Assume New Roles in the Health Sector: a Review of Experience.* Department of Public Health and Policy Publications, No. 22. London: London School of Hygiene and Tropical Medicine.

Berkley, S. (1996) 'Introduction', in *Enhancing the Performance of International Health Institutions.* Papers from the Pocantico Retreat, 1–3 February. Rockefeller Foundation, Social Science Research Council.

Berman, P. and Rose, L. (1996) 'The role of private providers in maternal and child health and family planning services in developing countries', *Health Policy and Planning* 11, 2: 142–55.

Berelson, B. (1969) 'Beyond family planning', *Science,* 163: 533–43.

Berman, P. (1995) 'Health sector reform: making health development sustainable', *Health Policy,* 32: 13–28.

Berwick, D. and Smith, R. (1995) 'Cooperating, not competing, to improve health care', *British Medical Journal,* 310: 1349–50.

Bidway, P. (1995) 'One step forward, many steps back: dismemberment of India's national drug policy', *Development Dialogue,* 1: 193–222.

Black, M. (1996) *Children First. The Story of UNICEF, Past and Present.* Published for UNICEF. Oxford University Press: Oxford and New York.

Blane, R., Brunner, E. and Wilkinson R. (eds) (1996) *Health and Social Organization.* London: Routledge.

Bloom, G. (1991) 'Managing health sector development: markets and institutional reform', in Colclough, C. and Manor, J. (eds) *States or Markets? Neoliberalism and the Development Policy Debate.* Oxford: Clarendon Press.

Bogg, L., Hengjin, D., Keli, W., Wenwel, C. and Diwan, V. (1996) 'The cost of coverage: rural health insurance in China', *Health Policy and Planning,* 11: 238–52.

Bond, P. and Weissman, R. (1997) 'The costs of mergers and acquisitions in the US health care sector', *International Journal of Health Services,* 27: 77–87.

Bongaarts, J. (1991) 'The KAP-gap and the unmet need for contraception', *Population and Development Review,* 17: 293–314.

Bose, A. (1988) *From Population to People.* Volume I. Delhi: BR Publishing Corporation.

Boyd, J. W., Himmelstein, D. U. and Woolhandler, S. (1995) 'The tobacco / health insurance connection', *Lancet,* 346: 64.

Bradlow, D. D. and Grossman, C. (1996) 'Adjusting the Bretton Woods institutions to contemporary realities', in Griesbarger, J. M.and Gunter, B. C., *Development. New Paradigms and Principles for the Twenty-first Century.* London: Pluto Press.

Bratton, M. (1989) 'The politics of government–NGO relations in Africa', *World Development,* 569–87.

Brohman, J. (1995) 'Universalism, eurocentrism, and ideological bias in development studies: from modernisation to neoliberalism', *Third World Quarterly,* 16:121–49.

Broomberg, J. (1994a) *Health Care Markets for Export? Lessons for Developing Countries from European and American Experience.* PHP Departmental Publication No 12. London School of Hygiene and Tropical Medicine.

Broomberg, J. (1994b) 'Managing the health care market in developing countries: prospects and problems', *Health Policy and Planning,* 9: 237–51.

Broun, D. (1995) 'Procurement of pharmaceuticals in World Bank projects'. World Bank PHNFLASH Archive document, Human Capital Development Working Papers, hrwp 034, received 8 November 1995.

Brown, B. (1992) *The United States and the Politicization of the World Bank. Issues of International Law and Policy.* London and New York: Kegan Paul International.

Brown, D. L. and Korten, D. (1991) 'Working more effectively with nongovermental organizations', in Paul, S. and Israel, A. (eds) *Nongovernmental Organizations and the World Bank.* Washington, DC: World Bank.

Brown, P. (1997) 'The WHO strikes mid-life crisis', *New Scientist,* 11 January: 12–13.

Browne, R. S. (1996) 'Rethinking the IMF on its fiftieth anniversary', in Griesbarger, J. M. and Gunter, B. G. (eds) *The World's Monetary System.* London: Pluto Press.

Brunet-Jailly, J. (1993) 'Macroeconomic adjustment and the health sector in Mali', *Macroeconomic Environment and Health, with Case Studies for Countries in Greatest Need.* Geneva: WHO.

Bruneton, C., van der Heide, B. and Naboulet, P. (1996) *Les échanges de médicamentes entre pays européens et pays en développement: efficacité des systèmes de régulation, problèmes et perspectives.* ReMed, PIMED and Wemos. English summary.

Bryant, J. H. (1988) 'Health for all: the dream and the reality', *World Health Forum,* 9: 291–302.

Budhoo, D. L. (1990) *Enough is Enough. Dear Mr Camdessus .... Open letter of Resignation to the Managing Director of the International Monetary Fund.* New York: New Horizons Press.

Buse, K. (1996) 'The World Bank', *Health Policy and Planning,* 9: 95–9.

Buse, K. and Walt, G. (1996) 'Aid coordination for health sector reform: a conceptual framework for analysis and assessment', *Health Policy and Planning,* 38: 173–87.

Cassels, A. (1996) 'Aid instruments and health systems development: an analysis of current practice', *Health Policy and Planning,* 11: 354–68.

Cassels, A.and Janovsky, K. (1992) 'A time of change: health policy, planning and organization in Ghana', *Health Policy,* 7: 144–54.

Cassen, R. and Bates, M. L. (1994) *Population Policy: a New Consensus.* Policy Essay No. 12. Washington: ODC.

Caufield, C. (1996) *Masters of Illusion. The World Bank and the Poverty of Nations.* London: MacMillan.

Centre for Reproductive Law and Policy. (1994) 'Reproductive freedom at the UN'. Cited in *WGNRR Newsletter* 48: 7–8.

Chabot, H. T. and Brenner, J. (1988) 'Government health services versus community: conflict or harmony', *Social Science and Medicine,* 26: 957–62.

Chabot, J. (1988) 'The Bamako Initiative', letter to the editor, *Lancet,* 10 December: 1366–7.

Chalker, J. (1995) 'Vietnam: profit and loss in health care', *World Health Forum,* 16: 194–5.

Chase, E. and Carr-Hill, R. (1994) 'The dangers of managerial perversion: quality assurance in primary health care', *Health Policy and Planning,* 9: 267–78.

Chatterjee, P. (1993) 'World Bank and UNDP', *InterPress Service,* 29 August 1993.

Chatterjee, P. and Finger, M. (1994) *The Earth Brokers. Power, Politics and World Development.* London: Routledge.

Chaudhuri, S. (1993) 'Dunkel draft on drug patents. Background and implications', *Economic and Political Weekly,* 28: 1861–5.

Chetley, A. (1990) *A Healthy Business. World Health and the Pharmaceutical Industry.* London and

New York: Zed Books Ltd.

Chetley, A. (1993) *Problem Drugs*. London and New York: Zed Books Ltd.

Chhabra R. and Nuna, S. (1993) *Abortion in India. An Overview*. New Delhi: Veerendra Printers.

Childers, E. and Urquhart, B. (1994) 'Renewing the United Nations system', *Development Dialogue*, 1.

Ching, P. (1995) 'User fees, demand for children's health care and access across income groups: the Philippine case', *Social Science and Medicine*, 41: 37–46.

Chowdhury, Z. (1995a) 'Bangladesh: A tough battle for a national drug policy', *Development Dialogue*, 1: 96–147.

Chowdhury, Z. (1995b) *The Politics of Essential Drugs. The Makings of a Successful Health Strategy. Lessons from Bangladesh*. London: Zed Books.

CIIR. (1996) *Continental shift. Europe's policies towards the South*. London: Catholic Institute for International Relations.

Ciszewski, R. L. and Harvey, P. D. (1994) 'The effect of price increases on contraceptive sales in Bangladesh', *Journal of Biosocial Science*, 26: 25–35.

Claeson, M. (1996) 'The World Bank's perspective on global health', *Current Issues in Public Health*, 2: 264–9.

Clark, J. (1995) 'The state, popular participation and the voluntary sector', *World Development*, 23: 593–601.

Clements, P. (1993) 'An approach to poverty alleviation for large international development agencies', *World Development*, 21: 1633–46.

Cohen, J. (1997) 'The Genomics gamble', *Science*, 275: 767–72.

Collier, C. (1996) 'NGOs, the poor, and local government', *Development in Practice*, 6: 244–9.

Collins, C. (1989) 'Decentralization and the need for political and critical analysis', *Health Policy and Planning*, 4: 168–71.

Collins, C. and Green, A. (1994) 'Decentralization and primary health care: some negative implications in developing countries', *International Journal of Health Services*, 24: 459–75.

Commission on health research for development. (1990) *Health Research: Essential Link to Equity in Development*. Oxford: Oxford University Press.

Conable, B. (1988) 'Barber Conable on the World Bank's view on poverty and population', *Population and Development Review*, 753–5.

Coney, S. (1992) 'A living laboratory: the New Zeeland connection in the marketing of Depo-Provera' in Davis, P. (ed.), *For Health or for Profit: Medicine, the Pharmaceutical Industry and the State in New Zealand*. Auckland, Oxford, New York and Melbourne: Oxford University Press. pp. 119–43.

Conly, S., Speidel, J. and Camp, S. (1991) *US Population Assistance: Issues for the 1990s*. Washington, DC: Population Crises Committee.

Conly, S. R and Speidel, J. J. (1993) *Global Population Assistance. A Report Card on the Major Donor Countries*. Washington DC: Population Action International.

Conly, S. and Rosen, J. E. (1996) 'International population assistance update: recent trends in donor contributions'. Population Action International, Occasional Paper No. 2.

Copenhagen Declaration and Programme of Action adopted by the World Summit for Social Development'. (1995) Copenhagen 6–12 March. In *World Summit for Social Development 6-12 March 1995*. Helsinki: Ministry of Foreign Affairs.

Coreil, J., Augustin, A., Halsey, N. A. and Holt, E. (1994) 'Social and psychological costs of preventive child health services in Haiti', *Social Science and Medicine*, 38: 231–8.

Cornia, G. A., Jolly, R. and Stewart, F. (1987) *Adjustment with a Human Face. Protecting the Vulnerable and Promoting Growth*. Vols 1–2. Oxford: Clarendon Press.

Correa, C. M. (1996) *The Uruguay Round on Drugs*. Discussion paper. Geneva: WHO, Action Programme on Essential Drugs.

Correa, S. and Petchesky, R. (1994) 'Reproductive and sexual rights. a feminist perspective', in Sen, G., Germain, A. and Chen, L. C. (eds), *Population Policies Reconsidered: Health, Empowerment and Rights*. Boston: Harvard School of Public Health.

Costello, A., Watson, F. and Woodward, D. (1994) *Human Face or Human Facade? Adjustment and the Health of Mothers and Children*. London: Centre for International Child Health.

Cottrell, K. (1996) 'Herbal products begin to attract the attention of brand-name drug companies', *Canada Medical Association Journal*, 155, 2: 216–19.

Courtois, X. and Dumoulin, J. (1995) 'Sale of drugs and health care utilization in a health care district in Zaire', *Health Policy and Planning*, 10: 181–5.

COWIconsult. (1991) *Effectiveness of Multilateral Agencies at Country Level*. Copenhagen: Danida.

Craft, N. (1995) 'Beijing and the future of women', *British Medical Journal*, 311: 580–1.
Crane, B. and Finkle, J. (1989) 'The United States, China, and the United Nations Population Fund: Dynamics of US policy-making', *Population and Development Review*, 15: 23–59.
Crane, B. (1994) 'The transnational politics of abortion', *Population and Development Review*, 20 (Suppl): 241–62.
Creese, A. L. (1991) 'User charges for health care: a review of recent experience', *Health Policy and Planning*, 6: 309–19.
Cross, P. N., Huff, M. A., Quick, J. D. and Bates, J. A. (1986) 'Revolving drug funds: conducting business in the public sector', *Social Science and Medicine*, 22: 335–43.
Culpeper, R. (1996) 'Multilateral development banks. Towards a new division of labor', in Griesgraber, J. M. and Gunter, B. C. (eds), *Development. New Paradigms and Principles for the Twenty-first Century*. London: Pluto Press.
Culpeper, R. (1997) *Titans or Behemoths? The Multilateral Development Banks*. Vol. 5. London: Intermediate Technology Publications Ltd.
Dahlgren, G. (1990) 'Strategies for health financing in Kenya – the difficult birth of a new policy', *Scandinavian Journal of Social Medicine*, Supplement 46: 67–81.
Dahlgren, G. (1994) *Framtidens sjukvårdsmarknader – vinnare och förlorare*. Bokförlaget Natur och Kultur i samarbete med Institutet för Framtidsstudier. Borås: Centraltryckeriet.
Daly, H. (1994) 'Farewell lecture to the World Bank', in Cavanagh, J., Wysham, D. and Arruda, M. (eds), *Beyond Bretton Woods. Alternatives to the Global Economic Order*. London, Washington DC and Amsterdam: Pluto Press, Institute for Policy Studies and Transnational Institute.
Davis, K. (1967) 'Population policy: will current programs succeed?', *Science*, 158: 730–9.
De Graff, D., Phillips, J., Simmons, R. and Chakraborty, J. (1986) 'Integrating health services into an MCH-FP program in Matlab, Bangladesh: an analytical update', *Studies in Family Planning*, 17, 5: 228–34.
De Kadt, E. (1982) 'Ideology, social policy, health and health services: a field of complex interactions', *Social Science and Medicine*, 16: 741–52.
De Kadt, E. (1989) 'Making health policy management intersectoral: issues of information analysis and use in less developed countries', *Social Science and Medicine*, 29: 503–14.
De Vries, B. A. (1996) 'The World Bank's focus on poverty', in Griesbarger, J. M. and Gunter, B. G., *The World Bank. Lending on a Global Scale*. London: Pluto Press.
Deacon, B. and Hulse, M. (1997) 'The making of post-communist social policy: the role of international agencies', *Journal of Social Policy*, 26: 43–62.
Dean, M. (1994) 'Prescription charges in the NHS', *Lancet*, 343: 531.
Development Dialogue. (1995) 'Health and drug policies: making them the top of agenda'. A strategy paper. *Development Dialogue*, 1: 5–24.
Dickson, D. (1994) 'Concern grows over China's plans to reduce number of "inferior births"', *Nature*, 367: 3.
Diop, F., Yazbeck, A. and Bitran, R. (1995) 'The impact of alternative cost recovery schemes on access and equity in Niger', *Health Policy and Planning*, 10: 223–40.
Donini, A. (1995) 'The bureaucracy and free spirits: stagnation and innovation in the relationship between the UN and NGOs', *Third World Quarterly*, 16: 421–39.
Doyal, L. (1996) 'The politics of women's health: setting a global agenda', *International Journal of Health Services*, 26: 47–65.
Drager, N *et al.* (1992) 'What determines aid for health: an empirical analysis of bilateral aid flows'. Paper delivered at International Conference on Macroeconomics and Health in Countries in Greatest Need. Document WHO/ICO/ME.CONF, 1992: 149–78. Cited in: Michaud, C. and Murray, C. J. L. (1994), 'External assistance to the health sector in developing countries. A detailed analysis 1972–1990', in Murray, C. J. L. and Lopez, A. D. (eds) *Global Comparative Assessments in the Health Sector: Disease Burden, Expenditure and Intervention Packages*. Geneva: WHO.
WHO Drug Monitor (1993) 'Drug Regulation and Developing Countries', *WHO Drug Monitor* 7, 1: 1–3.
Dunleavy, P. and O'Leary, B. (1987) *Theories of the State. The Politics of Liberal Democracy*. London: Macmillan Press Ltd.
Economist. (1995) 'Good intentions, road to hell?', *Economist*, 7 October: 121–2.
Edwards, M. and Hulme, D. (eds). (1995) *Non-governmental Organizations. Performance and Accountability*. London: Earthscan Ltd.
Eklöf, G. (1993) *Världsbanken och miljön*. Stockholm: Naturskyddsföreningen Förlag.
Engberg-Pedersen, P., Dohoo Faure, S. and Freeman, T. (1992) *Strategic Choices for UNICEF*.

Service Delivery, Capacity Building, Empowerment. Evaluation of UNICEF. Synthesis Report 1992. AIDAB, CIDA, DANIDA, SDC.

English, E. P.and Mule, H. M. (1996) *The African Development Bank.* London: Intermediate Technology Publications.

Enthoven, A. (1993a) 'The history and principles of managed competition', *Health Affairs* (supplement): 25–48.

Enthoven, A. (1993b) 'Why has managed care failed to control health costs', *Health Affairs (*Fall): 26–43.

Enthoven, A. (1994) 'On the ideal market structure for third-party purchasing of health care', *Social Science and Medicine,* 39: 1413–24.

Essential Drugs Monitor. (1996) 22.

Euromonitor. (1995) *The World Market for Pharmaceuticals.* London: Euromonitor.

Evans, I. (1995) 'SAPping maternal health', *Lancet,* 346: 1046.

Evans, R. (1996) Keynote address. The Ljubljana Conference on Health Care Reforms. WHO: Regional Office for Europe.

Evans, R. (1997) 'Health care reform: Who's selling the market and why?', *Public Health Medicine,* 19: 45–9.

Financial Times. (1997) 'Pharmaceuticals. Feelgood factor is back but industry stays wary', *Financial Times,* 24 April 1997.

Finger, W. (1994) 'Should family planning include STD services', *Network,* 19 May: 4–7.

Finkel, M. L. (1993) 'Managed care is not the answer', *Journal of Health Politics, Policy and Law,* 18: 105–11.

Finkle, J. and Crane, B. (1976) 'The World Health Organization and the population issue: organizational values in the United Nations', *Population and Development Review,* 2: 367–94.

Finkle, J. L. and Crane, B. B. (1975) 'The politics of Bucharest: population, development and the New International Economic Order', *Population and Development Review,* 1: 87–114.

Finkle, J. and Crane, B. (1985) 'Ideology and politics at Mexico City: the United States at the international conference on population', *Population and Development Review,* 11: 1–28.

Finkle, J. and McIntosh, A. (1994) 'The new politics of population', *Population and Development Review,* 20 (supplement): 3–34.

Fitzroy, H., Briend, A. and Fauveau, V. (1990) 'Child survival: should the strategy be redesigned? Experience from Bangladesh', *Health Policy and Planning,* 5: 226–34.

Foltz, A. M. (1994) 'Donor funding for health reforms in Africa: is non-project assistance the right prescription?', *Health Policy and Planning,* 9: 371–84.

Foster, G. M. (1987) 'Bureaucratic aspects of international health agencies', *Social Science and Medicine,* 25: 1039–48.

Fowler, A. (1995) 'NGOs and globalization of social welfare. Perspectives from East-Africa', in Drumboja and Therkildsen, O. (eds), *Service Provision under Stress in East Africa. The State, NGOs and People's Organizations in Kenya, Tanzania and Uganda.* Copenhagen, Nairobi, Kampala, Portsmouth and London: Centre for Development Research in association with EAEP, Fountain Publishers, Heinemann and James Currey.

Freed, R. and Freed, S. (1989) 'Beliefs and practices resulting in female deaths and fewer females than males in India', *Population and Environment,* 10, 3: 144–61.

Frenk, J., Sepulveda, J., Gomez-Dantes, O., McGuinnes, M. J. and Knaul, F. (1997) 'The new world order and the future of international health', *British Medical Journal,* 314: 1404–7.

Fuchs, W. R. (1997) 'Managed care and merger mania', *Journal of the American Medical Association,* 277: 920–1.

Fukuda-Parr, S. (1995) 'Redefining technical cooperation: challenge for the UN or let's dump the "technical cooperation" mandate', *IDS Bulletin,* 26: 64–7.

Gadomski, A., Black, R. and Mosley, W. H. (1990) 'Constraints to the potential impact of child survival in developing countries', *Health Policy and Planning,* 5: 236–45.

Gayi, S. K. (1995) 'Adjusting to social costs of adjustement in Ghana: problems and prospects', *The European Journal of Development Research,* 7: 77–101.

George, S. and Sabelli, F. (1994) *Faith and Credit. The World Bank's Secular Empire.* Harmondsworth: Penguin Books.

George, S. M., Latham, M. C., Ethirajan, N. and Frongillo, E. A. (1993) 'Evaluation of effectiveness of good growth monitoring in south Indian villages', *Lancet,* 342: 348–55.

Gerein, N. (1988) 'Is growth monitoring worthwhile?' *Health Policy and Planning,* 3: 181–94.

Gerein, N. and Ross, D. A. (1991) 'Is growth monitoring worthwhile ? An evaluation of its use in three child health programmmes in Zaire', *Social Science and Medicine,* 32: 667–75.

Gibbon, P. (1992) 'The World Bank and African poverty, 1973–1991', *Journal of Modern African Studies*, 30: 193–220.

Gibbon, P. (1993) 'The World Bank and the new politics of Aid', *The European Journal of Development Research*, 5: 35–61.

Giffin, K.(1994) 'Women's health and the privatization of fertility control in Brazil', *Social Science and Medicine*, 39: 355–60.

Gilbert, D. and Chetley, A. (1996) 'New trends in drug promotion', *Consumer Policy Review*, 6, 5: 162–7.

Gill, P. (1988) 'Helping is not enough', in Poulton and Harris (eds), *Putting People First. Voluntary Organizations and Third World Development*. London: MacMillan Publishers.

Gilson, L., Dave Sen, P., Mohammed, S. and Mujinja, P. (1994) 'The potential of health sector non-governmental organizations: policy options', *Health Policy and Planning*, 9: 14–24.

Gilson, L. and Mills, A. (1995) 'Health sector reforms in Sub-Saharan Africa: lessons of the past 10 years', *Health Policy*, 32: 215–43.

Gish, O. (1983) 'Forms of health service financing and their effect on the provision of care' *IDS Bulletin*, 14: 38–43.

Godal, T. (1994) 'Fighting the parasites of poverty: public research, private industry and tropical diseases', *Science*, 264:1864–5.

Godlee, F. (1993a) 'WHO at the crossroads', *British Medical Journal*,. 306: 1143–4.

Godlee, F. (1993b) 'WHO's election throws agency into bitter turmoil', *British Medical Journal*, 306:161.

Godlee, F. (1994a) 'The regions – too much power, too little effect', *British Medical Journal*, 309: 1566–70.

Godlee, F. (1994b) 'WHO in crisis', *British Medical Journal*, 309: 1424–8.

Godlee, F. (1994c) 'WHO in retreat: is it losing its influence ?', *British Medical Journal*, 309: 1491–5.

Godlee, F. (1994d) 'WHO at country level – a little impact, no strategy', *British Medical Journal*, 309: 1636–9.

Godlee, F. (1995a) 'Interview with the director general', *British Medical Journal*, 310: 583–6.

Godlee, F. (1995b) 'WHO in Europe: does it have a role?', *British Medical Journal*, 310: 389–93.

Godlee, F. (1995c) 'WHO fellowships – what do they achieve?', *British Medical Journal*, 310: 1490–1.

Godlee, F. (1995d) 'WHO special programmes: undermining from above', *British Medical Journal*, 310: 1781–2.

Godlee, F. (1997a) 'WHO director general faces leadership challenge', *British Medical Journal*, 314: 998.

Godlee, F. (1997b) ' WHO reform and global health', *British Medical Journal*, 314: 1359–60.

Godlee, F. and Carnall, D. (1995) 'WHO's head in controversy as auditor leaves', *British Medical Journal*, 310: 1221–2.

Gordenker, L. and Weiss, T. G. (1995a) 'NGO participation in the international policy process', *Third World Quarterly*, 16: 543–55.

Gordenker, L. and Weiss, T. G. (1995b) 'Pluralising global governance: analytical approaches and dimensions', *Third World Quarterly*, 16: 357–87.

Gore, A. (1995) *Remarks of the Vice President to the World Summit for Social Development*. World Summit for Social Development, 12 March 1995.

Goss, Gilroy and Associates Ltd. (1991) *Evaluation Assessment of the United Nations Population Fund: Final Report*. Ottawa.

Graham, W. and Campbell, O. (1992) 'Maternal mortality and the measurement trap', *Social Science and Medicine*, 35: 967–77.

Grant, J. (1982) *The State of the World's Children 1981–1982*. New York: UNICEF and Blackfriars Press.

Grant, J. (1983) *The State of the World's Children 1982–1983*. New York: UNICEF and Oxford University Press.

Grant, J. (1991) *The State of the World's Children 1991*. New York: Oxford University Press.

Grant, J. (1992) *The State of the World's Children 1992*. New York: UNICEF and Oxford University Press.

Grant, J. (1994) *The State of the World's Children 1994*. New York: UNICEF and Oxford University Press.

Gray, A. (ed.) (1993) *World Health and Disease*. Buckingham: Open University Press.

Green, A. (1987) 'The role of nongovernmental organization and the private sector in the provision of health care in developing countries', *International Journal of Health Planning and Management,* 2: 37–58.

Green, A. (1994) 'Decisions about health services should not be made purely on the basis of achieving efficient allocation and utilization of resources', *World Health Forum,* 15: 30–1.

Green, A. (1995) 'The state of health planning in the 1990s', *Health Policy and Planning,* 10: 22–8.

Green, A. and Barker, C. (1988) 'Priority setting and economic appraisal: whose priorities – the community or the economist', *Social Science and Medicine,* 26: 919–29.

Green, A. and Barker, C. (1996) 'Debating DALYs', *Health Policy and Planning,* 11: 179–83.

Green, A. and Matthias, A. (1995) 'NGOs – a policy panacea for the next millenium', *Journal of International Development,* 7: 565–73.

Green, A. and Matthias, A. (1997) *Nongovernmental Organizations and Health in Developing Countries.* London and New York: MacMillan Press and St Martin's Press.

Green, C. P. (1996) *Profiles of UN Organisations Working in Population.* Population Action International.

Green, M. (1977) 'New directions in US foreign assistance for population programs', *Population and Development Review,* 3: 319–52.

Green, R. H. (1978) 'Basic human needs: concept or slogan, synthesis or smokescreen?', *IDS Bulletin,* 9: 711.

Green, R. H. (1991) 'Politics, power and poverty: Health for All in 2000 in the Third World?', *Social Science and Medicine,* 32: 745–55.

Green, R. H. (1993) 'Better health for Africans?' Paper presented at a World Council of Churches Conference in Geneva in October 1993. World Council of Churches, PO Box 2100, 150 route de Ferney, 1211 Geneva 2.

Greenough, P. (1995) 'Intimidation, coercion and resistance in the final stages of the South Asian smallpox eradication campaign, 1973–1975', *Social Science and Medicine,* 41: 633–45.

Grimes, S. (1994) 'The ideology of population control in the UN draft plan for Cairo', *Population Research and Policy Review,* 13: 209–24.

Grosskurth, H., Mosha, F., Todd, J. *et al.* (1995) 'Impact of treatment of sexually transmitted diseases on HIV infection in rural Tanzania: randomised controlled trial', *Lancet,* 346: 530–6.

'Guiding principles for small national drug regulatory authorities'. (1989) *WHO Drug Information,* 3: 43–50.

Gunatilleke, G. (1984) *Intersectoral Linkages and Health Development. Case Studies in India, Jamaica, Norway, Sri Lanka and Thailand.* WHO Offset Publication No. 83. Geneva: WHO.

Gwatkin, D. (1979) 'Political will and family planning: the implications of India's emergency experience', *Population and Development Review,* 5: 29–59.

Gwin, C. (1994) *US Relations with the World Bank 1945–1992.* Brooking Occasional Papers.

Haddad, S. and Fournier, P. (1995) 'Quality, cost and utilization of health services in developing countries, a longitudinal study in Zaire', *Social Science and Medicine,* 40: 743–53.

Hagenfeldt, K. (1994) 'Contraceptive research and development today: an overview', in Van Look, P. and Pèrez-Palacios (eds), *Contraceptive Research and Development 1984 to 1994. The Road from Mexico City to Cairo and Beyond.* Delhi: WHO and Oxford University Press.

HAI-Lights. (1996) 'HAI protests World Bank/IFPMA fellowship'. *HAI-Lights,* September 1996.

Hammer, L. (1994) *What Happens to Welfare when User Fees Finance Health Care? The Impact of Gender on Policy Outcomes: Theory and Evidence from Zimbabwe.* Institute of Social Studies, Working Papers, August. The Hague: ISS.

Hamrell, S. and Nordberg, O. (1995) 'Editorial note', *Development Dialogue,* 1: 1–4.

Han, H.-J.(1994) 'Unwelcome daughters. Son preference and abortion in South Korea', in *Private Decisions, Public Debate. Women, Reproduction and Population.* London: Panos.

Harkavy, O. (1969) 'American foundations and the population problem', in Berelson, B. (ed.), *Population. Challenging World Crisis.* New York: Voice of America Forum Lectures.

Hancher, L. (1996) 'Pharmaceutical policy and regulation: setting the pace in the European Community', in Davis, P. (ed.), *Contested Ground. Public Purpose and Private Interest in the Regulation of Prescription Drugs.* New York and Oxford: Oxford University Press.

Hanson, A. and McPake, B. (1993) 'The Bamako Initiative: where is it going', *Health Policy and Planning,* 8: 267–74.

Hardon, A. (1992) 'Consumers versus producers: power play behind the scenes', in Kanji, N., Hardon, A., Harnmeijer, J., Mamdani, M. and Walt, G. (eds), *Drugs Policy in Developing Countries.* London and New York: Zed Books.

Hardon, A. and Kanji, N. (1992) 'New horizons in the 1990s', in Kanji, N., Hardon, A., Harnmeijer, J., Mamdani, M. and Walt, G. (eds), *Drugs Policy in Developing Countries.*

London and New York: Zed Books.

Harrison, S. (1995) 'Clinical autonomy and planned markets: the British case', in: Saltman R. and von Otter C. (eds), *Implementing Planned Markets in Health Care*. Buckingham: Open University Press.

Hartmann, B. (1987) *Reproductive Rights and Wrongs. The Global Politics of Population Control and Contraceptive Choice*. New York: Perennial Library, Harper & Row Publishers.

Hartmann, B. (1993) 'Population doublespeak', *Women's Global Network for Reproductive Rights Newsletter*, 42: 9–10.

Hartmann, B. (1995) *Reproductive Rights and Wrongs. The Global Politics of Birth Control*. Revised edition. Boston: South End Press.

Hartog, R. (1993) 'Essential and non-essential drugs marketed by the 20 largest European drug companies in developing countries', *Social Science and Medicine*, 37: 897–904.

Hayes, M. (1991) 'The risk approach: unassailable logic?', *Social Science and Medicine*, 33: 55–70.

Health Horizon. (1995) 'The World Bank: the pharmaceutical industry has a role to play', *Health Horizon*, 25: 10–11.

Heilbroner, R. and Milberg, W. (1995) *The Crisis of Vision in Modern Economic Thought*. New York: Cambridge University Press.

Helleneier, G. K. (1994) 'From adjustment to development in sub-Saharan Africa: consensus and continuing conflict', in Cornia, G. A. and Helleneier, G. K., *From Adjustment to Development in Africa*. New York: St Martin's Press, New York.

Hempel, M. (1996) 'Reproductive health and rights: origins of and challenges to the ICPD agenda', *Health Transition Review*, 6: 73–85.

Henshaw, S. (1990) 'Induced abortion: a world review', *International Family Planning Perspectives*, 16: 59–65.

Hernandez, D. (1985) 'Fertility reduction policies and poverty in Third World countries: ethical issues', *Studies in Family Planning*, 16: 76–87.

Hetzel, B. S. (1989) 'Healthy public policy and the Third World', *Health Promotion*, 4: 57–61.

Hewitt, A. P.and Killick, T. (1996) 'Bilateral aid conditionality and policy leverage', in Stokke, O. (ed.), *Foreign Aid towards the Year 2000: Experiences and Challenges*. EADI Book Series 18. London: Frank Cass.

Hien, N. T., Ha, L. T. T., Rifkin, S. and Wright, P. (1995) 'The pursuit of equity: a health sector case study from Vietnam', *Health Policy*, 33: 191–204.

Hildyard, N. (1993) 'Foxes in charge of the chickens', in Sachs, W. (ed.), *Global Ecology*. London and Halifax: Zed Books and Fernwood Books.

Hildyard, N. (1996) 'Public risk, private profit', *Ecologist*, 26: 176–8.

Hill, K. and Upchurch, D. M. (1995) 'Gender differences in child health: evidence from the demographic and health surveys', *Population and Development Review*, 21: 127–51.

Hodgkin, C. (1996) 'International harmonisation – the need for transparency', *International Journal of Risk Safety*, 9: 195–9.

Hsiao, W. C. L. (1995) 'The Chinese health care system: lessons for other nations', *Social Science and Medicine*, 41: 1047–55.

Hulme, D. and Edwards, M. (1997) 'Conclusion: too close to the powerful, too far from the powerless?', in Hulme, D. and Edwards, M. (eds), *NGOs, States and Donors. Too Close for Comfort?*, London and New York: Macmillan Press and St Martin's Press.

Hutchful, E. (1994) ' "Smoke and mirrors": the World Bank's social dimensions of adjustment (SDA) programme', *Review of African Political Economy*, 2: 569–84.

Hutton, W. (1995) *The State We're In*. London: Vintage Books.

ICO. (1995) *Division of Intensified Cooperation with Countries (ICO). Report on Activities 1990–1994*. Geneva: ICO/WHO.

IDA. (1960) *Articles of Agreement. As Approved for Submission to Governments by the Executive Directors of the International Bank for Reconstruction and Development*. Washington: IDA.

IFPMA. (1981) 'IFPMA code of pharmaceutical marketing practices', *World Development*, 11: 313–15.

Iglehart, J. K. (1994) 'The struggle between managed care and fee-for-service practice', *New England Journal of Medicine*, 331: 63–7.

Iliffe, S. and Freudenstein, U. (1994) 'Fundholding: from solution to problem', *British Medical Journal*, 308: 3–4.

Imersheim, A. W. and Estes, C. L. (1996) 'From health services to medical markets: the commodity transformation of medical production and the nonprofit sector', *International Journal of Health Services*, 26: 221–38.

IMF (1997) *International Monetary Fund Home Page.* Printed in April 1997. Internet: HTTP/
    WWW. IMF.ORG.
Information Research Ltd. (1980) *Opportunities for Pharmaceuticals in the Developing World over
    the Next Twenty Years.* Cited in Melrose, D. (1983).
Jain, A. (1995) 'Implementing the ICPD's message', *Studies in Family Planning,* 26,5: 296–8.
Jamison, D. T. and Jardel, J. P. (1993) 'Foreword: comparative health data and analyses', in
    Murray, C. J. L and Lopez, A. D. (eds), *Global Comparative Assessments in the Health Sector:
    Disease Burden, Expenditure and Intervention Packages.* Geneva: WHO.
Jarrett, S. and Ofusu-Amaah, S. (1992) 'Strengthening health services of MCH in Africa: the first
    five years of the "Bamako Initiative"', *Health Policy and Planning,* 7: 164–76.
Jaysena, K. (1985) 'Drugs – registration and marketing practices in the Third World', *Development
    Dialogue,* 2: 38–47.
Jensen, E., Kak, N., Satjawinate, K. *et al.* (1994) 'Contraceptive pricing and prevalence: family
    planning self-sufficiency in Indonesia', *International Journal of Health Planning and Manage-
    ment,* 9: 349–59.
Johnson, S. P. (1987) *World Population and the United Nations. Challenge and Response.* New York,
    Port Chester, Melbourne and Sydney: Cambridge University Press.
Johnson, S. P. (1995) *The Politics of Population. The International Conference on Population and
    Development. Cairo 1994.* London: Earthscan Publications.
Johnston, L. and Nicoll, R. (1997) 'Aids drugs cut to "guinea pigs"'. *The Observer,* 8 June 1997.
Jolly, R. and Cornia, G. A. (1984) 'The impact of world recession on children', *World Develop-
    ment,* 12: 3.
Jolly, R. (1988) 'From speeches to action: implementing what is agreed', *IDS Bulletin,* 49: 75–80.
Jolly, R. (1991a) 'UNICEF's real concerns with child health, population growth and ecological
    sustainability. Reply to Maurice King', *Nytt om U-lands Hälsovård,* 1: 10–16.
Jolly, R. (1991b) 'Adjustment with a human face: a UNICEF record and perspective on the
    1980s', *World Development,* 19: 1807–21.
Jolly, R. (1993) *UNICEF Support to Family Planning.* New York: UNICEF.
Jolly, R. and Singer, H. (1995) 'Fifty years on. The UN and economic and social development. An
    overview', *IDS Bulletin,* 26: 2–5.
Jolly, R. (1995) 'UN reform: focus for action', *IDS Bulletin,* 26,4: 8–14.
Jönsson, C. and Söderholm, P. (1996) 'IGO–NGO relation and HIV/AIDS: innovation or stale-
    mate ?', in Weiss, T. G. and Gordenker, L. (eds), *NGOS, the UN and Global Governance.*
    London: Lynne Rienner Publishers.
Joossens, L. and Raw, M. (1996) 'Are tobacco subsidies a misuse of public funds?' *British Medical
    Journal,* 312: 832–4.
Kane, N. M.(1995) 'Costs, productivity and financial outcomes of managed care', in Saltman, R.
    B. and von Otter, C. (eds), *Implementing Planned Markets in Health Care.* Buckingham: Open
    University Press.
Kanji, N. (1989) 'Charging drugs in Africa: UNICEF's Bamako initiative', *Health Policy and
    Planning,* 4: 110–20.
Kanji, N. (1992) 'Action at country level: the international and national influences', in Kanji, N.,
    Hardon, A., Harnmeijer, J., Mamdani, M. and Walt, G. (eds), *Drugs Policy in Developing
    Countries.* London and New York: Zed Books Ltd.
Kanji, N. and Hardon, A. (1992) 'What has been achieved and where are we now', in Kanji, N.,
    Hardon, A., Harnmeijer, J., Mamdani, M. and Walt, G. (eds), *Drugs Policy in Developing
    Countries.* London and New York: Zed Books Ltd.
Kanji, N and Jazdowska, N. (1993) 'Structural adjustment and women in Zimbabwe', *Review of
    African Political Economy,* 56: 11–26.
Kanji, N., Kanji, N. and Manji, F. (1991) 'From development to sustained crisis: structural adjust-
    ment, equity and health', *Social Science and Medicine,* 33: 948–93.
Kappagoda, N. (1995) *The Asian Development Bank.* London: Intermediate Technology
    Publications.
Kaprio, L. (1979) *Primary Health Care in Europe.* EURO Reports and Studies 14. Copenhagen:
    WHO.
Karcher, H. L. (1994) 'Germany hails health reforms as success', *British Medical Journal,* 308: 676.
Karkal, M. (1995) 'Politics of population at Cairo', *Economic and Political Weekly,* 30: 88–92.
Kessler, A. (1994) 'Family planning and the role of WHO', *World Health,* 3: 4–6.
Key, P. (1987) 'Women, health and development, with special reference to Indian women', *Health
    Policy and Planning,* 2: 58–69.

Khanna, J., Van Look, P. and Griffin, P. (1992) *Reproductive Health: a Key to a Brighter Future.* *Biennial Report 1990-1. Special 20th Anniversary Issue.* Geneva: WHO Special Programme of Research, Development and Research Training in Human Reproduction.

Khor, M. (1995a) ' "Don't tell me what to do" World Bank', *Third World Resurgence,* 60: 12–14.

Khor, M. (1995b) 'A worldwide fight against biopiracy and patents of life', *Third World Resurgence,* 63: 9–11.

Khor, M. (1997) 'WTO reform on the agenda? Competition policy: new threat to local firms', *Third World Resurgence,* 78: 20–7.

Kickbush, I. (1989) 'Healthy Cities: a working project and a growing movement', *Health Promotion International,* 4: 77–85.

Kickbush, I. (1995) 'World Health Organization: change and progress', *British Medical Journal,* 310: 1518–20.

Killick, T. (1995) *IMF Programmes in Developing Countries. Design and Impact.* London: Routledge.

Kimball, A. M. and Thant, M. (1996) 'A role for businesses in HIV prevention in Asia', *Lancet,* 347: 1670–2.

King, K. (1991) *Aid and Education in the Developing World. The Role of Donor Agencies in Educational Analysis.* Harlow: Longman.

King, M. (1990) 'Health is a sustainable state', *Lancet,* 336: 664–7.

King, M. (1991) 'An anomaly in the paradigm. The demographic trap. UNICEF's dilemma and its opportunities', *Nytt om U-lands Hålsovård,* 1: 5–9.

King, M. and Elliot, C. (1993) 'Legitimate double-think', *Lancet,* 341: 669–72.

King, M. and Elliot, C. (1994) 'Cairo: damp squid or Roman candle?', *Lancet,* 344: 528.

King, M. and Elliot, C. (1995) 'Double think – a reply', *World Health Forum,* 16: 293–8.

Kinnon, C. (1995) *WHO Task Force on Economics. WTO: What's in it for WHO?* Geneva: World Health Organization.

Kleckowski, B. M., Roemer, M. and van der Werff, A. (1984) *National Health Systems and their Reorientation towards Health for All. Guidance for Policy-making.* Public Health Papers No. 77. Geneva: WHO.

Klein, R. (1984) 'The politics of ideology vs reality of politics: the case of Britain's National Health Service in the 1980s', *Milbank Memorial Fund Quarterly/Health and Society,* 62: 82–109.

Klein, R. (1995a) 'Priorities and rationing: pragmatism or principles ?' *British Medical Journal,* 311:761–2.

Klein, R. (1995b) 'Big bang health care reform – does it work: the case of Britain's 1991 National Health Service reforms', *The Milbank Quarterly,* 73: 299–337.

Ko Ko, U. (1990) 'MCH in the context of primary health care: the WHO perspective', in Wallace, H. and Giri, K. (eds), *Health Care of Women and Children in Developing Countries.* Oakland: Third Party Publishing Company.

Kolodner, E. (1994) *Transnational Corporations: Impediments or Catalysts of Social Development?* UNRISD Occasional Paper 5. Geneva: UNRISD.

Korte, R., Richter, H., Merkle, F. and Görgen, H. (1992) 'Financing health services in sub-Saharan Africa: options for decision makers during adjustment', *Social Science and Medicine,* 34: 1–9.

Korten, D. (1991) 'The role of nongovernmental organizations in development: changing patterns and perspectives', in Paul, S. and Israel, A. (eds), *Nongovernmental Organizations and the World Bank.* Washington DC: World Bank.

Korten, D. (1995) *When Corporations Rule the World.* West Hartford and San Francisco: Kumarian Press Inc. and Berret-Koehler Publishers Inc.

Kothari, R. (1995) 'Globalization and "New World Order". What future for the United Nations?', *Economic and Political Weekly,* 30: 251–317.

Krugman, P. (1994) *Peddling Prosperity.* Massachusetts: Maid Press.

Krugman, P. (1996) *Pop Internationalism.* New York: WW. Norton.

Kuttner, R. (1996) *Everything for Sale.* New York: A. Knopf.

Kutzin, J. (1995) *Experience with Organizational and Financing Reform of the Health Sector.* Geneva: WHO Division of Strengthening of Health Services.

La Cheen, C. (1986) 'Population control and the pharmaceutical industry', in McDonnell, K. (ed.), *Adverse Effects. Women and the Pharmaceutical Industry.* Penang: IOCU. pp. 89–136.

Laga, M. (1995) 'STD control for HIV prevention – it works!', *Lancet,* 346: 518.

Lafond, A. (1994) 'UNICEF', *Health Policy and Planning,* 9: 343–6.

Lal, S. (1975) *Major Issues in Transfer of Technology to Developing Countries: a Case Study of the Pharmaceutical Industry.* TD/B/C.6/4. Geneva: UNCTAD.

Lancet. (1988) 'The Bamako Initiative', *Lancet,* 19 November: 1177–8.

Lancet. (1993a) 'World Bank cure for donor fatigue?', *Lancet,* 342: 63–4.

Lancet. (1993b) 'Whose future? Whose world?', *Lancet,* 342: 1125–6.

Lancet. (1994a) 'Structural adjustment too painful? ', *Lancet,* 344: 1377–8.

Lancet. (1994b) 'AIDS; The third wave', *Lancet,* 343: 186–8.

Lancet. (1995a) 'Fortress WHO: breaching the ramparts for health's sake', *Lancet,* 345: 203–4.

Lancet. (1995b) 'Turning to primary care', *Lancet,* 346: 1111.

Lancet. (1995c) 'European medicines in the 21st century', *Lancet,* 345: 1–2.

Lancet. (1995d) 'Bigger companies, better drugs?', *Lancet,* 346: 585.

Lancet. (1995e) 'Impact of HIV on delivery of health care in sub-Saharan Africa: a tale of secrecy and inertia', *Lancet,* 345: 1315–17.

Lancet. (1995f) 'Western eyes on China's eugenics law', *Lancet,* 346: 131.

Lancet. (1995g) 'Women in the world', *Lancet,* 346: 195.

Laurell, A. K. and Lopez-Arellano, O. (1996) 'Market commodities and poor relief: the World Bank proposal for health', *International Journal of Health Services,* 26: 1–18.

Lawrence, M. and Williams, T. (1996) 'Managed care and disease management in the NHS. What will be the role of the pharmaceutical industry', *British Medical Journal,* 13: 125–6.

Le Grand, A. (1992) 'The abortion pill: a solution for unsafe abortions in developing countries?', *Social Science and Medicine,* 35: 767–76.

Lee, K. (1994) 'The UNFPA: twenty-five years and beyond', *Health Policy and Planning,* 9: 223–8.

Lee, K. (1995) 'A neo-Gramscian approach to international organization: an expanded analysis of current reforms to UN development activities', in MacMillan, J. and Linklater, A. (eds), *Boundaries in Question: New Directions in International Relations.* London: Pinter.

Lee, K. and Walt, G. (1992) 'What role for WHO in the 1990s', *Health Policy and Planning,* 7: 387–90.

Lee, K. and Walt, G. (1995) 'Linking national and global population agendas: case studies from eight developing countries', *Third World Quarterly,* 16: 257–72.

Lee, K., Walt, G., Lush, L., Cleland, J., *et al.* (1994) *Population Policies and Programmes: Determinants and Consequences in Eight Developing Countries.* London School of Hygiene and Tropical Medicine and United Nations Population Fund.

Lee, K., Collinson, S., Walt, G. and Gilson, L. (1996) ' Who should be doing what in international health: a confusion of mandates in the United Nations?', *British Medical Journal,* 312: 302–6.

Lee, K. and Zwi, A. B.(1996) 'A global political economy approach to AIDS: ideology, interests and implications', *New Political Economy,* 1, 3: 355–73.

Leslie, J. (1992) 'Women's time and use of health services', *IDS Bulletin,* 23: 4–7.

Litvack, J. I. and Bodart, C. (1993) 'User fees plus quality equals improved access to health care: results of a field experiment in Cameroon', *Social Science and Medicine,* 37: 369–83.

Loewenson, R. (1993) 'Structural adjustment and health policy in Africa', *International Journal of Health Services,* 23: 717–30.

Logie, D. E., Woodroffe, J. (1993) 'Structural adjustment: the wrong prescription for Africa', *British Medical Journal,* 307: 41–44.

Lokayan Bulletin. (1994) 'Enough! 50 years of Bretton Woods institutions', *Lokayan Bulletin,* 11: 1–171.

London School of Hygiene and Tropical Medicine and Koninklijk Instituut voor de Tropen. (1989) *An Evaluation of WHO's Action Programme on Essential Drugs.* Submitted to the management advisory committee, the Action Programme on Essential Drugs. London and Amsterdam: School of Hygiene and Tropical Medicine and Koninklijk Instituut voor de Tropen.

Longford, M. (1996) 'NGOs and the rights of the child', in Willets (ed.), *The Conscience of the World. The Influence of the Non-governmental Organizations in the UN system.* London: Hurst and Company.

LSHTM/KIT. (1989) 'An Evaluation of WHO's Action Programme on Essential Drugs', London: LSHTM/KIT.

Lugalla, J. L. P. (1995) 'The impact of structural adjustment policies on women's and children's health in Tanzania', *Review of African Political Economy,* 63: 43–53.

Macintosh, M. (1992) 'Questioning the state', in Wyuts, M., Macintosh, M. and Hewitt, T. (eds), *Development Policy and Public Action.* Oxford: Oxford University Press and Open University.

Macintosh, M. (1995) 'Competition and contracting in selective social provisioning', *The European Journal of Development Research,* 7: 26–52.

Mahler, H. (1981) 'The meaning of "Health for all by the year 2000"', *World Health Forum,* 2: 5–22.

Mahler, H. (1984) 'The monitoring process has been set in motion', *World Health Forum,* 5: 99–103.

Mamdani, M. (1992) 'Early initiatives in essential drugs policy', in Kanji, N., Hardon, A., Harnmeijer, J., Mamdani, M. and Walt, G. (eds), *Drugs Policy in Developing Countries.* London and New York: Zed Books Ltd.

Mamdani, M., Garner, P., Harpham,T. and Campbell, O. (1993) 'Fertility and contraceptive use in poor urban areas of developing countries', *Health Policy and Planning,* 8: 1–18.

Mann, J. and Chin, J. (1988) 'AIDS: a global perspective', *New England Journal of Medicine,* 319: 302–3

Mangelsdorf, K. L., Luna, J. and Smith, H. L. (1988) 'Primary health care and public policy', *World Health Forum,* 3: 509–13.

Martines, J., Phillips, M. and Feachem, R. (1993) 'Diarrhoeal diseases', in Jamison, D. T., Mosley, W. H., Measham, A. R. and Bobadilla, J. L. (eds), *Disease Control Priorities in Developing Countries.* New York: World Bank and Oxford University Press.

Martins, H. (1983) 'Pharmaceutical policy in independent Mozambique: the first years', *IDS Bulletin,* 14, 4: 62–9.

Marwick. (1995) 'Growing use of medicinal botanicals forces assessment by drug regulators', *Journal of American Medical Association,* 273: 607–9.

Mason, E. S. and Asher, R. E. (1973) *The World Bank since Bretton Woods.* Washington, DC: The Brookings Institution.

Mastroianni, L., Donaldson, P. and Kane, T. (eds). (1990) *Developing New Contraceptives. Obstacles and Opportunities.* Washington, DC: National Academy Press.

May, N. (1995) 'Performance and accountability in the New World Order', *Development in Practice,* 5: 71–3.

Mayhew, S. (1996) 'Integrating MCH/FP and STD/HIV services: current debates and future directions', *Health Policy and Planning,* 11, 4: 339–53.

Maynard, A. (1993) 'Competition in the UK national health service: mission impossible?', *Health Policy,* 23:193–204.

Maynard, A. (1994) 'Can competition enhance efficiency in health care? Lessons from the reform of the UK national health service', *Social Science and Medicine,* 39: 1433–45.

Maynard, A. and Bloor, J. (1995) 'Health care reform. Informing difficult choices', *International Journal of Health Planning and Management,* 10: 247–64.

Mayor, S. (1997) 'Hong Kong University turns down tobacco money', *British Medical Journal,* 314: 169.

Mbugua, J. K., Bloom, G. H. and Segall, M. (1995) 'Impact of user charges on vulnerable groups: the case of Kibwezi in rural Kenya', *Social Science and Medicine,* 41: 829–35.

Mburu, F. M. (1989) 'Non-government organizations in the health field: collaboration, integration and contrasting aims in Africa', *Social Science and Medicine,* 29: 591–7.

McArthur, J. H. and Moore, F. D. (1997) 'The two cultures and the health care revolution. Commerce and professionalism in medical care', *Journal of American Medical Association,* 277: 985–9.

McCarthy, M. (1996)' Sponsors lose fight to stop thyroxine study publication', *Lancet,* 349: 1149.

McCarthy, M. (1994) 'US global population-control programme', *Lancet,* 343: 227.

McGillivray, M. (1991) 'The human development index: yet another redundant composite development indicator?' *World Development,* 19: 1461–8.

McIntosh, C. A. and Crane, J. L. (1995) 'The Cairo conference on population and development: a new paradigm?', *Population and Development Review,* 21: 223–61.

McIntosh, C. A. and Finkle, J. L. (1994) 'The politics of family planning: issues for the future', *Population and Development Review,* 20 (supplement): 265–75.

McIntosh, C. A. and Finkle, J.L.(1995) ' The Cairo conference on population and development: a new Paradigm?', *Population and Development Review,* 21: 223–61.

McNicoll, G. (1995) 'On population growth and revisionism: further questions', *Population and Development Review,* 21:307-40.

McPake, B., Hanson, K. and Mills, A. (1992) *Implementing the Bamako Initiative in Africa. A Review of Five Case Studies.* PHP Department Publications No. 8. London: London School of Hygiene and Tropical Medicine.

McPake, B., Ajuong, F., Forsberg, B., Liambilla, W. and Olenja, J. (1993) 'The Kenyan model of Bamako initiative: potential and limitations', International Journal of Health Planning and Management 8:123-8.

McPake, B. and Hongoro, C. (1995) 'Contracting out clinical services in Zimbabwe', *Social Science and Medicine,* 41: 13–24.

McPake, B. and Ngalande-Banda, E. (1994) 'Contracting out of health services in developing countries', *Health Policy and Planning,* 9: 25–30.

Melrose, D. (1982) *Bitter Pills. Medicines and the Third World Poor.* Oxford: OXFAM.

Melrose, D. (1983) 'Double deprivation: public and private drug distribution from the perspective of the Third World poor', *World Development,* 11: 181–6.

Mendehlson, S., Böll, W., Lehmann, L., Hirstiö-Snellman, P., Ward, S. and Toivonen, J. (1993) *Evaluation of the United Nations Population Fund (UNFPA). Synthesis Report.* CIDA, FINNIDA and BMZ.

Michaud, C. and Murray, C. J. L. (1994) 'External assistance to the health sector in developing countries. A detailed analysis 1972–1990', in Murray, C. J. L. and Lopez, A. D. (eds), *Global Comparative Assessments in the Health Sector: Disease Burden, Expenditure and Intervention Packages.* Geneva: WHO.

Mills, A. (1995) *Improving the Efficiency of Public Sector Health Services in Developing Countries: Bureaucratic versus Market Approaches.* PHP Departmental Publication No 17. London: London School of Hygiene and Tropical Medicine.

Mills, A., Vaughan, J. P., Smith, D. L. and Tabibzadeh, I. (1990) *Health System Decentralization. Concepts, Issues and Country Experience.* Geneva: WHO.

Mintzes, B., Hardon, A. and Hanhart, J. (1993) *Norplant: under Her Skin,* Amsterdam: WEMOS.

Miró, C.A. (1977) 'The World Population Plan of Action: a political instrument whose potential has not been realized', *Population and Development Review,* 3: 421–42.

Mistry, P. S. (1995) *Multilateral Development Banks. An Assessment of their Financial Structures, Policies and Practices.* The Hague: FONDAD.

Mnyika, K. S.and Killewo, J. Z. J.(1991) 'Irrational drug use in Tanzania', *Health Policy and Planning,* 6: 180–4.

Mohanty, M. (1995) 'On the concept of empowerment', *Economic and Political Weekly,* 30: 1434–6.

Moran, M. and Wood, B. (1996) 'The globalization of health care policy?', in Gummet, P. (ed.), *Globalization and Public Policy.* Cheltenham: Edgar Elgar Publishing Ltd.

Moses, S., Manji, F., Bradley, J. E., Nagelkerke, N. J. D., Malisa, M. A. and Plummer, F. A. (1992) 'Impact of user fees on attendance at a referral centre for sexually transmitted diseases in Kenya', *Lancet,* 340: 463–6.

Mosher, S. (1983) *Broken Earth: the Rural Chinese.* New York: The Free Press.

Mosley, W. H. (1985) 'Child survival: research and policy', *World Health Forum,* 6: 352–60.

Mosley, P., Harrigan, J. and Toye, J. (1991) *Aid and Power. The World Bank and Policy Based Lending.* Vol I–II. London: Routledge.

Muhuri, P. K. and Preston, S. H. (1991) 'Effects of family composition on mortality differentials by sex among children in Matlab, Bangladesh', *Population Development Review,* 17: 431–49.

Murray, C. J. L. (1994) 'Quantifying the burden of disease: the technical basis for disability-adjusted life years', *Bulletin of the World Health Organization,* 72: 429–45.

Murray, C. J. L. and Lopez, A. D. (1994) 'Quantifying disability: data, methods and results', *Bulletin of the World Health Organization,* 72: 481–94.

Murray, C. J. L. and Lopez, A. D. (1997) 'Mortality by cause for eight regions of the world: global burden of disease study', *Lancet,* 349: 1269–76.

Muschell, J. (1995) *Privatization in Health. Health Economics. Technical Briefing Note.* WHO Task Force on Health Economics. Geneva: WHO.

Nabarro, D. and Chinnock, P. (1988) 'Growth monitoring – inappropriate promotion of an appropriate technology', *Social Science and Medicine,* 26: 941–8.

Nandan, G. (1993) 'India to ban prenatal sex determination', *British Medical Journal,* 306: 353.

Nassim, J. and Sai, F. (1990) 'Family Planning and maternal and child health in the World Bank's population, health and nutrition program', in Wallace, H. and Giri, K. (eds), *Health Care of Women and Children in Developing Countries.* Oakland: Third Party Publishing Company.

Nature. (1994) 'China's misconception of eugenics', *Nature,* 367: 1–2.

Navarro, V. (1984) 'A critique of the ideological and political positions of the Brandt report and the Alma Ata Declaration', *International Journal of Health Services,* 14: 159–72.

Newell, K. W. (1988) 'Selective primary health care: the counter revolution', *Social Science and Medicine,* 26: 903–6.

Nichter, M. (1995) 'Vaccinations in the Third World: a consideration of community demand', *Social Science and Medicine,* 41: 617–32.

Nittayaramphong, S. and Tangcharoensathien, V. (1994) 'Thailand: private care out of control',

Health Policy and Planning, 9: 31–40.

Nord, E., Richardson, J., Street, A., Kuhse, H. and Singer, P. (1995) 'Who cares about cost? Does economic analysis impose or reflect social values', *Health Policy,* 34: 79–94.

Nordic UN project. (1991a) *The United Nations in Development.* Stockholm: Almqvist and Wiksell.

Nordic UN project. (1991b) *Perspectives on Multilateral Assistance.* Stockholm: Almqvist and Wiksell.

Nordic UN project. (1991c) *The United Nations, Issues and Options.* Stockholm: Almqvist and Wiksell.

Nordic UN Reform. (1996) *The United Nations in Development. Strengthening the UN through Change: Fulfilling its Economic and Social Mandate.* Oslo: The Nordic Reform Project, GCSM AS.

OECD. (1992a) *The Reform of Health Care. A Comparative Analysis of Seven OECD Countries.* Paris: OECD.

OECD. (1992b) *Development Assistance Manual. DAC Principles for Effective Aid.* Paris: OECD.

OECD. (1994) *The Reform of Health Care Systems. A Review of Seventeen OECD Countries.* OECD Health Policy Studies No. 5. Paris: OECD.

OECD. (1995) *New Directions in Health Policy.* Health Policy Studies No 7. Paris: OECD.

OECD. (1996a) *Beyond 2000: the New Social Policy Agenda.* Conference issues paper. Paris: OECD.

OECD (1996b) *Aid and Other Resource Flows to the Central and Eastern European Countries and the New Independent States of the Former Soviet Union (1990–1994).* Paris: OECD.

OECD (1996c) 'Multilateral investment negotiations on course', OECD letter, 5 June 1996.

OECD. (1997) *OECD Home Page.* HTTP://WWW. OECD.ORG. OECD: Paris.

Ofosu-Amaah, V. (1983) *National Experience in the Use of Community Health Workers. A Review of Current Issues and Problems.* WHO Offset Publication No 71. Geneva: WHO.

Okojie, C. (1994) 'Gender inequalities in health in the Third World', *Social Science and Medicine,* 39: 1237–47.

Okuonzi, S. A. and Macrae, J. (1995) 'Whose policy is it anyway? International and national influences on health policy development in Uganda', *Health Policy and Planning,* 10: 122–32.

Ollila, E. and Hemminki, E. (1996) 'Secrecy in drug regulation. Licensing documentation on the Norplant contraceptive', *Risk and Safety in Medicine,* 9: 161–72.

Opit, L. (1987) 'How should information on health care be generated and used?', *World Health Forum,* 8: 409–17.

OTA. (1993) *Drug Labelling in Developing Countries.* Congress of the United States, Office of Technology Assessment. Washington, DC: Government Printing Office.

Ottawa Charter on Health Promotion. (1986) An International Conference on Health Promotion. Organized by WHO, Health and Welfare in Canada and Canadian Public Health Association. 17–21 November. Ottawa, Canada.

Otting, A. (1994) 'The international labour organization and its standard-setting activity in the area of social security', *Journal of European Social Policy,* 4: 51–72.

Owoh, K. (1996) 'Fragmenting health care: the World Bank prescription in Africa', *Alternatives,* 21: 211–35.

Oxfam. (1995a) *The Oxfam Poverty Report.* Oxford: Oxfam Publications.

Oxfam. (1995b) *A Case for Reform. Fifty Years of the IMF and World Bank.* Oxford: Oxfam.

Packard, R. M., Wisner, B. and Bossert, T. 'Introduction', *Social Science and Medicine,* 1989, 28: 414–15.

Packard, R. and Epstein, P. (1991) 'Epidemiologists, social scientists, and the structure of medical research on AIDS in Africa', *Social Science and Medicine,* 33: 771–94.

PAHO/WHO. (1977) *PAHO's Cooperation in the Health Sector Reform Process.* PAHO/WHO.

Paker, D. and Jespersen, E. (1994) *20/20. Mobilizing Resources for Children in the 1990s.* UNICEF Staff Working Papers No. 12. New York: UNICEF.

Paphassarang, C., Tomson, G., Choprapawon, C. and Weerasuriya, K. (1995) 'The Lao national drug policy: lessons along the journey', *Lancet,* 345: 433–5.

Parnell, B., Lie, G., Hernandez, J. and Robins, C. (1996) 'Development and the HIV epidemic. A forward-looking evaluation of the approach of the UNDP HIV and development programme', http//www.undp.org/hiv/ toc.htm.

Patel, S. (1983a) 'Third World initiatives on pharmaceuticals: a documentation for the record', *IDS Bulletin,* 14,4: 71–8.

Patel, M. (1983b) 'Drug costs in developing countries and policies to reduce them', *World*

Development, 11,3: 195–204.

Patel, M. (1986) 'An economic evaluation of "Health for All"', *Health Policy and Planning,* 1: 37–47.

Paul, S. (1987) *Community Participation in Development Projects.* World Bank Discussion Papers 6. Washington, DC: World Bank.

Paul, S. and Israel, A. (1991) *Non-governmental Organizations and the World Bank. Cooperation for Development.* World Bank Regional and Sectoral Studies. Washington, DC: World Bank.

Paul, S. and Paul, J. A. (1995) 'The World Bank, pensions, and income (in)security in the global south', *International Journal of Health Services,* 25: 697–726.

Payer, C. (1982) *The World Bank. A Critical Analysis.* New York and London: Monthly Review Press.

Peabody, J. W. (1995) 'An organizational analysis of the World Health Organization: narrowing the gap between promise and performance', *Social Science and Medicine,* 40: 731–42.

Pearce, N. (1992) 'Adverse reactions: the fenoterol saga', in Davis, P. (ed.), *For Health or for Profit: Medicine, the Pharmaceutical Industry and the State in New Zealand.* Auckland, Oxford, New York and Melbourne: Oxford University Press, pp. 75–97.

Peretz, S. M. (1983) 'Pharmaceuticals in the Third World: the problem from the suppliers' point of view', *World Development,* 11,3: 259–64.

Petchesky, R. P. (1995) 'From population control to reproductive rights: feminist fault lines', *Reproductive Health Matters,* 6: 152–61.

Phillips, J., Simmons, R., Chakraborty, J., Chowdhury, A. (1984) 'Integrating health services in an MCH-FP program: lessons from Matlab, Bangladesh', *Studies in Family Planning,* 15,4: 153–61.

Pierotti, D., Blayo, C. (1994) 'The long march from abortion to contraception', *World Health,* 47, 3: 18–19.

Pietilä, H. (1985) UNDP. *YK:n kehitysyhteistyön sydän.* Suomen Helsinki: YK-liitto.

Prakash, P. (1994) 'Changing priorities in health care', *Economic and Political Weekly,* 29: 661–2.

Pritchett, L. (1994) 'Desired fertility and the impact on population policies', *Population and Development Review,* 20: 1–55.

Prost, A. and Jancloes, M. (1993) 'Rationales for choice in public health: The role of epidemiology', in Jamison, D. T., Mosley, W. H., Measham, A. R. and Bobadilla, J. L. (eds), *Disease Control Priorities in Developing Countries.* New York: World Bank and Oxford University Press. Appendix D.

Prudencio, I. and Tognoni, G. (1987) 'Essential drugs policy in Bolivia', *Health Policy and Planning,* 2: 301–8.

Puiggros, A. (1997) 'World Bank education policy: market liberalism meets ideological conservatism', *International Journal of Health Services,* 27: 217–26.

Qadeer, I. (1994) 'The brave new world of primary health care', *Social Scientist,* 22: 27–39.

Raghavan, C. (1995) 'Biopiracy reaches new heights', *Third World Resurgence,* 63: 12–15.

Razum, O. (1993) 'Mothers voice their opinion on immunization services', *World Health Forum,* 14: 282–6.

Reality of Aid 1995. (1995) An independent review of international aid. ICVA, Eurostep.

Reality of Aid 1996. (1996) *An Independent Review of International Aid.* ICVA, Eurostep, Earth-scan.

Reich, M. (1994) 'Bangladesh pharmaceutical policy and politics', *Health Policy and Planning,* 9,2: 130–43.

Relman, A. (1991) 'The health care industry: where is it taking us?', *New England Journal of Medicine,* 325: 854–9.

Ren, X. (1995) 'Sex differences in infant and child mortality in three provinces in China', *Social Science and Medicine,* 40: 1259–69.

Ribe, H. and Carvalho, S. (1990) *World Bank Treatment of the Social Impact of Adjustment Programs.* Working Papers 521. Washington, DC: World Bank.

Rich, B. (1989) 'The "greening" of development banks: rhetoric and reality', *Ecologist,* 19: 44–52.

Rich, B. (1994) *Mortgaging the Earth. The World Bank, Environmental Impoverishment and the Crisis of Development.* London: Earthscan.

Rich, B. (1995) *Statement of Bruce Rich on behalf of Environmental Defense Fund, National Wildlife Federation, Sierra Club and Greenpeace. March 27. 1995.* Washington, DC: Environmental Defense Fund

Richter, J. (1993) *Vaccination against Pregnancy. Miracle or Menace?* Bielefeld: HAI and BUKO.

Rifkin, S. and Walt, G. (1986) 'Why health improves: defining the issues concerning comprehensive primary health care and selective primary health care', *Social Science and Medicine*, 23: 559–66.

Righter, R. (1995) *Utopia Lost. The United Nations and World Order*. New York: Twentieth Century Fund Press.

Robinson, M. (1997) 'Privatising the voluntary sector: NGOs as public services contractors', in Hulme, D. and Edwards, M. (eds), *NGOs, States and Donors. Too Close for Comfort?* London and New York: MacMillan Press and St Martin's Press.

Robinson, J. C. (1996) 'The dynamics and limits of corporate growth in health care'. *Health Affairs* (Summer): 155–69.

Rockefeller Foundation. (1996) *Pocantico Retreat. Enhancing the Performance of International Health Institutions*. Cambridge, MA: Rockefeller Foundation, Social Science Research Council and Harvard School of Public Health.

Roemer, J. E. (1993) 'Distributing health: the allocation of resources by an international agency', in Sen, A. and Nussbaum, M. (eds), *The Quality of Life*. New York: Oxford University Press.

Rosenberg, S. A. (1996) 'Secrecy in medical research', *New England Journal of Medicine*, 6: 392–4.

Russel, S. and Gilson, L. (1995) *User Fees at Government Health Services: Is Equity Being Considered?* PHP Departmental Publication No 15. London: London School of Hygiene and Tropical Medicine.

Sachs, W. (1991) 'Environment and development. The story of a dangerous liaison', *Ecologist*, 21: 252–7.

Sadik, N. (1992) 'Public policy and private decisions: world population and world health in the 21st century', *Journal of Public Health Policy*, 13: 133–9.

Sadik, N (ed.) (1994) *Making a Difference: Twenty-five years of UNFPA Experience*. New York: PPC Group, UNFPA.

'Safe motherhood, reproductive health and population policies'. (1994) *Safe Motherhood Newsletter*, 14: 4–10.

Sai, F. T. and Chester, L. A. 'The role of the World Bank in shaping the Third World population policy', in Roberts, G. (ed.), *Population Policy: Contemporary Issues*. New York: Praeger.

Salmen, L. F. and Eaves, A. P. (1991) 'Interactions between non-governmental organizations, governments, and the World Bank: evidence from Bank projects', in Paul, S. and Israel, A. (eds), *Non-governmental Organizations and the World Bank. Cooperation for Development*. Washington, DC: World Bank Regional and Sectoral Studies.

Salmon, J. W. (1995) 'A perspective on the corporate transformation of health care', *International Journal of Health Services*, 25: 11–42.

Saltman, R. and von Otter, C.(1995) *Implementing Planned Markets in Health Care*. Buckingham: Open University Press.

Samba, E. M. (1981) 'Primary health care: unknowns, pitfalls, and hazards', *World Health Forum*, 2: 358–63.

Samson, K. T.(1995) 'The record of WHO and PAHO', *UN Special*, 1: 18–20.

Sanders, D. and Sambo, A. (1991) 'AIDS in Africa: the implications of economic recession and structural adjustment', *Health Policy and Planning*, 6: 157–65.

Sathyamala. (1989) Immunization. Seminar 354: 26–29.

Schieber, G. J. (1995) 'Preconditions for health reform: experiences from the OECD countries', *Health Policy*, 32: 279–93.

Schmidt, E. (1997) 'The World Bank and Russian oil', *Ecologist*, 27: 21–8.

Segall, M. (1983) 'The politics of primary health care', *IDS Bulletin*, 14: 27–37.

Selvaggio, K. (1984) 'World Health Organization bottles up alcohol study', *International Journal of Health Services*, 14: 303–9.

Sen, S. (1996) 'Debt, development and the International Monetary Fund', in Griesbarger, J. M. and Gunter, B. G. (eds), *The World's Monetary System. Toward Stability and Sustainability in the Twenty-first Century*. London: Pluto Press.

Seventh Consultative Committee on Primary Health Care Systems for the 21st Century. 'Health Care Systems for the 21st Century', *British Medical Journal*, 314: 1407–9.

Shaw, R. O. and Griffin, C. C. (1995) *Financing Health Care in Sub-Saharan Africa through User Fees and Insurance*. Washington, DC: World Bank.

Shelton, J. and Calla, C. (1991) Letter to the IPPF representing the views of USAID on IPPF draft, 'Medical and service delivery guidelines', 21 August.

Sherraden, M. S. and Wallace, S. P. (1992) 'Innovation in primary health care: community health services in Mexico and the United States', *Social Science and Medicine*, 35: 1433–43.

Shiva, V. (1994a) 'After 50 years, is the World Bank socially and environmentally responsible?' *Third World Resurgence*, 49: 22–4.

Shiva, V. (1994b) 'Whose choice? Whose life? Whose security?', *Third World Resurgence*, 49: 4–6.
Shiva, V. (1995) 'Who are the real pirates?', *Third World Resurgence*, 63: 16–17.
Siddiqi, J. (1995) *World Health and World Politics*. London: Hurst and Company.
Siegel-Itzkovich, J.(1997) 'WHO calls for tighter controls on Internet', *British Medical Journal*, 314: 1504.
Silverman, M., Lee, P. and Lydecker, M. (1986) 'Drug promotion: the Third World revisited', *International Journal of Health Services*, 16: 659–67.
Simons, H. (1995) 'Cairo: repacking population control', *International Journal of Health Services*, 25: 559–66.
Singer, H. W. (1995) 'Revitalizing United Nations: five proposals', *IDS Bulletin*, 26: 35–40.
Singer, H. V. (1995) 'Rethinking Bretton Woods from an historical perspective', in Griesbarger, J. M. and Gunther, B. G. (eds), *Promoting Development. Effective Global Institutions for the Twenty-first Century*. London: Pluto Press.
Singh, A. (1996) 'Pension reform, the stock market, capital formation and economic growth: a critical commentary on the World Bank proposals', *International Social Security Review*, 49: 21–41.
Skeet, M. (1984) 'Community health workers: promoters or inhibitors of primary health care ?', *World Health Forum*, 5: 291–5.
Smillie, I. (1995) *The Alms Bazaar. Altruism under Fire – Non-profit Organizations and International Development*. London: Intermediate Technology Publications Ltd.
Smith, D. and Bryant, J. H. (1988) 'Building the infrastructure for primary health care: an overview of vertical and integrated approaches', *Social Science and Medicine*, 26: 909–17.
Smith, R. (1993) 'Overpopulation and overconsumption', *British Medical Journal*, 306: 1285–6.
Smith, R. (1995) 'The WHO: change or die' (editorial), *British Medical Journal*, 310: 543–54.
Smith, R. (1996) 'Global competition in health care', (editorial) *British Medical Journal*, 313: 764–5.
Smith, R. and Leaning, J. (1993) 'Medicine and global survival. A new journal for the world's most pressing problems', *British Medical Journal*, 307: 693–4.
Smith, S. R. and Lipsky, M. (1992) 'Privatization in health and human services: a critique', *Journal of Health Politics, Policy and Law*, 17: 233–51.
South Centre. (1995) *The Uruguay Round. Intellectual Property Rights Regime. Implications for the Developing Countries*. Prepublication text. Geneva: South Centre.
South Centre. (1996) *A South Perspective on United Nations Reform*. Geneva: South Centre.
Sparr, P. (1994) *Mortgaging Women's Lives. Feminist Critiques of Structural Adjustment*. London: Zed Books.
Speth, J. G. (1994) 'Building a new UNDP: Agenda for Change'. Presentation to the UNDP Executive Board. 17 February.
Standing, H. (1997) 'Gender and equity in health sector reform programmes: a review', *Health Policy and Planning*, 12: 1–18.
Statement of the International Working Group on Transparency and Accountability in Drug Regulation. (1996) *Risk and Safety in Medicine*, 9: 211–17.
State's Role in Women's Empowerment. (1994) 'For better of for worse?', *Economic and Political Weekly*, 29: 3187–90.
Stefanini, A. (1995) 'Sustainability of NGOs', *World Health Forum*, 16: 42–6.
Stemerding, B. (1994) 'Reacting by WGNRR coordination office', *WGNRR Newsletter*, 48: 15–17.
Stenson, B. and Sterky, G. (1993) *SAREC/SIDA and WHO. A New Approach*. Stockholm: Department of International Health Care Research (ICHAR), Karolinska Institutet.
Stenzl, C. (1981) 'The role of international organizations in medicines policy', in Blum, C. *et al.* (eds), *Pharmaceuticals and Health Policy*. London: Croom Helm.
Stephenson, P., Wagner, M., Badea, M., Şerbanescu, F. (1992) 'Commentary: the public health consequences of restricted induced abortions: lessons from Romania', *American Journal of Public Health*, 82: 1328–31.
Sterky, G. (1985) 'Another development of pharmaceuticals: an introduction', *Development Dialogue*, 2: 5–13.
Sterky, G., Forss, K. and Stenson, B. (1996a) *Tomorrow's Global Health Organization: Ideas and Options*. Stockholm: Ministry of Foreign Affairs.
Sterky, G., Bidwai, P., Trung, T. T., Childers, E., Chunharas, S., Dan, Y. *et al.* (1996b) *Global Health Cooperation in the Twenty-first Century and the Role of the UN System*. Uppsala: Dag Hammarskjöld Foundation.

Stichele, M. (1994) 'Accountability and the World Trade Organization', in Cavanagh, J., Wysham, D. and Arruda, M. (eds), *Beyond Bretton Woods. Alternatives to the Global Economic Order*. London: Pluto Press.

Stichele, M. (1996) *The World Trade Organization. The Ministerial Conference in Singapore and the Developing Countries. An Introduction*. Amsterdam: Transnational Institute.

Stone, L. (1987) 'Cultural crossroads of community participation in development: a case from Nepal', cited in Foster, G. M. (1987), 'Bureaucratic aspects of international health agencies', *Social Science and Medicine*, 25: 1039–48.

Tarimo, E. and Webster, E. G. (1996) *Primary Health Care Concepts and Challenges in a Changing World*. Division of Strengthening of Health Services. Current Concerns. SHS Paper No. 7. Geneva: WHO.

Taylor, C. and Jolly, R. (1988) 'The straw men of primary health care', *Social Science and Medicine*, 26: 971–7.

Taylor, D. (1986) 'The pharmaceutical industry and health in the Third World', *Social Science and Medicine*, 22:1141-9.

Taylor, R. (1993) 'EC's medical markets are opened up', *British Medical Journal*, 306: 86.

The World Population Plan of Action. (1977) 'Documents', *Population and Development Review*, 1: 163–81.

Thomason, J., Mulou, N. and Bass, C. (1994) 'User charges for rural health services in Papua New Guinea', *Social Science and Medicine*, 39: 1105–15.

Thomason, J, Kolehmainen-Aitken, R.-L. and Newbrander, W. C. (1991) 'Decentralization of health services in Papua New Guinea: a critical review', in Thomason, J., Newbrander, W. C. and Kolehmainen-Aitken, R.-L. (eds), *Decentralization in a Developing Country: the Experience of Papua New Guinea and its Health Service*. Canberra: Australian National University, National Centre for Development Studies. Cited in Kutzin, J. (1995) *Experience with Organizational and Financing Reform of the Health Sector*. Current Concerns. SHS Paper No. 8. Geneva: WHO.

Tinker, A. and Koblinsky, M. (1993) *Making Motherhood Safe*. World Bank Discussion Papers 202. Washington, DC: World Bank.

Townsend, J. and Khan, M. (1993) 'Target setting in family planning programme: problems and potential alternatives', *Demography India*, 22: 113–25.

Tsouros, A. D. (1995) 'The WHO Healthy Cities project: state of the art and future plans', *Health Promotion International*, 10:133–41.

Tussie, D. (1995) *The Inter-American Development Bank*. London: Intermediary Technology Publications.

Ugalde, A. and Jackson, J. T. (1995) 'The World Bank and international health policy: A critical review', *Journal of International Development*, 7: 525–41.

UNDP. (1990) *Human Development Report*. New York: Oxford University Press.

UNDP. (1991) *Human Development Report*. New York: Oxford University Press.

UNDP. (1992) *Human Development Report*. New York: Oxford University Press.

UNDP. (1993a) *Heading for Change. UNDP Annual Report*. New York: UNDP.

UNDP. (1993b) *Human Development Report*. New York: Oxford University Press.

UNDP. (1994) *Human Development Report*. New York: Oxford University Press.

UNDP. (1995a) *Building a New UNDP. UNDP Annual Report 1994/1995*. New York: UNDP.

UNDP. (1995b). *Developing Countries Show Increasing Support for UNDP*. Press Release. New York: UNDP. 3 November.

UNDP. (1996) *Human Development Report*. New York: Oxford University Press.

UNFPA. (1990) *1990 Report*. New York: UNFPA.

UNFPA. (1994) *Report '94*. New York: Phoenix-Trykkeriet, UNFPA.

UNFPA. (1995a) *China*. A statement received on 30 August.

UNFPA. (1995b) *Programme Priorities and Future Directions of UNFPA in the Light of the International Conference on Population and Development (ICPD). Report of the Executive Director*. DP/1995/25. New York: UNFPA.

UNFPA. (1995c) *Report 1995*. New York: UNFPA.

UNFPA (1995d) *The State of the World's Population 1995*. New York: UNFPA.

UNFPA (1996a) *Mission Statement*. DP/1996/19, Adnex. New York: UNFPA.

UNFPA. (1996b) *A Revised Approach for the Allocation of UNFPA Resources to Country Programmes*. DP/FPA/1996/15. New York: UNFPA.

UNFPA. (1997a) 'Basic facts about UNFPA', internet: //www.unfpa.org/ facts.html. Printed in May 1997.

UNFPA. (1997b) *Report of the Executive Director for 1996. Programme Priorities.* DP/FPA/ 1997/10 (Part I). New York: UNFPA.

Unger, J. P., Mbaye, A. and Diao, M. (1990) 'From Bamako to Kolda: a case study of medicines and the financing of district health services', *Health Policy and Planning,* 5: 367–77.

Unger, J.-P.and Killingsworth, J. R. (1986) 'Selective primary health care: a critical review of methods and results', *Social Science and Medicine,* 22: 1001–13.

UNICEF. (1990) *Development Goals and Strategies for Children in the 1990s. A Unicef Policy Review.* New York: UNICEF.

UNICEF. (1993a) *UNICEF Annual Report.* New York: UNICEF.

UNICEF. (1993b) *UNICEF Policy on Family Planning.* UNICEF Executive Board. New York: UNICEF.

UNICEF. (1994) *UNICEF Annual Report.* New York: UNICEF.

UNICEF. (1995a) *UNICEF Annual Report.* New York: UNICEF.

UNICEF. (1995b) *UNICEF Management Study. Executive Summary.* E/ICEF/1995.

UNICEF. (1995c) *Health Strategy for UNICEF.* 1995 E/ICEF/1995/11/rev 1.

UNICEF. (1995d) *UNICEF Follow-up to the International Conference on Population and Development.* UNICEF, EB 29 June 1995. New York: UNICEF.

UNICEF. (1996a) *UNICEF Annual Report.* New York: UNICEF.

UNICEF. (1996b) *Management Excellence Progress Report: Recommendation on the Roles of Country, Regional and Headquarters Offices and Responsibility for Managing with National Committees.* UNICEF. E/ICEF/1996/AB/L.13. New York: UNICEF.

'UNICEF today'. (1994) *Child Health News and Review,* 2: 1–15.

Union of International Associations (ed.) (1992) *Yearbook of International Organisations 1992/1993.* München: Saur.

United Nations. (1992) *Basic Facts about the United Nations.* New York: United Nations.

United Nations. (1994a) *United Nations Handbook.* Wellington: New Zealand Ministry of Foreign Affairs and Trade.

United Nations. (1994b) *NGLS Handbook.* Geneva: United Nations Non-Governmental Liaison Service/UNCTAD.

United Nations. (1995) *Basic Facts.* Geneva: United Nations.

United States International Population Policy. (1982) Executive summary of 'Implications of worldwide population growth for US security and overseas interests', issued in December 1974. *Population and Development Review,* 8: 423–34.

UNRISD. (1995) States in Disarray. UNRISD: Geneva.

'Unsafe abortion'.(1993) *Planned Parenthood Challenges,* 1.

Use of WHO Certification Scheme on the Quality of Pharmaceutical Products Moving in International Commerce. (1994) Geneva: WHO, Action Programme on Essential Drugs.

Vågerö, D. (1994) 'Equity and efficiency in health reform: a European view', *Social Science and Medicine,* 39: 1203–10.

Van de Ven, W. P. M. M., Schut, F. and Rutten, F. H. (1994) 'Forming and reforming the market for third-party purchasing of health care', *Social Science of Medicine,* 39: 1405–12.

Van der Hoeven, R. (1991) 'Adjustment with a human face: still relevant or overtaken by events ?' *World Development,* 1991: 1835–45.

Van der Heide, B. (1991) *Exposed: Deadly exports. The Story of European Community Exports of Banned or Withdrawn Drugs to the Third World.* Amsterdam: WEMOS.

'Vatican withdraws support from UNICEF because of the pill'. (1993) *De Volkskrant,* 8 November 1993. Cited in *WGNRR Newsletter* (1993), 44: 15.

Vaughan, P., Mogedal, G., Kruse, S.-E., Lee, K., Walt, G. and de Wilde, K. (1995) *Cooperation for Health Development. Extrabudgetary Funds in the World Health Organization.* Australian Agency for International Development, Royal Ministry of Foreign Affairs, Norway and Overseas Development Administration, United Kingdom.

Vivian, J. (1994) 'NGOs and sustainable development in Zimbabwe: no magic bullets', *Development and Change,* 168–93.

Vivian, J. (1995) 'How safe are social safety nets ? Adjustment and social sector restructuring in developing countries', *The European Journal of Development Research,* 7: 1–25.

Vlassoff, C. (1994) 'Gender inequalities in health in the Third World: uncharted ground', *Social Science and Medicine,* 39: 1249–59.

Waddington, C. J. and Enyimayew, K. A. (1989) 'A price to pay: The impact of user charges in Ashanti-Akim district, Ghana', *International Journal of Health Planning and Management,* 4: 17–47.

Wagstaff, A. and Doorslaer, E. (1992) 'Equity in international finance of health care: some international comparisons', *Journal of Health Economics,* 11: 361–87.

Wagstaff, A. and Doorslaer, E. (1993) 'Equity in the finance and delivery of health care: concepts and definitions', in van Doorslaer, E., Wagstaff, A. and Rutten, F. (eds), *Equity in the Finance and Delivery of Health Care. An International Perspective.* European Community Health Services Research Series No 8. Oxford: Oxford University Press.

Waitzkin, H. (1994) 'The strange career of managed competition: from military failure to medical success?', *American Journal of Public Health,* 84: 482–9 (reply by Alan Enthoven on pp. 490–4.).

Wakhweya, A. M.(1995) 'Structural adjustment and health', *British Medical Journal,* 311: 71–2.

Walgate, R. (1997) 'World Health Organization leader to step down', *British Medical Journal,* 314: 1367.

Walsh, J. A. (1988) 'Selectivity within primary health care', *Social Science and Medicine,* 26: 899–902.

Walsh, J. A. and Simonet, M. (1995) 'Data analysis needs for health sector reform', *Health Policy,* 32:295–306.

Walsh, J. A. and Warren, K. S. (1979) 'Selective primary health care. An interim strategy for disease control in developing countries', *New England Journal of Medicine,* 301:967–74.

Walsh, J. A., Feifer, C. N., Measham, A. R. and Gertler, P. J. (1991) *Maternal and Perinatal Health Problems.* Washington, DC: World Bank.

Walt, G. (1993) 'WHO under stress: implications for health policy', *Health Policy,* 24: 125–44.

Walt, G. and Gilson, L. (1994) 'Reforming the health sector in developing countries: the central role of policy analysis', *Health Policy and Planning,* 9: 353–70.

Walt, G. and Harnmeijer, W. (1992) 'Formulating an essential drugs policy: WHO's role', in Kanji, N., Hardon, A., Harnmeijer, J., Mamdani, M. and Walt, G. (eds), *Drugs Policy in Developing Countries,* London and New York: Zed Books Ltd.

Warren, K. S. (1988) 'The evolution of selective primary health care', *Social Science and Medicine,* 26: 8491–8.

Warwick, D. (1982) *Bitter Pills. Population Policies and their Implementation in Eight Developing Countries.* Cambridge: Cambridge University Press.

Warwick, D. (1994) 'The politics of research fertility control', *Population and Development Review,* 20 (Supplement): 179–93.

Watkins, K. (1994) 'GATT: a victory for the North', *Review of African Political Economy,* 69: 60–134.

Watterson, A. (1993) 'Chemical hazards and public confidence', *Lancet,* 342: 131–2.

Watzman, N. and Woodall, P. (1995) 'Managed care companies "lobbying" frenzy', *International Journal of Health Services,* 25: 403–10.

Weerasuriya, K. (1996) 'Globalisation of drug registration and drug regulators in developing countries', *Risk and Safety in Medicine,* 9: 187–93.

Weil, D. E. C., Alicbusan, A. P., Wilson, J. F., Reich, M. R. and Bradley, D.J. (1990) *The Impact of Development Policies on Health. A Review of the Literature.* Geneva: WHO:

Weissman, R.(1996) 'A long, strange TRIPS. The pharmaceutical industry drive to harmonize global intellectual property rules, and the remaining WTO legal alternatives available to Third World countries', *Journal of International Economic Law,* 17, 4: 1069.

Werner, D. (1994) 'The life and death of primary health care', *Third World Resurgence,* 42/43: 10–14.

Werner, D. (1995) 'Turning health into an investment. Assaults on Third World health care', *Economic and Political Weekly,* 30: 147–51.

Werner, D., Sanders, D., Weston, J., Babb, S. and Rodriguez, B. (1997) *Questioning the Solution. The Politics of Primary Health Care and Child Survival with an In-depth Critique of Oral Rehydration Therapy.* Palo Alto: Healthwrights.

Westoff, C. (1988) 'Is the KAP-Gap real?', *Population and Development Review,* 14: 225–32.

Westoff, C. (1992) 'Measuring the unmet need for contraception: comment on Bongaarts', *Population and Development Review,* 18: 123–5.

White, J. (1993) 'Markets, budgets and health care cost control', *Health Affairs* (Fall): 44–57.

WHO. (1958) *The First Ten years of the World Health Organization.* Geneva: WHO.

WHO. (1975) *Executive Board. Fifty-fifth Session.* Official Records No 223. Geneva: WHO.

WHO. (1978) *Alma Ata 1978. Primary Health Care.* Geneva: WHO.

WHO. (1980) *Thirty-third World Health Assembly.* WHA33/1980/Rec/1. Geneva: WHO.

WHO. (1981a) *International Code of Marketing of Breast-milk Substitutes.* Geneva: WHO.

WHO. (1981b) *Global Strategy for Health for All by the Year 2000.* Geneva: WHO.

WHO. (1984) *Glossary of Terms used in the Health for All Series No. 1–8.* Geneva: WHO.

WHO. (1986) *Intersectoral Action for Health.* A 39/Technical Discussions No. 1–8. Geneva: WHO.

WHO. (1987a) *Handbook of Resolutions and Decisions of the World Health Assembly and the Executive Board.* Vol. III. First edition (1985/6). Geneva: WHO.

WHO. (1987b) *Economic Support for National Health for All Strategies.* A40/Technical Discussions No. 2. Geneva: WHO.

WHO. (1987c) *Evaluation of the Global Strategy for Health for All by the Year 2000. Vol 1. Global Review.* Geneva: WHO.

WHO. (1988a) *The Challenge of Implementation. District Health Systems for Primary Health Care.* WHO/SHS/DHS/88.1/Rev. 1. Geneva: WHO.

WHO. (1988b) *Alma Ata Reaffirmed at Riga.* WHO/SHS/88.2. Geneva: WHO.

WHO. (1988c) *The World Drug Situation.* Geneva: WHO.

WHO. (1988d) *Guidelines on National Drug Policies.* Geneva: WHO.

WHO. (1989) *Strengthening the Performance of Community Health Workers in Primary Health Care.* Report of a WHO study group. WHO Technical Report Series No. 780. Geneva: WHO.

WHO. (1990) *Management Development for Primary Health Care. Report of a Consultation.* WHO/SHS/DHS/90.4. Geneva: WHO.

WHO. (1991) *Interregional Meeting on the Public/Private Mix in National Health Systems and the Role of Ministries of Health.* Report. WHO/SHS/ NHP/91.2. Geneva: WHO.

WHO. (1992) *Women's Health: Across Age and Frontier.* Geneva: WHO.

WHO. (1993a) *Report of the Executive Board Working Group on the WHO Response to Global Change.* (Paper EB/92/4). Geneva: WHO.

WHO. (1993b) *Implementation of the Global Strategy for Health for All by the Year 2000. Vol. 1. Global Review.* Geneva: WHO.

WHO. (1993c) *Evaluation of Recent Changes in the Financing of Health Services. Report of a Study Group.* WHO Technical Report Series 829. Geneva: WHO.

WHO. (1994a) *Basic Documents.* Geneva: WHO.

WHO. (1994b) *The Work of WHO 1992–1993.* Geneva: WHO.

WHO. (1994c) *Pharmaceutical Companies Reinforce Partnership with WHO to Combat AIDS.* Press release WHO: 11, February 3. Geneva: WHO.

WHO. (1994d) *Health in Development. Prospects for the 21st Century.* Geneva: WHO.

WHO. (1994e) *Ninth General Programme of Work Covering the Period 1996–2001.* Geneva: WHO.

WHO. (1994f) *Health, Population and Development.* WHO position paper. Geneva: ICPD/WHO.

WHO. (1995a) *The World Health Report. Bridging the Gaps.* Geneva: WHO.

WHO. (1995b) *Programme Budget for the Financial Period 1996–1997.* Geneva: WHO.

WHO. (1995c) 'Working group on infant growth. An evaluation of infant growth: the uses and interpretation of anthropometry in infants', *Bulletin of WHO*, 73: 165–74.

WHO. (1995d) *Renewing the Health-for-All Strategy. Elaboration of a Policy for Equity, Solidarity and Health.* Consultation document. Geneva: WHO.

WHO. (1995e) *Achieving Reproductive Health for All. The Role of WHO.* Geneva: WHO.

WHO. (1996a) *Task Force on Health in Development.* WHO/HPD/96.10. Geneva: WHO.

WHO. (1996b) *European Health Care Reforms. The Ljubljana charter on Reforming Health Care.* Copenhagen: WHO Regional Office for Europe.

WHO. (1996c) *Equity in Health and Health Care: A WHO/SIDA Initiative.* Geneva: WHO.

WHO. (1996d) *European Health Care Reforms. Analysis of Current Strategies.* Copenhagen: WHO Regional Office for Europe.

WHO. (1996e) *Background Document: Eighth International Conference of Drugs Regulatory Authorities (ICDRA).* Support provided by WHO to drug regulatory activities, Bahrain, 10–13 November.

WHO. (1996f) *Revised Drug Strategy. Implementation of Resolutions.* WHA 1996/A49/4. Geneva: WHO.

WHO. (1997a) *Health Care Reforms. Analysis of Current Strategies.* Copenhagen: WHO Regional Office for Europe.

WHO. (1997b) *Reports of Advisory Bodies and Related Issues. Reflections of the Past – Visions of the Future. Report by the WHO Task Force on Health in Development.* WHO EB99/40. Geneva: WHO.

WHO/UNICEF. (1981) Joint Committee on Health Policy. National Decision-making for Primary Health Care. Geneva: WHO.
WHO/UNICEF. (1996) Revised 1990 Estimates of Maternal Mortality. a New Approach by WHO and UNICEF. Geneva: WHO.
Wilensky, H. L., Lambert, G. M., Hahn, S. R. and Jamieson, A. (1987) 'Comparative social policy: theories, methods, findings' , in Dierkes, M., Weiler, H. and Antal, A. (eds), Comparative Policy Research. Learning from Experience. Gower: WZB.
Wilkinson, R. (1996) Unhealthy Societies. The Afflictions of Inequality. London: Routledge.
Williams, D. (1987) The Specialized Agencies and the United Nations. The System in Crisis. London: C. Hurst and Company.
Wise, J. (1997) 'Baby milk companies accused of breaching marketing code', British Medical Journal, 18: 167.
Wisner, B. (1987) 'Doubts about "social marketing"', Health Policy and Planning, 2: 178–9.
Wisner, B. (1988a) 'GOBI versus PHC? Some dangers of selective versus primary health care', Social Science and Medicine, 26: 963–9.
Wisner, B. (1988b) Power and Need in Africa. Basic Human Needs and Development Policies. London: Earthscan Publications Ltd.
Woelk, G. B. (1994) 'Primary health care in Zimbabwe: can it survive?', Social Science and Medicine, 39: 1027–35.
Wolfensohn, J. D. (1996) 'Annual Meetings Speech', http://www.worldbank.org/html/ extmr/ jdwams96.htm, April 1997.
Wolffers, I. (1995) 'The role of pharmaceuticals in the privatization process in Vietnam's health-care system', Social Science and Medicine, 41: 1325–32.
Wolfson, M. (1983) Profiles in Population Assistance. A Comparative Review of the Principal Donor Agencies. Development Centre Studies. Paris: OECD.
Woodward, D. (1992) Debt, Adjustment and Poverty in Developing Countries. Vol II. The Impact of Debt and Adjustment at the Household Level in the Developing Countries. London: Pinter Publishers in association with Save the Children Fund.
World Bank. (1980) Health Sector Policy Paper. Washington, DC: World Bank.
World Bank. (1981) The World Bank. Washington, DC: World Bank.
World Bank (1986) Population Growth and Policies in Sub-Saharan Africa. Washington, DC: World Bank.
World Bank. (1987) Financing Health Services in Developing Countries. An Agenda for Reform. Washington, DC: World Bank.
World Bank. (1989) The World Development Report. New York: Oxford University Press.
World Bank. (1992a) The World Development Report. Washington, DC: Oxford University Press.
World Bank. (1992b) Population and the World Bank. Implications from Eight Case Studies. Operations Evaluations Department. Washington, DC: World Bank.
World Bank (1992c) National AIDS Control Project. India. Staff Appraisal Report. Washington, DC: World Bank.
World Bank. (1993a) World Development Report. Washington, DC: Oxford University Press.
World Bank. (1993b) Better Health in Africa. Washington, DC: World Bank.
World Bank. (1994a) Annual Report. Washington, DC: World Bank.
World Bank. (1994b) Better Health in Africa. Experience and Lessons Learned. Washington, DC: World Bank.
World Bank. (1994c) A New Agenda for Women's Health and Nutrition. Washington, DC: World Bank.
World Bank. (1994d) Population and Development. Implications for the World Bank. Washington, DC: World Bank.
World Bank. (1995a) Annual Report 1995. Washington, DC: World Bank.
World Bank. (1995b) Investing in People. The World Bank in Action. Washington, DC: World Bank.
World Bank. (1995c) ' FY95 population and reproductive lending up', World Bank PHNFLASH Electronic Newsletter on Population, Health, and Nutrition, Issue 97, received 22 November 1995.
World Bank. (1996a) World Development Report. New York: Oxford University Press.
World Bank. (1996b) Annual Report. Washington, DC: World Bank.
World Bank. (1996c) 'World Bank programs promote US export growth, job creation in Alabama'. Press release, 23 September. Washington, DC: World Bank.
World Bank. (1997) 'James D. Wolfensohn: World Bank President', http// www.worldbank.org/

html/extdr/ wolf/htm, April 1997.

World Population Plan of Action. Documents. (1975) *Population and Development Review,* 1: 163–81.

Wright, P. F. (1995) 'Global immunization – a medical perspective', *Social Science and Medicine,* 41: 609–16.

WTO. (1995) *Trading into the Future. World Trade Organization.* Geneva: WTO.

WTO. (1997) World Trade Organization Home Page. 11 April. HTTP/ WWW. WTO.ORG. Geneva: WTO.

Xu, B., Rimpelä, A., Järvelin, M.-R. and Nieminen, M. (1994) 'Sex differences in infant and child mortality in China', *Scandinavian Journal of Social Medicine,* 22: 242–8.

Yach, D. (1996) 'Renewal of the Health-for-All strategy. Round Table', *World Health Forum,* 17: 321–6.

Yang, B. M. (1993) 'Medical technology and inequity in health care: the case of Korea', *Health Policy and Planning,* 8: 385–93.

Yang, B. M. (1991) 'Health insurance in Korea: opportunities and challenges', *Health Policy and Planning,* 6: 119–29.

Yesudian, C. A. (1994) 'Behaviour of the private sector in the health market of Bombay', *Health Policy and Planning,* 9: 72–80.

Yi, Z., Ping, T., Baochang, G. *et al.* (1993) 'Causes and implications of the increase in China's reported sex ratio at birth', *Population and Development Review,* 19: 283.

Yoder, R. (1989) 'Are people willing and able to pay for health services?', *Social Science and Medicine,* 29: 35–42.

Yuval-Davis, N. (1995) 'From Cairo to Beijing: feminist and transversal politics', *WGNRR Newsletter,* 50: 7–9.

Zaidi, S. A. (1986) 'Why medical students will not practice in rural areas: evidence from a survey', *Social Science and Medicine,* 22: 527–33.

Zaidi, S. A. (1994) 'Planning in the health sector: for whom, by whom ?', *Social Science and Medicine,* 39: 1385–93.

Zeidenstein, G. (1977) 'Strategic issues in population', *Population and Development Review,* 3: 307–18.

Index

254